our children
live on

About the Author

Elissa Al-Chokhachy, MA, RN, CHPN, FT, is a certified hospice and palliative care nurse and a fellow in thanatology. The recipient of the Boston College Award for Excellence in Nursing and the American Red Cross Healthcare Hero Award, Elissa is the author of four hope-filled books to help with loss and grief.

miraculous
moments *for the bereaved*

Elissa Al-Chokhachy

Llewellyn Publications
Woodbury, Minnesota

FIRST EDITION
First Printing, 2012

Cover design by Adrienne Zimiga
Cover images: Hands: vlad_star/Shutterstock.com
Butterflies: iStockphoto.com/Jordan McCullough
Edited by Andrea Neff

Llewellyn Publications is a registered trademark of Llewellyn Worldwide Ltd.

Library of Congress Cataloging-in-Publication Data
Our children live on : miraculous moments for the bereaved / [edited] by Elissa Al-Chokhachy. — 1st ed.
    p. cm.
  ISBN 978-0-7387-3135-3
1. Future life. 2. Children—Death—Religious aspects. 3. Miracles. I. Al-Chokhachy, Elissa.
  BL535O97 2012
  133.901'3—dc23
                              2012020553

Llewellyn Publications
A Division of Llewellyn Worldwide Ltd.
2143 Wooddale Drive
Woodbury, MN 55125-2989
www.llewellyn.com

Printed in the United States of America

Contents

Acknowledgments   xiii

Introduction   1

◟ 1 *Visions* 7

Sharing Gifts with My Son   NANCIE FELD   •   9

A Given Name   GEORGIA BOURNE   •   14

Peter's Parting Gifts   FRANK A. BUTLER   •   17

The Blue Coat   ELISSA AL-CHOKHACHY   •   24

Ballet Slippers   JOAN ENRIQUEZ   •   26

Families Are Forever   NANCY CLOUTIER   •   28

Children Coming Back from Beyond   DOREEN NEILLEY   •   36

My Wish Fulfilled   BEVERLY F. WALKER   •   38

Joey   ELISSA AL-CHOKHACHY   •   40

A Gift from Ana   KRISTIE CULLUM   •   41

Miracles from Daniel   KIM POKROY   •   44

Grampy Will   TERI ERAMO   •   50

∿ 2 Sounds 57

Baby Jake   CLARE BURHOE   •   59

I Feel Great   ALISON ROBERTO   •   65

I'm Here   BONNIE DOANE MOODY   •   67

Forgiven   JOE GOODSPEED   •   69

Coincidences and Cooperation   ELISSA AL-CHOKHACHY   •   73

From Your Heart to Mine   PATRICIA CERRUTTI   •   75

Moments of Grace   BETSY WALTER   •   79

∿ 3 Smells 85

Together   JEANNETTE LUPOLI   •   87

Signs from Brandon   KIMBERLY MARINO   •   90

Just Believe   ANDREA GODWIN   •   97

The Light of My Life   KRYSTA O'NEILL   •   104

Comforting Signs from Claudia   JULIE SMITH   •   110

∿ 4 Touch 117

Signs from Kim   CINDY TAGLINI   •   119

A Life Saved   DAVID KEITH LAVOIE   •   121

Dream Baby   MARTHA W. BRANDT   •   125

My Body Is in Heaven   GWEN BURNS   •   130

Our Christmas Angel   LAURETTE A. POTTER   •   132

∿ 5 A Sense of Presence 139

Birthday Wishes   GINA FIMBEL   •   141

Hope from Beyond   ELISSA BISHOP-BECKER   •   143

Checking Things Out   JUDITH KONG   •   147

Signs from Beyond   DARLENE GOODWIN   •   149

Miracles of Healing   RICHARD FULLER   •   153

Holding On to Hope and Love   MICHELE A. HARRIS   •   155

～ 6 *Signs* *157*

Rainbow Blessing   JOANNE HADLEY   •   159

Messages from Meghan   NANCY KUHN   •   160

Heaven on Earth: It's a Camp Thing   ALI LERNER DOYLE   •   163

April Snow Squall   REGIS MCDUFFEE   •   166

Sean's Surprise Visit   BONNIE O'NEIL   •   173

Kristen's Butterflies   LAURA OUELLETTE LAURIA   •   175

Miss Mischief   ELISSA DAVEY   •   181

Angel Whispers on the Wings of a Dragonfly

   ANGELA RODRIGUEZ   •   183

Our Eternal Bond   BARBARA DESCLOS   •   185

Life Is Good   DONNA CRAIG   •   189

Confirmation from Mom   MARY BETH SWEET   •   193

Lucas, a.k.a. Turtle   NANCE WELLES   •   196

Glitter Girl   NANCY CINCOTTA   •   198

Butterfly Effect   PAMELA HEALEY   •   201

Love from Matthew   JAMES TROLAND   •   204

And the Curtain Gently Fluttered   R. JILL BILLER   •   206

I Love You to the Moon and Back   FRAN SAWDEI   •   211

A Shooting Star   MARIA CLEARY   •   214

Gifts from My Boy   TERRY LATHAN   •   216

~ 7 Dreams 221

Dancing with David MELISSA CRITCHLEY • 223

Jell-O Wrestling SHERRI H. EPSTEIN • 225

A Potted Plant and Puppy KIM JIN-WOO • 230

In Papa's Care DEBRA SUE RICHTERS • 234

Miracle Moment LAURA ALCAZAR-VIZCARRA • 235

Meeting an Unborn Son BRENT LEDGERWOOD • 238

Our Children Live On Forever ELISSA AL-CHOKHACHY • 241

Aunt Mickey MICHELLE ZACCARIA • 242

Our Treasure ANN MORELLI • 246

Finally Free ELISSA AL-CHOKHACHY • 251

~ 8 Angels 255

Heaven ELISSA AL-CHOKHACHY • 257

ICU Angel LAURIN BELLG • 259

Pink Carnations from Angel VINETTE SILVERS • 262

Surprising Sisters EILEEN KEARNEY • 267

Gratitude ELISSA AL-CHOKHACHY • 269

God's Messenger ROSA VIGLAS • 271

And the Cradle Rocked AMI & MATTHEW ROMERO • 277

Angel Visitors ELISSA AL-CHOKHACHY • 283

Baby Cherub Healing ANDIE HIGHT • 284

Isabella's Kiss ANGELA AMOROSO & DREW SKINNER • 286

Inspiration Angel ELISSA AL-CHOKHACHY • 289

~ 9 Near-Death Experiences 293

Walking the Rainbow THERESA BURKE MELNIKAS • 295

The Light That Shines Forever JOAN MEESE • 298

Passing into the Light on the Isle of Guernsey
RENEE L. COLLAS • 301

Second Chance ROBIN FRANK • 304

Into the Light MARY J. WASIELAK SKAGGS • 307

Morgan and Jesus MARLENE LEEDS • 313

Saved by the Light OWL MEDICINE WOMAN • 314

Conclusion 317

A Parent's Lullaby: A Song of Hope for Bereaved Parents 319

Share a Story 321

Acknowledgments

I offer my deepest gratitude to all of my contributors who have willingly shared their stories of love and loss in this anthology. May your beautiful stories bring tremendous hope and healing to many.

Thank you to all of my dearest friends, family members, and co-workers who have lovingly supported me along the journey. Special thanks to my editor and friend, Lori Monaco, and my dear friend Brianne Duff, who have helped these stories to shine.

Thank you to all of the beloved angels who are honored within these pages. You are our teachers and guides. Thank you for showing the way.

Most of all, I offer my sincerest gratitude to God, Creator and Source, for the opportunity to serve in this way.

Introduction

As for myself, I believe in miracles.

—SHAKESPEARE

HUMANKIND HAS CONTEMPLATED THE existence of life after death throughout the ages. Whether facing one's own mortality or the loss of a loved one, people need to know if life continues on. Will they see their deceased loved ones again? As an experienced hospice nurse, I have had the honor of caring for hundreds of dying patients and their loved ones. During one of the most difficult times in their lives, they have been my greatest teachers. These individuals, more than anyone, need to know if there is life after death. Based on my experience, I can say without hesitation that there is.

An unexpected visit from my beloved cousin Steffan two weeks after he died absolutely convinced me that life is eternal. As young children, my brother and I lived with our aunt, uncle, and six cousins for nine years while growing up in Knoxville, Tennessee. Many years later, when I was twenty-three, our eldest cousin Steffan was tragically killed in a car accident at the age of twenty-nine. As horrific as that was, my cousin came to visit me in the early morning hours two weeks later. In a dreamlike state, I experienced colors that were brighter than anything in this reality. All my emotions were amplified. I saw Steffan totally healed, happier and more at peace than I ever knew him in this life. I even held him in my arms. Miraculously, that experience healed my grief because I knew that my cousin was alive and well. My greatest wish is that everyone could have that same certainty.

There are many experiences that dispel the myth that death is the final chapter of life. People who are nearing death often see deceased loved ones in the room with them during the last days and weeks of life. Bereaved individuals commonly experience after-death communication with deceased loved ones. Those who have had near-death experiences offer the most extraordinary validation of all. They may be able to describe what happened to their physical body during resuscitation efforts. They may also be able to report what happened to them on the other side when their spirit or soul left their human form. This book is a compilation of all three types of experiences. It is an extraordinary book of hope for anyone who has experienced the loss of a child. Also, it will offer reassurance to anyone who has lost a loved one or who wonders if there is life after death.

As a hospice nurse and the author of four books, I am passionate about bringing comfort, hope, and healing to the dying and the bereaved. My first two illustrated children's books were written to help guide children and the adults in their lives through loss and grief. Yet, from my early days as a hospice nurse in 1991, I sensed a strong need for an anthology. People facing death or the loss of a loved one needed a collection of true life-affirming stories, which didn't exist at the time. For years I collected testimonials wherever I went for my third book, *Miraculous Moments: True Stories Affirming That Life Goes On.* I am grateful that this resource has been so well received by nurses, counselors, social workers, chaplains, hospice professionals, and the bereaved. Grief support groups are now utilizing it on a regular basis. Because the original manuscript had grown so large over the years, I divided it into two books. This book is the companion volume, with one third of the stories coming from the original manuscript.

Our Children Live On was written to bring hope and healing to anyone who has lost a child, grandchild, or young person. These individuals need hope and reassurance that their loved ones live on. The loss of a child is unfathomable. How can parents and grandparents possibly go forward when all of their hopes, dreams, and plans for their child and grandchild have suddenly vanished? It doesn't matter whether the child died in utero, at birth, or afterward; the loss is still an inconceivable one. Depending on the circumstances, the impact of that loss can be even greater. Children are supposed to outlive their parents and grandparents, at least that is what we were taught as children. But what happens when this natural cycle of life is interrupted? Those left behind are forced to find a way to navigate through heart-wrenching loss and grief.

Bereaved parents and grandparents often need to talk about their children who have died, yet many well-meaning individuals avoid the topic entirely. Not only do they feel uneasy discussing children who have died, but they may also feel uncomfortable with outward expressions of grief. Yet, tears help some people work through heartache, pain, and loss. The value of being a supportive, listening presence should never be underestimated.

I remember one young mother who told me how hard it was when people asked her how many children she had. If she said two, she felt that she was negating the existence and importance of her third child, her two-year-old son who had died from a brain tumor five years earlier. But if she told them three, she would be asked where the child was or what the child was doing. The conversation would end abruptly as soon as she said that her son had died from a brain tumor at age two. Now, whenever she is asked, she says, "I have two children and an angel." In this way, she is able to acknowledge her son while, at the same time, giving the individual an opportunity to explore further, if desired.

The devastating impact of a child's loss can be lifelong. Ongoing support from family members, friends, clergy, medical professionals, grief support groups, and organizations that address the loss of a child can make an important difference. Finding ways to acknowledge the child helps create a legacy, so the child will be remembered. It is also important to address the spiritual dimensions of the relationship. Many bereaved individuals report transcendent spiritual experiences that occurred prior to the death of their loved one and afterward. These experiences are real and valid and bring healing to grief. The realization that a deceased loved one is still in one's life can transform an experience of absence into one of loving presence.

Bereaved parents often see their deceased children in dreams and occasionally in visions; almost always, these children appear happy, healthy, and without any physical limitations. Some parents receive invisible hugs, hear their child's voice, or experience a comforting sense of presence. Others notice beautiful butterflies hovering nearby or rainbows that appear at poignant moments in their grief journey. Transcendent moments such as these occur commonly and serve as beacons of hope for the bereaved.

Our Children Live On contains eighty-two heartfelt testimonials written by bereaved mothers, fathers, grandparents, family members, friends, and those in the helping professions. Their stories of love, loss, and healing have been divided into nine chapters according to their experiences and the hope-filled signs they received. Because each of us experiences the world through the senses, there are chapters on visions, sounds, smells, touch, and a sense of presence, as in the format of the first book, *Miraculous Moments*. Since bereaved individuals commonly see their deceased loved ones during dreamtime, there is a chapter on dreams. There are also chapters on angels, signs received from loved ones in spirit, and near-death experiences of children. Some stories describing multiple experiences could easily have been placed in more than one chapter. Every story is true, although a few names and locations have been changed in order to protect the confidentiality of the individuals and family members. Although most contributors have written their own stories, I have worked with each in the writing and editing of these accounts.

Healing from grief can be a lifelong process. It is unique for each individual. Everyone grieves differently. Some of the contributors in this book share their grief openly, while others prefer to keep their feelings more private. Some cope by being in touch with their feelings, while others need more distance. There are those who have made it through loss and grief on pure faith alone. Fortunately, spiritual encounters such as the ones shared in this book can provide hope and reassurance for the bereaved. Death is not the end. It is simply a doorway to our spiritual home where we will all be together again.

Wherever I go, people tell me about life-affirming experiences with their deceased loved ones and children who have passed on. In my heart, I know the children who have left this world far sooner than we had planned are alive and well, and they come close in times of need. They hear our thoughts and prayers and send miraculous signs of hope. They want us to be happy. These children are our guardian angels, teachers, and catalysts for growth as we struggle to make sense out of that which seems senseless and purposeless. Even though they may not be physically present, they can be spiritually present at any moment so that we are never alone. Through the blessings of faith, prayer, and loving support, especially from our children and loved ones in spirit, we find our way to a new day.

May the angels who are honored within these pages offer hope, healing, and comfort to those who are hurting. May their courageous journeys help show the way. May God, the Creator and Source of All

That Is, heal the hearts of those who are suffering. Remember always that love and life are eternal, and one day, you will see your children again. Until that blessed day of reunion, may you be blessed with God's healing, grace, and peace.

I

Visions

And while I stood there
I saw more than I can tell
and I understood more than I saw;
for I was seeing in a sacred manner
the shapes of things in the spirit,
and the shape of all shapes as they must
live together like one being.

—BLACK ELK

THERE ARE MYSTERIES THAT occur in this physical realm that cannot be explained scientifically. One of those mysteries is the gift of vision that occurs for dying individuals and the bereaved. During the last days and weeks of life, people who are dying often have visions of beloved family members who have already passed on. They may talk about seeing other people in the room with them, spiritual beings, or even deceased pets. Sometimes they talk about seeing "the light" or going home or on a trip. They may also share an awareness of when they will die.

Family members who witness terminally ill loved ones speaking to unseen visitors may easily dismiss this behavior as confusion caused by medications they have taken. Yet dying individuals are able to see spiritual helpers, invisible to ordinary sight, who have come to transition them home. Three of the stories in this chapter describe visions shared in the final days of life. Experience the awe-inspiring last images seen by an adult son. Be uplifted by a teenager's dreamlike vision months before he died. Feel comforted by a young grandson's appearance next to his dying grandmother and the solace it provided his mother.

Bereaved individuals also experience visions of loved ones who have died. Seeing their deceased loved ones totally healed and happy again can be so reassuring and life-affirming. The nine remaining stories in this chapter address this type of vision. Imagine the joy of seeing one's disabled child now able to dance freely. Experience a mother's hope when her young son reveals that he just played his favorite video game with his brother who had passed years before. Some of the stories describe assistance given in naming a child, locating missing pets, and even preventing an auto theft. How amazing it is that those in spirit can assist the dying and also provide comfort and help to those grieving their loss.

Sharing Gifts with My Son

Nancie Feld

The year 1996 was a long time ago, and yet I clearly remember the pain of losing my fourteen-year-old son, Ryan, to a malignant brain tumor. I remember the elation of seeing him again after his death and the miracles we experienced throughout the process. Ryan was diagnosed with a medulloblastoma on his thirteenth birthday in October of 1994.

One morning in early autumn of 1995, Ryan awoke and shared a strange dream that he'd had. He told me that we were on separate planes. I thought he meant astral planes. "Planes, Ryan?"

"Yeah, like separate vacations."

"Oh, airplanes."

He continued. "Yeah, and I was sad because you couldn't go with me. But when we landed, I got off the plane, and everyone was very happy and knew my name! They were all calling out, 'Ryan, Ryan!'"

"What did it look like, Ryan?" I asked.

"It was beautiful. Everything was very clean and the colors...the colors were so bright!"

"Where did you think you were, Ry?" I asked, expecting his response to be "heaven." Instead, he replied, "Well, I don't know. I think it was Disney World!" With that, I understood that my son had been taken on a preview visit of his new home, one that I was not permitted to see or enter at this time.

I attempted to keep my child's life as normal as possible. When Ryan wanted to go to the mall in November for Christmas shopping, I medicated him, connected his mobile pain management controller, and packed his wheelchair in the car. In what proved to be Ryan's last Christmas season, I wheeled him around the mall, recalling how I had wheeled him in his stroller many years earlier as a cuddly little mass of love. Ryan dozed off and on during our adventure. However, when we stopped in front of his favorite store, the Discovery Store, he sat straight up and wanted to go directly into the middle of the crowded shop. Having grown very interested in American Indian lore, he quickly focused on a pair of dream-catcher earrings for me for Christmas. The store was crowded, though, and his energy was waning, so we decided to come back another day. I was very touched that above all the other things in that store, he wanted those earrings for me.

I went to bed later that night confident in the fact that my boyfriend, Doug, was sleeping with Ryan in his room. I still had the baby monitor turned on so I would be able to respond to any emergency that might occur. Very early the next morning, I awoke to the sound of a calm, conversational tone. It sounded as if Ryan and Doug were in the midst of a prolonged conversation. I walked downstairs and then stopped outside Ryan's bedroom. From the doorway I could see Ryan sitting up in bed, with his arms crossed behind the back of his head. His emaciated right leg, hooked over his left knee, swung back and forth. It was clear that Ryan was in conversation with someone, although I couldn't see anyone else in the room except Doug, who was fast asleep on the couch. Normally I would have interrupted Ryan and asked with whom he was speaking, but somehow I knew not to interfere.

The next day, I noticed how thin and wasted Ryan had become, especially in the last week. I began to cry at my helplessness for the child I loved so dearly, repeatedly apologizing for my weakness and lack of control over the situation. I kept telling Ryan, "I'm so sorry, baby. I'm so sorry." I dropped down onto his bed and hugged him.

"Don't worry, Mom," he said. "It will not be much longer. I won't be suffering much longer they said."

"Who said?" I couldn't help but ask.

"Never mind," he muttered softly. "The only thing I'm worried about is, who is gonna take care of you?" Two days later, on January 12, 1996, at 5:53 PM, my only son left this world, just as he had foretold.

As I gazed at my child minutes before his transition, I noticed that Ryan seemed to arch his back as he tried to sit up. Up until this point he had exhibited only minimal responsiveness. All I recall saying was, "What, baby? What's the matter?"

Then Ryan flung both his arms around my neck for what was to be our last hug. "I love you, too, Ryan," I said, not noticing anything unusual at the time. However, the hushed voices of all the friends and family members in the room who had come to say goodbye immediately changed to gasps. Everyone in the room began to cry and pray, as if witnessing a miracle. They told me later that when Ryan began to sit up, the front of his T-shirt was pulled upward, as if some invisible force was pulling him up by his shirt to say one last goodbye to his mom.

The next morning, I awoke to silence. There were no whirring noises or electronic beeping sounds coming from his monitoring equipment. There were no more whispers or TV sounds either. I found myself lying alone on the couch, quickly reviewing the previous night's events, when I glanced over at the coffee table. Scattered around the table were candies from a nearby bowl, along with several crumpled-up candy wrappers. Just then, Doug came down the stairs. I asked, "Did you eat candy last night?"

He replied, "No, no one did. Everyone left after you fell asleep."

"Then who did this?" I asked, as I pointed at the table.

"I don't know," he said. "I don't remember it being like that last night when I covered you with the blanket." We both stared at the violated candies and empty wrappers. Then, at the same time, we both said, "Did you notice these are all Ryan's favorite candies?" Small smiles crossed our faces and then faded as we remembered how Ryan loved those candies, yet had been unable to eat them because of the feeding tube inserted into his stomach.

Several months later, I had a dream visitation from Ryan. In the dream, I found myself wandering on a beautiful mountainside with snow-capped mountain peaks in the distance. It was a heavily wooded area, with oversized pine trees speckling the site. I turned to the left and saw several picnic tables with teenagers sitting on the benches. Some of the teens were walking around deep in discussion, while others were teasing one another. It seemed as though they were all waiting for someone or something.

I remember catching a glimpse of a sparkle in the sun. The sparkle was an earring, an earring from Ryan's ear that he had pierced in an effort to remain an ordinary teenager. I saw Ryan sitting on top of a picnic table, with his feet resting on the bench. With his head hanging low, he looked sad as he fiddled with his hands. I took a few more steps forward. Then Ryan got up, turned around, and saw me. No words came from him, just a huge smile. We ran to each another and hugged and kissed. I said, "Ryan, I love you. I miss you so much." He just hugged me, hanging on tightly.

"Mom, Mom, wake up! Come on, wake up, Mom!" I heard these words, but I was not quite sure that I wanted to comply with this command. I pulled the covers down from my face, opened my eyes, and saw a squiggly blur before me. I blinked and rubbed my eyes, and there on the bed before me sat Ryan. Smiling and appearing as healthy as could be, he looked down at me and said, "Mom, I knew that you knew I was okay, but I needed to show you that I was okay." We spoke for a while until I finally drifted off to sleep. I awoke the next morning with a sense of excitement and relief. The weight of the world was off my shoulders. I didn't have to worry about my son anymore.

Many months later while working as an office nurse, an established patient came in for her annual visit. In her hand she held a small box. "Something made me stop and get this for you," she said, "because

I know this will be your first Mother's Day without your son." My hands trembled as I accepted her gift; tears welled up in my eyes as I unwrapped it. When I opened the box, I gasped. Inside sat the same exact dream-catcher earrings that Ryan had picked out for me during his last Christmas!

Through this small miracle, my son was letting me know, "Mom, I am still watching over you." Ryan had wanted to give me those earrings for Christmas, but he was never well enough to go back and get them. I had forgotten all about them, but I will never forget any of the miracles or messages that I received from my child. Engraved in my memories are those experiences that will sustain me through every day of this existence until the day finally comes when Ryan will welcome me home.

Nancie Feld, MSN, MHA, RN, mother and wife, works as an occupational health nurse in Round Rock, Texas. Crafts, pets, and her granddaughter, Lola, propel her on her joyful path of love, laughter, and faith that she will reunite with her son one day.

A Given Name

Georgia Bourne

My brother died when he was fifteen years old. He was the apple of my eye; I adored him. He made me laugh—not an easy thing to do, especially at that time in my life. His golden hair, always in ringlets, drove all the girls crazy, even though my brother didn't really care for those curls. His name was Jimmy, or rather James George Bourne, and his birthplace was Plymouth, Massachusetts. Jimmy landed in my family by adoption when I was thirteen years old. He was a beautiful, healthy newborn, no more than two weeks old. Jimmy brought such joy to our family. In fact, he brought joy wherever he went throughout his entire life. Always laughing, my young brother had an ever-present smile on his freckled face. He had the most amazing deep blue eyes that continually sparkled.

Jimmy was all alone when my father found his lifeless body upstairs in the attic. Finding him with a rope around his neck was shocking. All the *whys* we had at that time still remain in our minds to this day. My brother had every reason in the world to live. Why did he have to die? Jimmy had plans to become a sports writer and a news sportscaster. To this day, I cannot watch a game without thinking of him as I listen to the sportscaster excitedly reporting play-by-play details from a booth somewhere out of sight. Jimmy would have been so good at it. No, he would have been great at it. He would have become a legend, like Sam Cohen, who wrote for the *Boston Herald American*, or his pal, general manager Red Auerbach of the Boston Celtics, both of whom were friends of our family.

Jimmy's death was a deep loss for all of us. I knew Jimmy first as my baby brother, then as my friend, and later as my confidant. Whenever I speak of him nowadays, I tell people, "I loved him dearly." Jimmy touched my wounded heart in ways that kept me going.

The intense pain and despair I felt after his tragic death caused me to do my own inner work, the slow and painstaking healing from the numerous losses in my own life.

Jimmy's death also brought us face to face with each other eight years later. It was early in my pregnancy when my obstetrician told me I was having a baby girl. In hopes of finding a suitable name for her, I endlessly searched documented family histories on both sides of my family. I searched, speaking every name I came across to no avail. None seemed fitting, not even close.

I remember one night feeling so frustrated at the seemingly endless search for my baby's name that I finally went to bed, still trying to tell myself it would be okay. My little girl would just have to bring her name with her when she came. Sometime during the night, an amazing, life-changing event took place, to which I awoke in awe. My beautiful younger brother with those gorgeous blond, curly locks was standing right in front of me! It felt so natural and normal to be with him. "Aren't you excited?" Jimmy asked as he smiled, referring to the child I was carrying within.

"I'm thrilled!" I answered, returning his smile.

"Have you found a name yet?" he questioned, intently studying my response.

"No. I've looked and looked, but haven't found one yet."

Then, all of a sudden, I realized that Jimmy and I were conversing telepathically. It seemed perfectly normal to be communicating this way. The experience didn't feel at all like a dream. It felt as if we were simply shooting the breeze with one another.

"Do you like the name 'Maggie'?" Jimmy asked, watching closely for my initial reaction.

With a huge smile, I enthusiastically told him, "I love it! I do. *I just love it!*"

Returning one of his big, remarkable grins, Jimmy said, "Well, that's her name: Maggie."

I passed over this suggestion rather quickly, as I was suddenly overcome by a bittersweet realization. "The only thing that bothers me, Jimmy," I said, "is that you're not going to know her."

Again, my brother smiled a patient, all-knowing smile. Jimmy said calmly, "But I already do know her. *She's Maggie.*"

Our eyes met just one more time before he was gone. Once again, I felt overwhelmed by the astonishing experience of our meeting. Then I was brought back from wherever we were to the present. I hadn't been asleep. It hadn't been a dream. Greeted by the early morning light of dawn, I found I wasn't the least bit tired or groggy. I was filled up, *spiritually lifted* into the day. My daughter's given name stayed with me. From that moment on, she was Maggie to me, Maggie Leigh. I loved it then, and I love it now. She is a perfect Maggie, if ever there was one.

Jimmy's visit was as real as can be, as if the two of us were standing together and having a conversation. Perhaps it was more real than that. Perhaps, in a sense, it was what we all have to look forward to on our inevitable journey home. One thing I know for sure is that my brother has been with me every step of the way in my raising of Maggie and is within me every time I speak her name. I look forward to the journey home, having known great joy here on this earth and having been allowed to raise my daughter with the knowledge of my brother's constant, steady hand upon her life. Great joys abound; some call this bliss and rightly so.

Georgia Bourne, MS, RN, LMHC, mother of Maggie, works on Cape Cod as an operating room nurse and licensed professional counselor specializing in trauma work using Eye Movement Desensitization and Reprocessing (EMDR). She enjoys helping her clients achieve a high level of mental health, wholeness, and self-actualization.

Peter's Parting Gifts

Frank A. Butler

⌒

Our firstborn child and only son, Peter Arthur Butler, was a charmer from the moment he was born on August 17, 1955. He was a good baby, easy to live with, and sensitive to people and the world around him. Peter was bright and alert but did not enjoy school until he entered the Harley School in Rochester, New York, in 1970, while I was on a yearlong training assignment at Eastman Kodak's Kodak Park Works. Our son thrived in the warm and challenging environment at Harley, with its bright, caring teachers and small classes.

When our family moved back to Massachusetts in 1971, Peter attended the Governor Dummer Academy in Byfield as a day student. From there, he went on to Earlham College, an excellent, small Quaker college in Richmond, Indiana. While at Earlham, he met the lovely and vibrant Tania Armstrong, and the two married shortly after graduation.

Peter was employed by W. R. Grace in the Construction Products Division and received his initial training at their headquarters in Cambridge, Massachusetts. After that, he had assignments in Wisconsin and Illinois. While living in Chicago, he earned his MBA at the Keller Graduate School of Business. In the mid-'80s, Peter received a job promotion and the opportunity to return to the division headquarters in Cambridge, Massachusetts. Although it meant Tania would be leaving her family behind in Indiana, the two of them were excited, as were my wife and I, about his promotion and having their family nearby. Just after they arrived, Peter was diagnosed with Hodgkin's disease at thirty years of age. His physician in Chicago had missed the initial symptoms. By the time Peter's primary care physician in Massachusetts recognized the problem, the Hodgkin's had already progressed to stage II, which meant it had spread to two or more lymph node regions. The cure rate was less than 50 percent. Peter, Tania, and our entire family felt stunned and upset to receive such unsettling news.

Peter received the standard chemotherapy and radiation treatments. When he went into remission, we all hoped he was cured. However, that was not to be the case, and the cancer reappeared. This time, the medical decision was made to do an autologous bone marrow transplant. The procedure was quite an extensive ordeal, but Peter seemed to respond very well. After several weeks of much prayer and bated breath, we were all sure we'd seen a veritable rebirth as he emerged from the sterile room.

The following months were exhilarating as each new "first" was successfully accomplished by Peter. It was about six months before he could return to work again. As a product manager for roofing materials at Grace, his work took him as far away as Saudi Arabia. Peter also resumed the recreational activities he loved doing with Tania and their six-year-old son, Jamie. They played tennis, hiked, camped, rode their bikes, and relaxed at our family cottage on Peaks Island off the Maine coast in Casco Bay.

Our son had a tremendous love for music. His mom, Ruth, is a fine musician and violinist and had been concertmistress of her high school orchestra. Peter picked up his deep appreciation for music from his mother, who constantly played classical music as well as big band music on our stereo throughout his childhood. He enjoyed all kinds of music and had a very good sound system of his own, with a great collection of records and CDs. Ruth and I will never forget the first time we visited Peter and Tania after Jamie was born in 1985; we were intrigued by how carefully Peter would place Jamie, just weeks old, on the floor between the speakers so that Jamie would get the full and balanced effect of the stereo speakers.

Then, in the summer of 1995, Peter's symptoms started to reappear. After Peter submitted himself to the most extreme treatments known and approved, the consulting team of doctors from Brigham and Women's Hospital, the Dana-Farber Cancer Institute, and the Beth Israel Deaconess Medical Center in Boston could not offer him any new, currently approved protocol. So Peter was offered an opportunity to participate in an experimental treatment with monoclonal antibodies. This procedure involved a weekly infusion followed by a CAT scan to monitor the progress and results of the antibodies attacking the cancer. Tania was a teacher at a local elementary school. Ruth and I were retired, living only twenty miles away from their home; naturally, we volunteered to drive Peter to Boston for his treatments.

On Friday, October 27, 1995, Peter awoke early because of some disturbing dreams. Tania called and asked if we could come earlier than usual so that Peter would not be alone when she left to take Jamie to school. When we got there, Ruth and I sat on either side of Peter and hugged him. He responded with a radiant smile and said, "Ah, a nice sandwich hug!"

Peter was not hungry that morning and didn't even want to eat breakfast before we left for Boston. Though it was not evident, he must have been feeling short of breath; for the first time ever, Peter asked if we could bring the emergency portable oxygen cylinder in the car as a precaution. The medical staff was waiting for Peter, ready to do the scan as soon as we arrived. Ruth and I settled in the reception area to wait.

After just a short time, the technician operating the scanner came in to tell us that Peter was asking for us. Apparently, Peter did not want to continue the scan unless we could be with him and hold his hands, which we did. As the scan progressed, Peter shared some thoughts with us. He talked about several things, including how bad things can happen to good people, and how he would never give up. Ruth and I were standing on either side, holding his hands and listening as he continued to share his feelings and thoughts with us. We had no idea that our son was dying.

After the scan, the three of us walked to the infusion area, where caring and skilled nurses routinely drew blood samples to monitor a patient's progress prior to the next infusion. For some inexplicable reason, despite numerous painful attempts, the nurses were not able to draw a blood sample. At noon, the staff brought Peter some lunch, but he was still not interested in eating. He calmly informed his doctor, nurses, Ruth, and me that he was feeling confused and dizzy. Therefore, a decision was made to let him rest a little while longer before making any further attempts to draw blood or administer his infusion.

On a typical day, everything would have been completed in time for the three of us to be able to share a late lunch together at home. Yet the afternoon seemed to drag on with no progress being made. We stayed with Peter the whole time. Finally, the decision was made to send Peter to the emergency room at Brigham and Women's Hospital, where he would be admitted for observation and further testing to determine what was going on. The staff would not allow Peter to walk the short distance and had him transported by ambulance to the emergency room.

Once Peter arrived, he clearly and strongly refused to be admitted or to have any routine checks performed. Fortunately, his oncologist and good friend from all the years of treatment arrived in time to shield him from the institutional bureaucracy. She compassionately moved Peter to a small, private examination room. There, Peter confided that he was dying and just wanted to go home. The oncologist responded, "I don't think you are dying, Peter, but often patients do know best."

Peter thanked the doctor for her care and asked her to please thank Vicki and all the other nursing staff for their great care as well. Then he said he did not want to be rude, but requested that she please leave to take care of the necessary actions to get him moved home. The doctor assured Peter that he had never been rude and left the room to make the arrangements. At that point, Ruth and I found ourselves alone in the examination room with our son on either side of his bed. He was quiet for a few moments and seemed to relax somehow. Peter asked us to raise his bed so he would be in a sitting position.

When we did, Peter's eyes opened wide and a beautiful smile came over his face. He went on to share with us an amazing experience, one that is impossible to record exactly. There are no words that can possible convey the impact of that moment, what it meant and still means to Ruth and me. As best as we can report them, the highlights are as follows.

"Cool...that's so cool...the light is *so bright* and the colors are *so beautiful*," Peter said.

Ruth asked if it was like fireworks. Peter replied, "No, much better, Mom. And the music, it's *so lovely*."

He turned to me with his impish smile that always melted my heart and said, "You were right all along, Dad...Mom, please put my glasses on. It is *so beautiful*. All the colors...you won't believe this, but I'm the luckiest person...this is so cool...it's so beautiful...the door is opening...people are coming to greet me, friends."

I asked if Grammy and Grandpa were there. Peter said, "Yes, yes, but others, many more. There are windows...beautiful windows...windows are opening...lots of windows...and a door...Where is Jamie? I hope Jamie can see this. Where are Tania and Jamie? Be sure to tell Tania's parents how proud I am of her. Be sure to tell them." In those days, there were no cell phones. Jamie was still in school, and Tania had not yet arrived home from work to pick up our message on the answering machine to join us right away at the hospital. We reassured our son that they would arrive shortly.

With another nice smile, Peter said some words about something that we did not understand...something about crystal, perhaps in connection to the windows. "This is *so cool*." Then Peter shared some thoughts about some practical things, such as telling us that he had tried to organize things clearly and it was all filed on his computer under "Estate." Peter shared this reality with us for perhaps another ten or twenty minutes with his eyes open wide, just looking at something in an intense way before asking again where Jamie and Tania were. Then he said, "The door is closing... It is so sad... so sad."

Ruth and I felt numbed by the fact that our son was dying, yet we were awed by the visions he had shared. A few times, we thought he stopped breathing, but then he would ask for Jamie and Tania, what time it was, or where they were. By the time Jamie and Tania arrived, it was a little before 7:00 PM. Almost immediately, Peter became revitalized and alert. Jamie climbed onto the examination table into Peter's arms, and Tania hugged them both.

Peter talked with Jamie very lucidly for about ten or fifteen minutes. He told Jamie how he had always been there for him and how sorry he was that he would not be there any longer. Peter told Jamie how important it was for him to ask for help if he needed it, and that there would always be others to help him, like Mommy, Grammy, and Grandpa. Our son wanted to assure Jamie that he would never be alone. His ten-year-old son stoically listened to his father's final comforting words and advice.

Then the ambulance arrived and transported Peter back home. Once he was in his own bed, we gathered around him. Jamie and Tania hugged Peter and gave him a backrub. We all shared affirmations of our love. Ruth, Tania, Jamie, and I each kissed Peter, affirmed our love again, and said goodnight. Peter slipped off to sleep, never to wake up again in this reality. But he left us all with a glorious glimpse of another and even greater reality.

Saturday began with a fierce, windy, slashing rain. Just before Peter died, as we all gathered around his bedside, a thunderstorm started. It felt like the very heavens were raging with our grief and loss. Then, at sunset, the clouds parted to the west and produced the most spectacular sunset with the fullest and brightest rainbow we had ever seen here in the Northeast. We were uplifted by the rainbow's magnificence, which lasted five or ten minutes and seemed like a benediction, a reminder of God's promise to us all.

Frank A. Butler is a retired CEO of the Eastman Gelatine Corporation, a wholly owned subsidiary of Eastman Kodak. He and his wife, Ruth, have two daughters and three grandchildren. Frank remains active in many church and service organizations.

The Blue Coat

Elissa Al-Chokhachy

———

Over the years, many individuals have excitedly shared with me about signs of hope they have received from deceased loved ones. Yet, curiously, others have reported receiving no signs at all. Part of me has to wonder if perhaps signs had been given but were not recognized as such at the time. Loved ones in spirit do not always reach out in the ways we might want, expect, or imagine. The following remarkable experience, told to me by several nuns, clearly demonstrates that divine intervention from loved ones in spirit can occur at any time.

When Sister Theresa was twelve years old, her mother gave birth to twins, Emily and Emilio. Just before the twins's third birthday, they received matching blue snowsuits in the mail. Theresa asked if the twins could wear the snowsuits to Mass the next day, but her mother said no, it was too warm outside. Four days later, Emilio became quite ill and died unexpectedly from a severe respiratory infection. His family deeply grieved the untimely death of this beautiful, little boy. In the years that followed, his mother would say with regret, "Why didn't I just let the twins wear their snowsuits?" After that, the family never postponed anything. They had learned the hard way that tomorrow may never come.

Sister Theresa eventually joined the convent and served God in many ways, particularly through her mission work in a poor, urban setting. Late one night on Holy Saturday many years later, she had a close call at a dimly lit intersection while driving home from the rectory. Her car was the only one on the road. She had just slowed down in preparation to turn left when three men in their twenties surrounded the car. The man on her right opened the passenger door, which turned on the overhead light. "We won't hurt you," he said gruffly. "We just want the car." As she started to get out of the driver's seat, the man next to her reached behind her to unlock the back door. All of a sudden, he shouted to the others, "Hey guys, leave her alone! She's got a kid!" The man on her right yelled, "Where?"

"Right there with the blue coat!" he said, pointing to the back seat. Instantly, the three men stopped in their tracks and took off, disappearing just as quickly as they had come. Sister Theresa didn't dare look back. Petrified and awestruck, she drove away in silence knowing it could have been so much worse. She could have been hurt; they could have stolen her car and left her stranded in a rough neighborhood. She felt so comforted knowing that her little brother, her angel in spirit, had come to her rescue, even thirty-five years after his death.

Sister Theresa has always wished that her little brother could have been in her life and that he could have had an opportunity to wear his birthday suit. Yet it wasn't meant to be, at least not in the way she had thought. Sister Theresa feels grateful for all the gifts that God brings, and especially for the divine intervention of her little brother.

Ballet Slippers

Joan Enriquez

Angela Monica, our beautiful blond, blue-eyed daughter, was the youngest of our five children. We were so happy to have another girl since there were three boys between our oldest daughter and her. Soon after Angie's birth we realized that something was seriously wrong. We were heartbroken when we learned that not only did Angie have severe retardation, but she also had multiple disabilities and an uncontrollable seizure disorder. Despite our ongoing efforts to provide her with the best medical and educational care possible, our little girl never progressed beyond a six-month developmental level. Her older siblings loved her dearly and encouraged her, delighting in her accomplishments no matter how small. They even learned how to care for her when she had seizures. Angie never stood, walked, or talked, but she had a very special sound that she made for each of us in the family.

Angie brought so much goodness into our lives through her gentle nature and patience in the suffering she endured. She loved us unconditionally, and we loved her in return, not in spite of her limitations but just because she was who she was. Because of her, we were kinder to one another, since she would get upset if voices were raised in anger in our house.

The medicines that Angie took over the years in an attempt to control her seizures did a job on her system. Her health was fragile, and in my heart I knew during the last year of her life that we would soon be losing her. It was so painful to watch her decline because we loved her so much and we wanted her to stay with us for as long as we could have her. Often when I held Angie in my lap, I would look down and find her staring at my face. I had the feeling that she was trying to memorize it so she wouldn't forget it when she left us.

For Angie's tenth birthday on December 2, her seventeen-year-old sister, Maryellen, gave her a pair of black leather ballet slippers. She told Angie that every little girl should have her very own pair of dancing shoes. Angie became quite sick that Christmas, and by December 30 it was evident that she needed to be hospitalized. Almost as soon as she arrived at the hospital, Angie stopped breathing. She was resuscitated, and her pediatrician worked all night long to stabilize her, but I knew that God was calling her home. While the doctor was working on her, suddenly her eyes opened wider and clearer than I had ever seen them, and I knew that she was seeing beyond this world to someplace beautiful. Soon after that she died.

We buried Angie in her new ballet slippers and smocked Polly Flinders dress that I had bought her for Christmas. A few days after the burial, while I was fully awake, I was gifted with a vision of my daughter. I felt so comforted to see Angie dancing in her pretty new dress and ballet slippers in the most exquisite field of flowers imaginable. The flowers were more vivid in color than I had ever seen and more richly fragrant than any I had ever smelled. Angie was as happy and joyful as any little girl should be, and she was completely free from all her pain and disabilities. I felt that I was being told that I had done a good job taking care of her on this earth, and now I could let her go into God's loving care. It is so hard for a mother to lose her child. However, I know that my daughter Angie is waiting for me in heaven, and one day she will dance across that beautiful field of flowers into my arms.

Joan Enriquez, a retired children's librarian, lives in Kingston, Massachusetts, with Armando, her husband of forty-eight years. They have four children and eight grandchildren. Joan enjoys Armando's Mexican cooking, reading, knitting, water aerobics, and spending time with friends and family.

Families Are Forever

Nancy Cloutier

———

Heaven and earth are not distant enough
to separate the hearts which our Lord has joined.

—St. Francis de Sales

This is one of my favorite quotes from the Catholic theologian St. Francis de Sales. Growing up Catholic, I had been introduced to his writings and found them both enlightening and comforting. Little did I know how often I would come to refer to this quote for comfort many years later.

The youngest of four children, I grew up on a farm in Iowa during the sixties. My mom was mostly Irish, while my dad was German. Both were hard working and very loving in their own way. Mom was much more demonstrative in her love, constantly wanting to hold and kiss us, while Dad seemed a bit dismissive, as he jokingly brushed off our hugs and kisses. We all understood that Dad loved us by the way he provided for our family, but I don't ever remember hearing him say "I love you" or initiating a kiss or hug. It just wasn't his way.

From my parents, I learned to be pragmatic about life but also to embrace it warmly. My mother was a firm believer in God and instilled in us the need to serve Him and others. My dad was also a believer, though at times was more skeptical. He went along with Mom's earnest attempts at making sure all their children attended Mass and said the rosary nightly, especially during the months of October and May, the months devoted to Mary, the mother of God. Despite my mother's insistence that no one should ever miss Sunday Mass under any circumstances, I do remember my dad somehow managing to beg off on attending during planting or harvesting seasons. My siblings and I never thought much of it until years later, when we realized that Dad just needed a break from "all that religion stuff."

As time went on, I left for college and eventually decided to major in social work. Later, I earned a Master of Social Work degree and began working at a hospital as a social worker in the pediatric oncology department. At first I was terrified of this assignment, but I quickly began to love my patients and their families as I became involved in their lives.

For the next several years, I worked side by side with the nurses, doctors, and other professionals. We helped the pediatric patients and their families adjust to their diagnoses and cope with the various treatments. Sometimes we also helped them say goodbye when treatment sadly failed. It was such an honor and blessing to be there with them during those times. Only later would I realize how much I had learned from these patients and their families about how to handle loss through unexpected death and all the grief that would follow. I owe them all a tremendous debt of gratitude.

During this period of time, I met the man I would marry. Michael had been a single parent to a young boy named Tyler, so when we married, we both knew we wanted to have more children. Sadly, our first pregnancy ended in a miscarriage, but shortly thereafter, we had a son, Zachary. While I was pregnant with Zachary, my mother died suddenly of a heart attack. I was devastated by this loss and missed my mother so much. We had always been close, and I had hoped to rely on her motherly wisdom and practical help in raising my own children. My miscarriage and the loss of my mother were the first of a series of losses for our young family.

Seven months after my mother's death and only one month after Zachary was born, my dad suffered a serious stroke. He was eighty-four years old at the time. The medical staff on his rehabilitation unit felt he should go into a nursing home, but my siblings and I knew he would lose any desire to live if forced to move there.

Fortunately, after a month of rehabilitation, it was agreed that Dad could return to his home with twenty-four-hour supervision. I lived an hour and a half away from Dad and had a young boy and small infant at home to care for; I knew I would not be able to care for Dad in his home, as he desired. I had one week to arrange round-the-clock care for him. With God's help, I was able to find some very reliable and wonderful ladies to take care of Dad.

As life fell into a new rhythm, I became pregnant with another son, Brandon. We were delighted that God was giving us new life after so much loss. All was going well until two months before I was due to give birth. Michael learned that the factory he worked for was going to close in six months, and he would need to look for work elsewhere. I became worried because we had just moved into a new home a year earlier. We were having another baby, and I was not employed outside the home. How would we manage financially?

Fortunately, my worries were soon put to rest when my husband received an offer to go to work for a major company in Florida. I had mixed emotions about leaving my father, although by this time he had recovered enough that he was living independently in his own home. Also, I had never left my home state of Iowa and was nervous about what our new life might be like. Still, as the snow fell outside, I felt like Florida just might be the opportunity we were looking for. We moved in February, when Zachary had just turned two and Brandon was five months old. Tyler, at the age of ten, was actually looking forward to starting at his new school. It appeared to us that life was looking up.

Once in Florida, we quickly settled into our home and new life, all the while feeling so blessed to have a healthy family and a wonderful (and warm) new home to enjoy. As is common in Florida, our home came with a swimming pool. I wasn't happy about the pool. Although my husband and Tyler loved the water, we had two small children who weren't able to swim. It was difficult to find a home without a pool. My only stipulation when buying our home was that we would install a fence around the pool as soon as possible. From a neighbor, I had learned that drowning was the most common cause of death among small children there. Once the pool fence was installed, I breathed a little easier but never really let my guard down.

Time moved along, and our three sons flourished in the Florida sunshine. Brandon, our youngest, was a sweet and handsome little boy. He had darker features than his older brothers, with straight brown hair and beautiful sparkly brown eyes that spelled mischief. Although he was on the thinner side and had a smaller frame, I can still recall the long and muscular shape of his legs from all the running and chasing he did after his brothers.

Our lives were full and busy. As a family, we created many memories together, mostly wonderful ones. Yet one devastating event changed everything. That was the unexpected death of my twenty-two-month-old son, Brandon. On a seemingly typical Saturday morning, I was busy catching up on laundry and cleaning the house. My husband was outside doing yard work. Our two youngest boys were outside with their dad playing in the yard. As so often happens with small children, Brandon wandered off. A few minutes later, my husband realized he wasn't playing with his brothers and went looking for him. All I remember was hearing the panic-stricken yell from my husband to call 911, and the image of him carrying Brandon, lifeless and turning blue, out of the pool. My husband and the emergency rescue workers all tried in vain to bring Brandon back to life, but I knew even before we got to the hospital that he was gone.

Michael and I were shattered by this loss. We found it extremely painful to get through the days that followed. Had it not been for our faith and the ongoing needs of our other children, I believe I would have crawled under the covers and never come out again. It was like being in a dark abyss, not being able to find one's way out. On another level, I did not want to. Everywhere we turned, there were memories and reminders of our family now broken and lost. While the professional side of me knew what grieving entails and the work that we had before us, the grieving mother side of me just wanted to die with my child. The thought of Brandon being all alone when he died haunted me.

Gradually Michael and I were forced to return to our previous normal activities. The pain was still so raw and exposed, but we knew our other children were counting on us to be there for them, too. What a blessing that we had them! Another blessing came in a phone call I received from my dad a few weeks after Brandon died. Dad was anxious to tell me something but wasn't sure how receptive I would be. He was slightly afraid I might think he was crazy. I urged him to please tell me.

Dad explained that the night before, he had been lying in bed, not yet asleep, but relaxed. He had just finished saying his prayers when suddenly a bright light glowed at the foot of his bed. In that light, he saw my mother holding Brandon! Next to Mom and Brandon was my nephew Danny, who had died several years earlier at the age of twelve. All of them were dressed in beautiful white, flowing gowns, and they all were smiling and laughing.

My dad, who suffers from hearing loss, could not understand what they were saying to him, but a feeling of complete happiness and peace came over him. He did not feel any fear or confusion at all. Also, Dad said that my mother looked young again, like in the days when they were first married. The colors surrounding the three of them were so bright and beautiful. My dad felt that he needed to call me as soon as possible to tell me of this vision; he was certain that they were all in heaven together, and that my mother was now taking caring of Danny and Brandon.

I began to cry tears of joy and relief that all of them were together. My baby was being so well taken care of by my very own mother! I trusted her more than anyone to be loving and attentive to him. I can't explain the peace I had when I learned of this vision. After I relayed it to Michael, we both marveled at how they were able to appear to my dad when he had always been somewhat skeptical of spiritual events. But, in a very real sense, it made the vision that much more genuine. If Dad believed it was real, then I believed it, too. God is so good! He knew what it would take to make us believe in Him and be comforted.

After this happened, Michael and I experienced a real turning point in our grief. It still hurt, but we now felt confident that Brandon was in heaven and that we would see him again someday. As time went by, I was a bit curious why I had not seen a vision of Brandon myself, but for whatever reason, it hasn't yet happened for me. I still keep praying to hear from him.

Ironically, when Zachary was six years old, he was lucky enough to see his little brother, Brandon. The day after it happened, Zachary told me about it while he was preparing to take his bath. He first asked if telling me something about Brandon would make me cry. When I said I didn't think so, Zachary relayed his experience. The night before, a bright light had awakened him outside his closed bedroom door. Curious about it, he walked out to the family room and saw a small but very bright light surrounding Brandon as he sat on the floor facing the television. Brandon looked up at Zachary and said, "Hi, Zachy." That was exactly how Brandon had pronounced Zachary's name. He was playing a favorite video game that the two used to play together. Zachary said he was a bit frightened, but Brandon told him everything was going to be okay.

Then, Zachary fell asleep on the couch, and that is where I found him the next morning. I had been curious about why he was on the couch, but he refused to tell me at the time. His behavior that day had seemed a bit strange to me. However, after he told me about Brandon's nighttime visit, it all made sense. I asked Zachary how he felt during his brief time with Brandon. He said he was frightened at first, but then he felt better when Brandon told him everything would be okay. I was surprised that he hadn't come to wake me up when this happened, but Zachary said he just remembered feeling tired and falling asleep on the couch.

In the years since Brandon died, our family has experienced many ups and downs emotionally and spiritually. Our oldest son, Tyler, went through a time of depression, believing that if only he'd been home at the time of Brandon's death, he could've somehow prevented it. Fortunately, he worked through these emotions and now has a very deep spiritual side.

Zachary, however, had the most difficult time coping with Brandon's death. He was three and a half years old at the time and had a lot of anger, which he aimed especially at me. With my professional background, I understood that I was a safe target for these strong emotions because I was his mother and loved him unconditionally. Still, this was particularly distressing for me, because it was just Zachary and me at home after Brandon died. My own grief made me want to draw him in even closer, yet he refused my overtures and fought me physically. We sought counseling for him, which helped tremendously. Now it doesn't bother Zachary to talk about Brandon.

We also went on to have another son whose name is Ryan. He looks a great deal like Brandon, although they have distinctly different personalities. It amazes me how one little boy has had such a healing presence in our family life. While Ryan could never replace Brandon, he certainly has been a wonderful addition.

One of the things many parents fear after they lose a child is that their child's memory will be forgotten. We have tried to keep Brandon's memory alive in our family by talking about him and remembering favorite little stories. We still celebrate Brandon's birthday each year with his favorite chocolate cake and comment on how old he would be. We also like to think about what he would be interested in or what grade he would be in school.

We have made sure that Ryan knows about his older brother and has seen pictures and videos of him. We are proud that all our boys can share their thoughts and feelings about Brandon openly with us and with others. In many ways, it has been a long road to healing, but like a broken bone, I believe we have grown even stronger. After all, families are forever.

Nancy Cloutier, MSW, lives in Fort Myers, Florida, with her husband and three living sons. She hopes that by sharing her story, others may find hope and peace.

Children Coming Back from Beyond

Doreen Neilley

Six years after my brother died in a vehicle accident in Canada, I lost my only son, Dean, in a vehicle accident in Australia, where we were living. The pain from their combined losses felt unbearable. The following year, my husband, daughter, and I relocated back to Canada, and we brought our two dogs with us. When our Rhodesian Ridgeback dog, Shaka, went missing a few months later, I searched for him for three days. On the third night, my son appeared to me when I was sitting at the computer trying to make a missing-dog flyer. It was incredible! Here I was struggling to find Shaka's picture and there he was telling me I didn't have to—someone had shot Shaka and hidden him down by the river near our home. Sure enough, that's just where I found him. It all felt surreal. Even though I was happy to have seen my son, I was deeply saddened that Shaka had died. But Dean had been able to comfort me by finally ending my search.

Shortly after that, I got another dog whom I named Bear. He was a lively yellow Labrador–sled dog cross who loved to go for gallops in our rural area. That winter, Bear went missing, too. With a heavy heart, I searched and searched for days, to no avail. Then Dean came to visit me again, only this time he was carrying my huge Bear easily in his arms. I couldn't believe it. Bear grinned at me and wagged his tail, then swiped Dean with his tongue. Dean told me that Bear had fallen through the ice, but that he was okay, and he would see me again one day. Just knowing that, I no longer felt the need to search any further. Dean and Bear had brought me peace.

Finally, when my only grandchild, six-month-old Dakota, died of SIDS three years later, I could barely hold myself together. I had to, though, at least for a couple of weeks, to help my daughter, who needed my support so much. When I returned home, I sobbed and sobbed and questioned why God didn't want the women in my family to have any sons. I also remember lying in bed wondering if my grandson was okay. Did Dakota have someone to look after him?

At that moment, my son and my brother appeared to me, gently smiling and holding Dakota in their arms between them. Together they said, "It's okay, we've got him!" I was very, very thankful and relieved to know that Dakota wasn't alone, and at least the three of them were together. I can only think that God must have something very important for all of them to do. I haven't had any visitations since then, but thanks to that visit, I know they are all okay. One day, when my husband and I join the three of them, we know that our dogs will be waiting for us, too.

Doreen Neilley was born in Edmonton, Alberta, Canada. She married her pen pal of eight years and then went to live with him in Australia. Doreen and her husband now reside in Alberta, Canada, where they have a daughter and a wonderful granddaughter.

My Wish Fulfilled

Beverly F. Walker

⎯⎯

My whole world fell apart the day my son, Don Jr., fell asleep at the wheel while driving in North Carolina. Our family went through the heartbreaking task of bringing his twenty-eight-year-old body back to his home state of Tennessee for burial. We also acquired Donnie's much-loved cat, Audrey, in the process. You can imagine how very special this gray-and-black-striped tabby became to all of us.

My son and I shared a love for red-tailed hawks. Alongside a country road one day on a walk near our home, we even saw a pair of red-tailed hawks up close. Needless to say, it did not surprise me when hawks started showing up after his death just at the appropriate times when I needed them. I knew the hawks were signs from God and from my son, letting me know Donnie was fine in His care. I also believed that the many feathers I kept finding were tangible signs of hope from my son.

Yet I so longed for a vision of Donnie, especially during the early months and years of my grief. I read numerous books by renowned mediums and psychics in my spiritual quest for answers, and I truly believed these visions could occur. At the same time, I knew I would probably fall apart at the seams if it ever actually happened to me.

Over the years, I experienced the shock, the denial, the anger, and the not wanting to accept the truth of what had happened. After seven years, I finally realized that I would survive and come out a better person in the end. I also learned to take my son with me in a new, spiritual way. I realized that Donnie is always with me, especially through those hawk sightings and "feather treasures."

By the ninth year of my grief journey, I was having more good days than bad, as generally happens with the passing of time. Then, on one ordinary evening at home, it happened. I had not yet thought about

Donnie that day or cried any tears. Once I finished making supper, I turned and called out to my husband to come eat. Just as I turned, I noticed Donnie's cat on the back of the easy chair to my right. In that very instant, as I looked at Audrey, I saw my son! He had the biggest smile ever on his face. I could see Donnie from the waist up, floating above Audrey, with his hand outstretched to pet her. Although the colors appeared misty and washed out, my son was wearing the same brown patchwork vest that he was wearing in a picture I still kept on my kitchen windowsill. I could feel my son radiating such peace. As soon as I called out to my husband, Audrey jumped to the floor and ran to the table, and the vision disappeared. Even though the vision had lasted for only two or three seconds, I knew I had just witnessed something spectacular. All I could emotionally handle at that moment was to sit down, let it sink in, and say out loud, "Cool!"

It took me ten minutes or so before I could divulge to my husband what had just occurred. First, I had to convince myself that what I had seen with my own eyes was real and not just my imagination. When I shared what I had seen, my husband was just as happy as I was that Donnie had sent us another sign. Our son had managed to miraculously reach out to Audrey and me and let all of us know he was fine. I'm not sure if Donnie had found a way to open the portal on that day or if I had somehow managed to connect to it, although I wasn't meditating or praying at the time. Most likely it was simply God who had made it possible. In the end, it doesn't matter how it happened. All I know is that I am so grateful for the miracle that occurred and for the confirmations that my husband and I continue to receive from our son. They are constant reminders that the love we share with Donnie continues on.

Beverly F. Walker resides in Greenbrier, Tennessee. She is a writer with many stories published in Chicken Soup for the Soul, *including four stories in their* Grieving and Recovery *edition. Beverly loves scrapbooking, photography, and spending time with her grandchildren.*

JOEY

Elissa Al-Chokhachy

———

I'll never forget the conversation I had with Mary, the spouse of one of our hospice patients. As we sat together with her dying husband, I gently questioned her about her spiritual orientation, or if she believed in life after death. Mary responded affirmatively and then went on to describe the life-changing event that had convinced her of this.

Many years earlier, a tragic accident had occurred in her home. Two of her sons had secretly removed their father's hunting gun from the cabinet. The boys were unaware that the gun was still loaded. When the older son jokingly pointed the rifle at his younger brother and pulled the trigger, five-year-old Joey was instantly killed. The family was overcome with immeasurable despair, angst, grief, and regret. For years Joey's needless death haunted them, especially Joey's guilt-ridden older brother.

When Mary's mother was dying several years later, she shared that Joey was right there, standing at the foot of her bed. Her grandson appeared happy, smiling, and wearing his baseball cap. Mary felt so relieved and thrilled to finally know that her son was alive and well. Excitedly, she contacted the family priest to relay the incredible news about Joey. However, the priest responded in a less than supportive manner. Attempting to dispel the vision, he said, "Disregard what your mother said. Her hallucinations are from the morphine she is taking."

"No, Father. You're wrong," Mary replied adamantly. "My mother is not taking any morphine. In fact, Mom hasn't been taking any medications for quite some time." In her heart, Mary knew the truth. Joey was alive, and her mother had seen him. And how reassuring to know her mom would look after her son. The Creator works in mysterious ways. It is amazing that a dying woman's vision could bring a grieving mother such solace, hope, and peace.

A Gift from Ana

Kristie Cullum

In the spring of 1995 while working as a hospice nurse in San Antonio, Texas, I met a child named Ana. She was a two-and-a-half-year-old child with big, chocolate brown eyes, short, tousled brown hair, and a contagious smile. Ana lived in a Catholic foster home for children with AIDS. When she was just six months old, her mother brought Ana to this house of hope because she was too ill to care for her any longer. Ana's mother died from AIDS three months later.

The foster home assigned Sister Mary Claire to be Ana's foster mother. Sister Mary Claire was sixty-eight years old, but she had the energy of someone half her age. She was very loving and very determined that Ana have as normal a life as she could for as long as possible. When I met Ana, she was at the end stage of her disease, and hospice had been called to provide comfort and emotional support. She was fed through a tube in her stomach. Ana could not walk, talk, or roll over. But she could smile and laugh, and she did both often. In spite of all her misfortunes, Ana was a happy, content, and loving child. She loved watching the activity of the other children in the home and would squeal with excitement when they ran past her. Sister Mary Claire and I often commented that we just knew Ana would be running with the others if only she could. One day as I walked up to the front door, I could hear laughing and squealing and lots of activity coming from inside. I looked in through the window and saw Sister Mary Claire holding Ana in her arms, chasing the other children through the house. Ana was laughing so hard she was practically breathless. It was quite a scene to witness.

Another love of Ana's was music and having people sing to her. She would watch our faces intently as we sang, almost as if she was trying to learn how we did that. When she liked a particular song, she would smile her beautiful smile and wave her arms. We discovered at Christmas time that her favorite song was "Deck the Halls," especially the "fa la la la la" part. We were still singing that song when Valentine's Day came, just to see her smile.

Over the months, I grew very close to Ana and Sister Mary Claire. The idea that this child was dying and did not have a mother to hold and cuddle her ignited my maternal instincts. I adopted Ana into my heart. Late one night a year and two months after I met her, Ana died. It was a very emotional event for all of us who had come to love her. When I arrived back at my home, I wept about the unfairness of this hideous disease. I cried that Ana had been cheated out of having a normal life; I cried that she was never able to walk or talk or play. I cried for our loss of such a sweet spirit. I cried myself to sleep.

Several hours later, something woke me from my sleep. I opened my eyes to the early morning light coming through my window... and to Ana standing at the foot of my bed! I propped myself up on my elbows and all I could say was, "Ana! You're standing!" She stood right there, smiling that familiar smile at me. Then she raised her right hand, waved at me, and turned and skipped away. I did not move for several minutes. I just stared at the place where she had been standing. Then my mind started trying to process the experience. Was she really just here? Was I dreaming? Was this a vision? I found myself crying again, but this time they were tears of relief, happiness, and reassurance. I believe Ana came back to tell me she was okay. Ana was happy now. She came to say goodbye and to tell me that I could let go. I felt a sense of peace that is hard to explain. I felt comforted.

It has been four and a half years since Ana died. Sister Mary Claire worked at the foster home for two more years before retiring to Michigan to be with her family. I am still working as a hospice nurse. Hospice work can be very tiring emotionally. Ask anyone who knows me, and they will tell you my mantra is *Give me strength*. Stories like Ana's are what give me strength to continue my work.

Kristie Cullum, RN, pediatric care manager for the Houston Hospice Butterfly Program, also travels to Africa to work with children with AIDS. Recipient of the Good Samaritan Foundation Excellence in Nursing Award, Kristie is married with two grown children and one precious grandson, Devin.

Miracles from Daniel

Kim Pokroy

After giving birth to my first child and falling in love with him every single day, I never, ever imagined Daniel would be taken away from me. For the first year of his life, my adorable blond-haired, blue-eyed son was healthy. I thought he would be forever mine. As a first-time mother, I had dreamt of watching him go off to school, play team sports, and get married, and I had looked forward to being the grand-mother of his children one day. Yet none of these dreams would be realized for me or my son.

As a baby, Daniel appeared perfectly healthy. However, by the time he was six months old, I noticed that he didn't seem to be able to sit up or focus like other babies his age. After months of uncertainty and testing, our infant son at ten months old was diagnosed with Tay-Sachs disease, a progressive neurological genetic disorder. Stunned and angry, my husband, Jerome, and I now faced the heartbreaking, unexpected loss of our child.

Prior to making the decision to conceive our first child, Jerome and I had gone for genetic counseling, as most married Jewish couples do. We needed to determine if we were Tay-Sachs carriers due to the high risk of incidence in Jewish Ashkenazi couples. In order for Tay-Sachs to be passed on to a child, both parents must carry the gene. Because of the lab results, we felt comfortable moving forward with starting our family. However, what we didn't know was that the lab had made an error and had reported one false negative result; we were both Tay-Sachs carriers after all.

For the next year of Daniel's life, I watched his healthy body grad-ually deteriorate and eventually begin to shut down. The end of his life was fast approaching. As his mother, I felt helpless. There was nothing I could do other than to make my son as comfortable as possible and to love him with all my heart. Jerome was wonderful. My family was a tremendous help. The best doctors and nurses cared for Daniel. But nobody could save Daniel, as there is no cure.

How could my baby's life be almost over when it had barely just begun? How could my life go on without my child? A few days before Daniel died, I panicked. I found myself screaming intensely at my husband, telling him that I wasn't going to be able to let go of Daniel's body from my arms. I would not survive the pain of losing him. After all, I had given birth to him. He had grown inside of me. I had nursed him, held him, and loved him. He was so much a part of me. I loved my precious baby more than words can say. I could never let him go ... never!

My loving husband kept trying to calm me down by telling me that Daniel's body was merely the shell that housed our precious son and that once his body died, the shell was nothing. Daniel's spirit— his love inside the shell—would come out and go straight to heaven. And heaven was a beautiful, peaceful, healthy place for Daniel to live forever. One day, we would be together again. I tried so hard to listen to Jerome, but I just couldn't grasp the concept of eternal life.

For the last nine months of his young life, Daniel had been completely paralyzed. He was unable to voluntarily move any muscles. He could no longer sit, smile, swallow, laugh, or talk. However, during the last moments of his life, our little son gave me a miracle that changed my life.

Minutes before Daniel died on October 15, 1998, our twenty-two-month-old son was lying between his daddy and me on our bed. The three of us were surrounded by Daniel's grandparents, uncles, and the hospice nurse. All of a sudden, Daniel lifted his right hand into the air and, in the process, stretched his right arm out in front of him as if *he was reaching out to someone.* Our son held his hand there for a few moments. He then slowly lowered his hand and arm back down by his side. Daniel turned his head to the right to face me and looked into my eyes. *He smiled and squeezed my hand,* neither of which he had been able to do for months. In that moment, I knew he was going to be okay, and he would not be alone when he left this earth. After that, Daniel took his last breath … and he was gone.

It was truly a miracle that Daniel had showed me *he could move again* just before he left his sick body. If others had not been present, I don't think anyone would have ever believed it possible. All of us gasped in shock at the same time as we witnessed Daniel's miracle! Jerome cried as he held me, saying, "Kim, he did this for you."

Through the tears and agony of saying goodbye, I thanked Daniel for this miracle. I was also deeply grateful that my parents were able to be there to help us. They loved their grandson so very much. Twenty-four hours a day, Mom and Dad took shifts holding Daniel during seizures, giving him oxygen and loving him. We were so blessed to have them at our side.

As I look back to those last few days, I believe our son actually knew of my pain and confusion during that devastating time. Daniel's miracle helped me survive his loss. He taught me to believe that when our loved ones die, they are not gone forever. Just like Daniel, they leave their earthly bodies to become angels in heaven. Now I know Daniel is in a better place. I believe he is happy and watching over our family. I share this story so you, too, can believe in miracles and in the power of love.

Daniel's second miracle occurred on Mother's Day in 1999. It came to me through a dear friend I had met at the national Tay-Sachs conference in New York a year earlier. During the most painful time in our lives, I connected instantly with a beautifully spiritual Japanese woman, Chie Sasaki. We shared a common bond: our only children and firstborn sons suffered from Tay-Sachs disease.

When Chie and I met, Daniel was sixteen months old, and I was struggling with the progression of his failing health. Chie was grieving the recent loss of her son, Yasuhiro, from the same devastating disease. He was five years old at the time of his death. Having already gone through the unthinkable loss of a child from Tay-Sachs, Chie was able to help me in so many ways. As Daniel became progressively sicker, we spoke more often on the telephone. Chie guided and supported me through each step of the journey. At one point, she even came to our home for two weeks to help care for Daniel. Jerome and I will be forever grateful for her ongoing kindness, generosity, strength, and friendship.

I was dreading that Mother's Day, my first Mother's Day without Daniel. On that day, seven months after Daniel died, I received an amazing phone call from Chie in Japan. "Kim!" she exclaimed. "Daniel just came to me!" Chie had awoken early that morning to see Daniel at the foot of her bed. He was standing up and smiling, both of which were impossible for him to do while he was alive. Daniel was also proudly holding a purple tube-shaped pillow. Chie had the sense that Daniel had come to tell her something, yet he did not say a word. Chie thought perhaps his message was for me, since she had no idea why he had come to see her. Daniel just stood there looking so happy as he proudly displayed his tube-shaped pillow to Chie. "Oh my gosh!" I said to Chie, suddenly realizing exactly what Daniel was trying to say. "Daniel was holding a Torah!"

"What is that?" Chie inquired.

"It is the holy scroll of sacred Jewish laws and tradition, which is read every Saturday on the Sabbath." Daniel had died during Simchat Torah, the Jewish holiday celebrating the completion of the annual reading of the Torah. Jerome and I had decided to bury him with a special gift honoring the holiday—a little, purple, pillow-shaped toy Torah made for babies. In traditional Jewish custom, nothing is placed inside the casket of a deceased person. Yet Jerome and I had secretly agreed that we would place the toy Torah in Daniel's arms when he was buried. He was only a small child, and we hoped the symbol of the Torah would give our son extra protection.

Jerome and I had not told anyone besides our parents about our plan. In fact, Jerome's father was the only person who saw the toy Torah with Daniel, as he had stayed the night with Daniel, watching over him at the funeral home. According to Jewish tradition, the body of a Jewish person who has died is never left alone until it is buried; this is done out of respect for the body that housed the soul. Jerome's father had stayed with Daniel. Because it was a personal matter, none of our parents had discussed the Torah incident with anyone, including Chie. For this reason, Chie's vision was an incredible confirmation for our family.

Chie's vision affirmed that Daniel is alive, healthy, and happy. It brought us so much comfort to know that he still has the toy Torah. I believe our young son came to Chie to convey a powerful message. Because she was previously unaware of our gift or even what the Torah meant, her vision was living proof that Daniel truly is okay. What an amazing Mother's Day gift! Daniel had found his messenger.

My beloved friend Chie is remarkable. Since the death of her son, she speaks with Yasuhiro, and the two of them work as a team to help others. Chie shares her story of Daniel and her experiences with other children in her book, *My Little Angel, Yasuhiro*. She helps so many families communicate with loved ones who are sick or dying before and after transition. I do not know what I would have done without her.

Since then, I have been fortunate to have been given a second chance at motherhood. It was important for Jerome and me to have a healthy child. Thankfully, we have been blessed with two healthy children. Yes, I still miss Daniel every single day. I love him so much. My sincerest hope for everyone who reads this story is to be able to receive the strength and love necessary to move through the pain and heartache of grief.

Daniel changed me. I live with pain, but I live a happy life, too. I am deeply grateful for the miracles of hope I have received. Every year I speak with first-year medical students at Baylor Medical School on a panel with other parents who have lost children. From the perspective of the patient's family, I am able to teach them about compassion. Through Daniel's life and death, I am privileged to help raise awareness of Tay-Sachs disease. Every other year, Baylor Medical Center and Jewish Family Services come together to bring reduced-cost screening for Tay-Sachs and other genetic disorders to the Houston community.

Even thirteen years later, I still miss my son. I am stronger as a result of having had him in my life. In the past, I underestimated my strength. But, having gone through all I did with Daniel and the grief that followed, I now realize how strong I really am. I have found myself through it all. Jerome has, too. I am so thankful for my loving husband and my family. Daniel, we will love and miss you forever.

Kim Pokroy is married to her childhood sweetheart and friend, Jerome. As former South Africans, they feel blessed to live in Houston, Texas, with their two wonderful children, Zack and Samantha, and have the loving support of family.

GRAMPY WILL

Teri Eramo

In some ways this story resembles a few already shared. Yet in other ways it does not. The only thing I know is that it is real and true and so full of spirit that whenever I think of it and Grampy Will, I cannot help but smile.

Just a few weeks shy of his ninety-first birthday, Wilbur Andrews, affectionately known to our family as Grampy Will, became ill and needed gastrointestinal surgery. Believing that he was strong enough to recover, my grandfather-in-law opted to have it done. Instead, that surgery was the beginning of the end of his physical life. During the time he spent hospitalized and in rehab, my husband, Michael, and I visited Grampy Will nearly every day. We talked with him and tried to comfort him as best we could. He was the one who had helped walk us through this world; surely we could help him when he needed us most.

Grampy Will was a major player in our lives and especially in the life of our young son, Benjamin. Always ready to go for a drive or to knock down block towers with Benjamin, he was a part of us like no other. Grampy Will brought laughter and stories of times past on his almost daily visits with our family. He would tell us often that our son, Benjamin, was the thing that kept him going. I think the innocence and laughter of a small child in his life made Grampy Will feel alive and needed. When Grampy Will became sick and was hospitalized, we regularly brought Benjamin to visit because it always cheered him up. Our young son would stand next to his bed and sing all the new songs that he had learned in school to his great-grandfather. I can still see Grampy Will smiling widely and clapping at Benjamin's endearing renditions!

After weeks spent in the hospital and in rehab, it became evident that Grampy Will was soon going to be leaving this world. He had started to share with us about the choirs in heaven that were singing in preparation for his arrival. It was joyful singing, he told us, with birds fluttering all about. Grampy Will would ask if we could see them or hear them. Sadly, we couldn't, for those glimpses of the spiritual world were being shown only to him. By the look of astonishment on his face, we knew he was truly seeing these images and was comforted by them.

Grampy Will was extremely devoted to his church, the Second Congregational Church in Beverly, Massachusetts. Never having lived more than a few blocks away his entire life, he had been born and raised there. Grampy Will honored this church so much that he was the silent and sometimes not-so-silent steward of its doors. He was not a hired hand, but he was surely a willing hand. He was in charge of opening the church for all weddings and funerals. Then he would close its doors late at night after its purpose had been served for the day. Grampy Will opened the doors for Mike and me at our early evening winter wedding. I can still see him smiling as he stood at the top of the stairs waiting for us to arrive—a few minutes late!

It was an honor for Grampy Will to serve wherever he was needed. What better way to experience the cycle of life on earth than to be present for both the happiest and the saddest of occasions for any human being. Grampy Will enjoyed giving back. Almost daily, he would stop by the church office to sit in *his* chair as he visited with staff and ministers. Because this incredible man selflessly gave so much of his time, love, and energy to the church, it only seemed right and appropriate that he would be graced to hear choirs of angels in heaven singing in preparation for his arrival. He surely deserved it.

One evening while Michael and I were visiting with Grampy Will at the rehab hospital, his dear friend Elissa and another friend were visiting as well. Grampy Will had a high fever and was in a good deal of pain. I placed cool cloths on his forehead to help bring down the fever while Elissa sat on the bed and talked with him. After a while, I rejoined my husband, who was standing just a few feet away.

In an effort to provide some comfort, Elissa offered Grampy Will a backrub. He agreed. She turned him onto his right side and began massaging his back. My husband and I were talking quietly with each other when one of the most incredible and spiritual moments I have ever experienced occurred. Michael and I were standing at the foot of the bed, leaning against the wall. Grampy Will was still lying on his right side, turned away from us. In between long pauses, he was quietly talking with Elissa when he suddenly began asking about the baby. "What happened to the baby?" he asked her.

Elissa looked at us quickly, somewhat puzzled, and asked, "What baby, Will? Whom are you talking about?"

"Mike and Teri's baby," he answered. My heart jumped as Michael turned to look at me. We could hardly believe what he was saying.

Elissa looked at us again, confused. Thinking that Grampy Will must be referring to Benjamin, our four-year-old son, she asked, "Do you mean Benjamin, Will? He's okay. He's doing just fine."

"No," he said. "The *other* baby…the little boy." This time she looked at us with surprise. Our eyes immediately filled with tears, for the one thing that we had *never* shared with Grampy Will was that I had had a miscarriage; I had lost the baby a year before Benjamin was born. More than that, Mike and I had never known the sex of the baby. We had so often wondered if our first baby was a boy or a girl. And even though Elissa had been a longtime friend of Grampy Will's, she hadn't known our story either.

For years I had grieved the loss of this child, never having openly shared my feelings with anyone other than my parents and Mike's mother. Daily, I silently spoke to our child. And every night I'd write to my baby in a journal in the form of a prayer, sharing my thoughts and feelings of both sadness and hope. Tucked away inside my journal was the sonogram picture of our baby. The only identifiable thing in that photo was his tiny little heart, which was white, surrounded by the shadowy gray and black of the film. Having this photo of our baby, as well as a private place to keep it, allowed me to be able to grieve, cry, and work through the pain of our loss. But all of this I did alone.

Grampy Will waved hurriedly for me to come to his side. It was so apparent that he had something to say. Crying, I walked over to him, took his hands in mine, and then knelt beside him. He started to cry. "Teri," he said, with small tears rolling down from his eyes, *what happened to the baby?"* Almost pleading, he asked me, *"Why didn't we have a funeral?"*

Grampy Will was obviously upset. My heart broke, as I told him that we had lost the baby early on in the pregnancy, so there was no infant for us to be able to have a funeral. He was *so* sad. Not only had we lost a baby, but Grampy Will had also lost a great-grandchild. And, as steward, he wanted to be able to honor that baby as he had done for so many others who had passed through our church doors on their way home.

I told him that I was so sorry, and we cried as he held my hand for what seemed a very long time. I asked Grampy Will to take care of the baby, our little boy, and he assured me that he would. This gave me *such* peace, as I knew that Grampy Will would always watch over and protect both our children ... on earth ... and in heaven. The shock and surprise of what he had seen moved all of us with such powerful emotion that evening. His vision clarified that the spirit does, in fact, live on. What a beautiful gift to have received, and one we will never forget. Grampy Will gave Michael and me the chance to honor and acknowledge our baby in a way that had never before been possible.

In the summer of 1997, the year that I had miscarried, I started the tradition of annually planting a miniature rose bush in our garden in memory of our little baby. One day on a walk, without even searching, I found a flat rock in the shape of a mother holding a baby. I instantly knew that rock was meant to grace the spot where the roses were planted. And, year after year, it does beautifully. Nowadays I sit on the stone wall adjacent to that spot in the garden and talk to Grampy Will and our little son. My heart is filled with so much peace knowing that the two of them are together.

Since Grampy Will's passing, I have often dreamt of him. Yet there is one dream in particular that has been especially comforting to me over the years. The dream began on a hot, sunny, summer morning. Grampy Will was driving down an old brick road in his old, silvery blue station wagon. I was alone, walking down the sidewalk of the same road, when Grampy Will pulled his car up alongside me. I bent down to peer in the window. He leaned toward me and flashed a huge smile. With his left hand still on the steering wheel, he said, "Get in! We're going to a family picnic!"

Grampy Will was wearing a light blue, short-sleeved shirt and his typical dark brown pants. He looked healthy and the same as he did prior to becoming sick. "Grampy Will!" I exclaimed, as I slid onto the front bench seat right next to him. I was beside myself with so much excitement and surprise. "It's you!" I exclaimed. "You're back!"

"Yes," Grampy Will said, grinning, "but just for this."

"You look *so* happy."

"I am! *Very* happy! I just came to tell everybody." Knowingly, we smiled at each other with a very clear understanding that all was well. As we drove happily down the bumpy street together, Grampy Will said to me, "Let's stop for pastries."

Once inside the bakery, we stood side by side, as we had done many times over the years. With his hands in his pockets, Grampy Will happily chatted with a short woman behind the counter in his usual manner. The woman started to hand us the familiar white box of homemade pastries tied with a string. As I reached to take the box out of her hands, the dream ended. I woke up *so* thrilled and excited to know that he was, without a doubt, rejoicing happily in heaven. Thank you, Grampy Will, for your gift of love and your continued support. We love you and miss you always.

Teri Eramo, wife and mother, is a graphic designer and artist. She feels blessed to be able to share about her beloved Grampy Will and the healing awareness he brought about her son. Teri will never forget her memorable road trips with Grampy Will.

2

Sounds

Let us be silent that we may hear the whisper of God.
—RALPH WALDO EMERSON

SOME PEOPLE VIEW DEATH as the end of one's existence. If this were true, then how would it be possible for bereaved individuals to hear the sounds of their deceased loved ones' voices after they have died? Imagine how reassured a grieving parent would feel to hear their child's voice one more time. This would be the last thing one would expect, and yet it miraculously happens. The only plausible explanation is that the soul is able to transcend physical death. Truly, death is not the end. Our departed loved ones in spirit live on.

What if a parent grieving the loss of a child were to hear little footsteps running down an empty hallway when their child had never been able to walk? The awareness that their child in spirit no longer has physical limitations can be a transformative and healing experience. Instead of worrying about whether their child continues to struggle, the bereaved parent can hold on to new hope. At least their child can enjoy doing the things in the spiritual realm that they had envisioned for him or her while here on earth.

Following a child's death, sometimes a toy will start to play the child's favorite song or might speak a message of comfort to a loved one who is bereft. Think about how comforting these playful and childlike messages from spirit can be. Within this chapter are seven stories with examples of various sounds heard following the death of a child. These sounds, which cannot be logically explained, are music to the ears of all those who deeply grieve. They are some of the many ways children in spirit reach out to their parents and loved ones from beyond. In their own way, these children are saying, "Please don't be sad. I love you. I am with you. You are not alone."

BABY JAKE

Clare Burhoe

———

Jake was our first child and our only child at the time, and we loved him more than we could have ever imagined. When we lost him at eighteen months old, we were devastated. Unexpectedly and seemingly peacefully, Jake died in his sleep. We will probably never know the reason he died, but we believe that his passing was seamless. Our son went to sleep here, and he woke up in heaven. This belief is based on several experiences my husband and I have had since his death.

Jake was larger than life in both body and spirit. From just a couple of weeks after his birth, his height and weight were literally off the charts. People who saw him always marveled at his size and beauty. He had a cherubic face with big blue eyes, curly blond hair that glinted in the sunlight, and an ever-present gap-toothed smile that could melt your heart.

When Jake was just ten months old, he was diagnosed with a rare genetic seizure disorder called tuberous sclerosis complex. Although he was not expected to die from the disease, his physicians told us that Jake could suffer uncontrollable seizures and severe developmental delays. Fortunately, his seizures were completely controlled with medication. And although the experts told us he was developmentally delayed, Jake was perfect to us and to everyone who knew him. He was happy, fun, and beautiful. Jake loved everyone. He truly was an angel with a golden glow.

Jake loved music and singing. Just a few weeks before he died, he learned how to whistle and also had started humming random tunes to himself. His favorite toys were those that played music or made sounds. He particularly loved the Mozart Magic Cube and his First Steps musical walker. Both of these toys would actually hold Jake's attention for several minutes until the moment arrived when he felt compelled to suddenly run around the house roaring like a lion, pull all the toilet paper off the roll, or climb on top of the furniture.

Nothing seemed out of the ordinary on the night of April 15, 2003. Jake had fallen asleep in my arms on the sofa after an evening of robust play. My husband, Peter, carried our eighteen-month-old son up to his bedroom and laid him down in his crib fast asleep. His grandmother (affectionately known as *Nushka*, the Hungarian word for "grandmother") was staying overnight as usual. She babysat our son on Mondays and Tuesdays while my husband and I were at work. Each morning Jake woke up sometime between 6:00 and 7:00 and played with his Elmo phone or the musical mobile attached to his crib until someone came to get him. Nushka would get up as soon as she heard Jake stir, change his diaper, and feed him breakfast so that we could stay in bed a little longer. Because I am a light sleeper, I normally woke up anyway when I heard Jake playing with his toys over the baby monitor, but I would drift back to sleep for thirty minutes or so as soon as I heard the two of them go downstairs.

However, on that Tuesday morning, I woke up much later than usual with an unexplainable feeling of dread. I hadn't heard Jake or Nushka. I ran into Jake's room to check on him, and I saw him in his usual sleeping position on his right side with his back to the door. As I approached my son, I couldn't detect the gentle rise and fall of his back from breathing. I called out Jake's name several times and placed my hand on his back. I felt nothing. I turned him over and instantly knew that Jake had left us, taking our hearts with him. Our pain was unbearable.

The days and weeks that followed are hazy now. However, some events do stand out, and those have made all the difference. There was a steady stream of family and friends coming and going from the house up until the funeral, with the exception of one evening a couple days after Jake's death. On that particular night, my husband, Nushka, and I found ourselves at home alone together for the first time. Earlier in the day, we had picked "Twinkle, Twinkle Little Star" as the opening song for Jake's funeral service because it was one of the songs that his favorite Mozart Magic Cube played. It was also one of the songs I used to sing to him if he was upset or trying to fall asleep.

As Nushka, my husband, and I were tearfully sharing stories and writing remembrances for the funeral, out of the blue Jake's First Steps walker started playing "Twinkle, Twinkle Little Star" on its own! The toy was sitting alone next to a wall. Nothing and no one was touching it. Surprisingly, we had never known "Twinkle, Twinkle" to be part of its repertoire. In fact, it took me quite some time to figure out how to get the First Steps walker to play the song again. Initially we were a little taken aback by the music playing spontaneously, but as soon as we realized which song was playing, we were awestruck! Without a doubt, Jake had chosen this private moment and particular song to let his three primary caregivers know he was alive, well, and watching over us. We were greatly comforted to know that our baby had not left us completely. For the first time since his death, I did not feel like dying myself. That toy had never played music or sounds on its own before and has never played any since. I will never forget the hope instilled in me as a result of Jake's musical message.

A couple weeks after the funeral, one of Jake's daycare teachers, Christine, called to see how we were doing. "I hope you don't think I'm crazy," she said. Christine then went on to share a similar experience. On her first day back at the center after Jake's service, Christine and her co-teacher had just finished picking up the toys in the toddler room and were getting ready to leave for the day. Suddenly they both began to hear strange sounds. They soon discovered that the source was a plastic cash register, which was making noise from inside the toy cabinet where it had been put away. Christine told me that this toy had never made noise on its own before and hasn't since. The two of them were amazed and believed this was a tangible sign from Jake to let them know he was okay. Peter and I agreed. It was one more confirmation of Jake's original message. We were extremely grateful for Christine's willingness and courage to share her experience. Just knowing that Jakey was all right helped ease my pain.

About a month after Jake's death, several members of our family went to a workshop in Boston with James Van Praagh, the famous psychic medium, in hopes of having some further contact with Jake. As part of the workshop, James taught us how to do specific meditation exercises. During one of the exercises, he instructed us to visualize our own spirit guides. Afterward, both my husband and my mother independently said that their spirit guide was Jake. What was surprising was that they both saw him as a young man and not as a small child.

The following month, my husband and I took a trip out of state to visit our dear friends, who have four children. Their two youngest girls, Cassidy, age five, and Hadley, age seven, loved "Baby Jake" dearly. Cassidy was especially affected by his death. Her mom told us she had been talking about Baby Jake a lot and drawing pictures of him, and she made sure her mom mailed us one, along with a letter telling us how much she missed him.

During our visit, Cassidy spent a lot of time drawing pictures with magic markers and then showing them to us. Because I had been reading books on spirituality and life after death, I learned that, during dreamtime, everyone maintains a connection with the spirit world, especially children. I asked Cassidy if she'd had any dreams about Baby Jake. Cassidy told us that she'd had two dreams about her little friend. In the first dream, a *scary* one, which happened shortly after Jake's death, Cassidy told me, "I heard Baby Jake crying in his crib, and when I went to get him, he was dead." In the second dream, which she'd had the night before our conversation, Cassidy told me that she and Jake "went all over the world together." When I asked her if it was a nice dream or a scary dream, she told me it was nice and then moved on to other topics.

The next day, my husband and I were sharing a quiet moment alone when, for the first time, it occurred to me to ask for more details regarding his vision of Jake as his spirit guide. He described Jake as a young man with the same facial features he'd had as a child, with slightly straighter hair and wearing an ethereal robe-like garment that covered his feet. That same afternoon, when Cassidy presented us with her latest stack of drawings, we asked her to tell us about each of them. She explained that the scribbles were a path or road. When we came to the drawing of a tiny, smiling face with a long, stretched-out triangle underneath, she said very matter-of-factly, "That's Baby Jake as a teenager wearing a dress." Notably, some of the new pictures had drawings of Baby Jake and Teenager Jake side by side. The similarity of Cassidy's drawing of Jake to my husband's description just minutes earlier was striking. I asked Cassidy if the Jake in her "going around the world" dream was a baby or a teenager. She confidently informed me that he was a teenager. My husband and I were heartened to know that our son was well, and also that he was able to spend time with his friend.

The fact that my husband, mother, and Cassidy all independently saw Jake as a teenage young man and not as an eighteen-month-old child is indisputable evidence that Jake's spiritual life continues on. I know he still watches over us. I am comforted that our child's existence is much greater than the little time he had on earth, and that he continues to have a presence in our lives.

Prior to Jake's death, my husband and I were not at all religious. We went to church only for weddings and funerals, spending very little time if any pondering questions of a spiritual nature. We still don't go to church. Yet these remarkable experiences with Jake have deeply awakened our spirituality. We still miss our Jakey more than we can express, and we will always grieve his loss and the life we had hoped we would have together. Yet our hearts are happy to know that he is well and in a place of peace, love, and joy. And we look forward to being reunited with our son Jakey one day.

Clare Burhoe is the mother of Baby Jake and twins, Raef and Joshua, who have brought so much joy. She is grateful to her family, friends, and her dog, Wilson, who provided the strength and support to finally feel hope for the future.

I Feel Great

Alison Roberto

⌒

When Ryan David Roberto was born, I remember feeling like Superwoman. It was such a high. I loved every part of being a mom. I had finally found my purpose. What a great child to get purpose from, too. Ryan was a blue-eyed, towheaded baby who loved to smile and laugh. He also loved to eat. Many a passerby at the local store would comment on Ryan not missing too many meals. His rolls had rolls. He was chubby and cute and a gift from God. Our lives were moving along as normally as could be until, at fifteen months old, our perfect little baby was diagnosed with a brain tumor.

Despite all our best efforts, which included multiple surgeries, chemotherapy, radiation, and even experimental therapies, our sweet, precious, four-year-old child lost his battle to cancer. Supported by family, friends, and hospice workers, Ryan passed away at home in the arms of his mother and father. It was so hard to believe this was the end. For three long years, I had been waiting for the other shoe to drop while at the same time hoping it never would. Now, my worst fear was a reality. I remember giving Ryan a kiss, the last kiss I would ever give my son.

Ryan's funeral was held on June 4, 2001. In many ways, it felt like that was the last day that so many people thought about him. It was his last big deal, his last birthday, his last Christmas, his last everything. Then, it was over. The phone calls stopped. So did the cards. No one really asked any more questions. Although John and I were able to talk about our happy memories of Ryan, it was way too difficult to share anything more than that. For a while, I attended a support group for people who had lost a child, but I still felt very much alone. I read a lot of books on grief to keep me sane. The ones I liked most were the books about a parent losing a child. Those parents understood my grief, and I understood their grief as well.

I eventually returned to work. One night after work, I found John and our second son, Jacob, already asleep. I sat in bed praying and talking to Ryan. I did this often after his death. It made me feel like he wasn't so far away. I remember saying, "Ryan, I wish I knew how you felt." After uttering those words, the most amazing thing happened. I couldn't believe it, but I actually heard a response! I heard the words *"I feel great!"* come from Ryan's bedroom. I was stunned. What had just happened? It took me a moment to figure out that Ryan's Sleep and Snore Ernie lying on the top shelf in his bedroom, a toy that had not uttered a word for two years, had just answered my question! Those words were part of Ernie's repertoire. I excitedly woke up my husband and described what I had heard. John listened and, just like I did, felt stunned and happy. Whatever the explanation, it doesn't really matter. It made *me* feel wonderful. It made *me* feel great.

Nine months after Ryan's death, I became pregnant with our third child. Fortunately, the birth of Noah brought a lot of healing. I started to feel happiness again. My baby reminded me of God's love. Five years later, we were blessed with another son, Nicholas, bringing more healing.

As for today, life has once again become humdrum. Yes, my humdrum is a little different than most. On every anniversary of Ryan's death, I keep myself very busy. Every year for his birthday our family goes to Chuck E. Cheese's, Ryan's favorite place, after a day of giving gifts to local charities. Every Christmas card has a picture of three little boys with the names of four inscribed. Every Christmas morning there is an empty stocking with Ryan's name on it. Every September there is a new conversation with a teacher about our family situation. Every so often someone asks, "How many children do you have?" and there is a pause.

Alison Roberto, wife of John and mother of Ryan, Jacob, Noah, and Nicholas, resides in Clovis, California. A substitute teacher, Alison enjoys helping in her sons' classrooms, being a team mom, and spending time with her family.

I'm Here

Bonnie Doane Moody

Our son David faced multiple medical challenges his entire life. Severe asthma, pain from neurofibromatosis, and frequent hospitalizations made his life an uphill battle. It was hard to watch him struggle to keep his head above water. At twenty-one years old, David wanted to live independently, and he tried renting a room in a neighboring town. We owned a large home, which we shared with our daughter, Cindy, her two children, and David's younger brother. My husband and I lived in a second-floor in-law apartment, with a metal gate at the top of the winding staircase to keep our dogs inside.

David visited us often, generally for a meal and conversation, which we enjoyed. Whenever he did, he usually surprised me by walking up behind me while I was busy concentrating on something else. I found his surprises unsettling, so I asked David not to do that anymore. I requested that he please just bang the metal gate and call out "I'm here!" whenever he arrived.

Shortly after that, our son went missing for three days. Worried sick, I was afraid he had taken his life. On a gut level, I sensed it because I knew that he had struggled so. Then, on the second night of the search, his sister, Cindy, had an unusual experience while driving home from work. Mysteriously, numerous bright lights surrounded her car in the darkness. With the largest light remaining on the driver's side, the lights, bigger than fireflies, danced alongside her as she drove. They disappeared as soon as she arrived home. Cindy hurried upstairs to our apartment to tell us that she felt her brother had died. She sensed that the large bright light had been David dancing with all the spirits. We were somewhat comforted by that thought. The police found his body the next day in the woods. Our hearts were broken. David had taken his own life. His note said that his declining health had become too much to bear. He even wrote his own obituary. He thanked us and assured us that we had been good parents.

A couple weeks later, my husband happened to be outside working on the yard. I was sitting alone in the apartment watching TV when I heard the metal gate bang. Then David's voice called out loud and clear, *"I'm here!"* I felt shocked, excited, and elated all at the same time. Our son was letting us know that he was okay. His struggle was over, and David was still with us. What incredible assurance he brought us that day. I still miss him, though, in the same way I signed all the cards that I wrote to him throughout the years: "Love you always, David."

Bonnie Doane Moody, wife, mother of four, grandmother of fourteen, and great-grandmother of two, has been married to her high school sweetheart, Richard, for fifty-two years. Happily retired in Texas together, they are thankful for the love received and patience learned from David.

FORGIVEN

Joe Goodspeed

There is comfort in weeping. Yet some people believe that people of faith should never weep, especially when someone dies. As a clergyman, I am viewed as a grief expert, and I am expected to maintain composure when dealing with situations such as the horrible death of one's child. However, I know from personal experience that there is great comfort in weeping. The death of my thirty-year-old son, Harry, moved me to tears, numbness, and disbelief. Even though I am a Methodist minister, I could not hold back my tears. I now know that two hurtful, divisive attitudes that I held in my heart for a decade made my heartache even greater.

The first divisive attitude started in the early '80s when Harry informed his mother, sister, and me that he was gay. I lost control of myself. I was as angry as could be, and I sent him packing. I literally kicked my son out of my home and told him to go live with his gay friends. Afterward, I cried privately. I could not let anyone see me weep or know that I had just made the worst mistake of my life. My pride prevented me from taking back anything I had said to my son. The second divisive attitude involved my reluctance to speak with him. For almost ten years, I barely even remember talking to Harry on the phone. Now I realize how truly unkind I was to my son.

I'll never forget the telephone call my wife and I received from Harry on the Monday after Easter of 1990. It changed my life. Harry told us that he had been hospitalized twice in the last month, and he had just been released. He had something to tell us, and he wanted to see us in the next few days. Fearing the worst, we drove to his apartment two days later.

The moment we saw Harry, his mother and I both knew something was dreadfully wrong. His skin was yellowish in color, and he was extremely thin, almost skin and bones. As we talked for a few minutes about small stuff, I could feel so much fear building up inside of me. Then, Harry told us he had been diagnosed with AIDS, otherwise known as acquired immune deficiency syndrome. This was the reason he had been hospitalized. My heart skipped a beat; I was horrified. My son was dying of AIDS.

Amidst my anguish, I told Harry that I loved him in spite of all the things I had said and done ten years prior. I was humbled, fearful, and full of regret. It took all the grit I could muster to speak those words. It was at that time that I realized the meaning of 1 John 4:18: "There is no fear in love, but perfect love casts out fear for fear has to do with punishment, and whoever fears has not reached in perfection." I put aside my fear of catching AIDS. In that moment, all I wanted to do was to take care of my son, to save him if possible, and to make up for the years he was away. I asked, "What do you need, Harry? What can we do for you?"

"I would like to come home and be with you and Mother," he replied.

"Good. That's what we want, too."

After his doctor's visit two days later, Harry came home to live with us. Our time together lasted almost three weeks. He felt sick all the time, and he suffered often with pain. Early one morning around 4:30, Harry was having difficulty breathing, and he was also in a great deal of pain. After giving him some medicine, we decided it was time to take him to the hospital, where he was admitted. The emergency room doctor helped ease his discomfort with stronger pain medication. Harry remained in the hospital for five more days.

Nighttime seemed to be the most difficult for him, so his mother, sister, and I would stay with him late into the night. We would talk about all the fun times we had had together and even about the hard times. Harry shared his feelings with us; he didn't want to die. All we could do was try to help him overcome his fears and to let him know that we loved him. One evening, he said, "Mom, Dad, I am sorry that I took this road. I only wish I could have taken a higher road and made something out of my life." How I wished I could turn back the hands of time; I, too, would have made a different choice.

One day while Harry was talking with his sister, he asked if she would pray with him. His sister agreed, and they prayed the Lord's Prayer together. Afterward, Harry told her that he was making a statement of faith to his Lord Jesus; he was sorry for having turned away from Him. They both cried a lot. Following one last night of struggle, my son, Harry, died. A few days later, we held a simple graveside service. Many of his friends were there, and many of my friends were there. I wept openly for my son. So did other family members and friends. From that moment on, all we could do was try to heal from this enormous loss in our lives.

For the next year, I found myself volunteering at a home for men diagnosed with AIDS. By sharing my journey with Harry, I was able to provide solace to these young men. We would often talk about Harry. Even though I still felt bad for the way I had treated him, at least I was able to offer some kindness to other individuals struggling with the same disease.

About a year after Harry's death, something strange happened to me. I was driving in my car one afternoon on the way to the hospital to see a church member. Suddenly I thought I heard someone talking to me, but I was alone in the car. The voice said, "I'm all right. Everything is fine with me." Instantly I recognized the voice. It was my son! *Harry was speaking to me!* Although I could not see him, I could definitely hear his voice. What an assurance! Complete peace filled my body and my mind.

Harry's words were soft and quiet. He did not mention anything about what I had said ten years earlier. All he said was that everything was fine, and he was okay. Any fear I had been holding on to instantly dissolved. I felt comforted and so encouraged. Harry was safe.

And not only was my son safe, but I felt my own redemption; just as the Psalmist had written in the Bible, I, too, had been forgiven. In my prayers, I give thanks to God for Harry and for the memorable experience of him speaking to me. Yet even today I would like to see my son again, hold him in my arms, and talk with him.

As I look back, I wish I had told Harry that I loved him instead of telling him to get out. Now, I would work hard at resolving those feelings of homophobia, which proved to be so divisive to our family. I would help my son so much more. Thank God that my son, Harry, forgave me. He told me so before he died. Perhaps if I had made a different choice, if I had done things differently, maybe Harry would be with us today. I have learned the hard way to be patient. I have learned to let God guide my actions rather than let myself be controlled by my fear and my emotions. I am forever grateful to God that my son, Harry, is still with me in spirit.

Joe Goodspeed is a retired United Methodist minister.

COINCIDENCES AND COOPERATION

Elissa Al-Chokhachy

I remember being deeply moved when a woman, Sarah, shared a heavy burden with me. Her life had been forever changed by the loss of a child in her care. While she was babysitting, the child had become entangled in a string that ended up around his neck, which took his life. For years upon years, she carried tremendous guilt and angst for the death of the sweet little boy, Antonio, whom she had come to love. How could she ever forgive herself for that moment of irresponsibility and the needless loss of this child's life? Would the parents and family ever forgive her for not properly supervising the child in her care?

This young woman had been raised in a Spiritualist tradition where messages and communication from spirit were commonly given during church services. Sarah assumed that she would hear from Antonio a lot, but she actually heard very little from him. One of the games they had played together was called "Coincidences and Cooperation," a silly game the two of them had made up. Although Sarah never described the game to me, she did share that after Antonio died, she would randomly see each of those words. They were the only signs that Sarah received until many years later, when one of her friends from church gave her a spirit message. Her friend saw a young boy in spirit who was very tired from carrying a large pack on his back. Sarah asked if the boy could possibly be Antonio. The friend replied, "All I know is that the little boy says the bag on his back is filled with your tears."

Was it just a coincidence that a boy on the other side had sent this message to her through a friend? Sarah believed it was Antonio letting her know it was time to let go of the heavy burden. Her sadness and remorse had been weighing them both down, and he was tired; it was time to forgive herself and move on. Although mistakes happen to the best of us, rarely do they have such life-altering ramifications. Yet Antonio had blessed Sarah with a rare gift of how to live the rest of her life. She could either continue to carry the burden and weigh Antonio down in the process, or she could help Antonio, forgive herself, and perhaps do something to help others.

Although Sarah could not bring Antonio back or change what happened that day, she could do something to help others on his behalf. She could turn the tragedy into a lesson to help teach children about the enormous responsibility they take into their hands whenever they agree to babysit someone's child. Babysitters need to pay attention and be aware of what the child or children are doing at every moment—a child's life could depend on it. In that way, Antonio and Sarah would be working together to help make the world a safer place for others.

From Your Heart to Mine

Patricia Cerrutti

⌐———⌐

Our middle son, Christopher, was easygoing, kind, and fun-loving. Because all three of our boys played football, basketball, baseball, and lacrosse, our lives were busy, hectic, and fun-filled. Chris, who was fifteen months older than his younger brother, Jerry, also loved the outdoors. He went to scout camp every summer, and on one occasion he even did a hundred-mile canoe trip in Maine with his fellow scouts.

Chris was a good listener, too. He had many friends, and his one-liners always kept everyone laughing. Even today, fifteen years later, his friends stop by to visit my husband and me, and we never get tired of hearing their Chris stories. Our son loved to joke around, even with me. Often when I would be cooking or hurrying somewhere, Chris would decide that I needed a hug. He would pick me up, hug me, and carry me around the downstairs of our home. Chris would say, "Mom, this hug is going to last you." How I miss those hugs.

Our son and his friend ran a landscaping business together. After working for twelve hours landscaping, he would come home for dinner and then leave for his second job on the weekends. Chris worked at a restaurant in order to save up money for a new truck. On March 26, 1995, Chris fell asleep on his way home from work less than two miles from our home. His car struck a tree. Although Chris was airlifted to Boston Medical Center, they could not save his life. His sudden death was impossible to comprehend.

Our family was devastated; our grief was overwhelming. However, we were surrounded by love from family, friends, neighbors, and church members. Somehow we kept going. One dear friend, Lorraine, called me every day. She would patiently listen to me cry and ramble on with all of my "if onlys": if only we had helped him buy a truck, if only he hadn't worked that night, if only his friend had picked him up that night instead... Other times Lorraine did the talking when it was just too hard for me to say anything. My two sisters also listened to all of my Chris stories, and they encouraged me to talk about him. My son Chris lived for twenty-two years; it felt as though it would take me at least another twenty-two to grieve his loss.

In my roles as wife and mother, I felt that it was important for me to move forward, and to help the other members of my saddened family do the same. It felt as though we were pieces of driftwood in the ocean; on some days we were aimlessly floating, while on other days we were crashing into the sand. I had no energy, and I wanted to stay in bed forever. I would beg God for help, saying, "Please, God, just get me out of this bed so I can make it through this day." So many raw emotions swirled with the suddenness of my son's death. I encouraged my children and husband to find purpose in their lives again. I returned to work the week after Chris died in order to set an example. Our son Chuck went back to work, and I insisted that our son Jerry return to college to finish his sophomore year. My husband, Pat, who had retired just before Chris died, also found a part-time job, which helped.

My husband and I joined a grief support group at the home of our neighbor Penny Wigglesworth. Five of us had lost a child. The group was wonderful because we could listen to and understand one another's pain. We shed many tears and told heartfelt stories together under the guidance of Reverend Patricia Long from Old North Church in Marblehead, Massachusetts. One day, as we were discussing the subject of letting go, it felt as if there were a knife inside of my heart. I told them that although I knew Chris was in heaven, I was still "holding on to his leg"; I just couldn't let him go. They understood my pain and tried to reassure me that someday I would be able to let go. Defiantly, I told them that I would never let him go. Although the group never formally discussed this again, I did in my conversations with God. I talked to God day and night. I prayed to Him, argued with Him, begged Him, and pounded on His shoulders to please give me my Chris back.

Several months into my grieving, I saw Chris in a dream. He was running up the stairs on an outdoor fire escape. Even though I ran after him, I couldn't catch him. Finally he stopped, turned around, and smiled his beautiful smile at me. Chris told me to please take care of Dad. I was hurt and disappointed that there were no kind words for me. However, from that time forward, I made sure to be gentler with my husband, Pat.

The second year after Christopher's death was much harder than the first. The denial was going away, and I now realized that God was not going to send Chris back; perhaps Chris didn't want to come back either. Also, most people assumed that I was better. My sleep pattern was still a mess; I would go to bed exhausted and wake up in the middle of the night thinking about Chris.

By this time, I had met several people outside my group who had also lost a child. Because this type of loss is difficult to bring up, I began thinking that we needed something to connect us and to identify us to one another. I discussed my idea with my neighbor Haviv Shaul, a jeweler. I told him how I felt Chris was our star, and gave him my idea about a bereavement necklace. With a little help from his wife, Haviv designed a beautiful openhearted pendant with a star hanging down inside; a blue sapphire stone on the star would represent the loss of a boy and a pink sapphire would be for a girl. He also designed a lapel pin for men. We named the pendant and the pin set "Loving Consolation." Loving consolation is what I want to give to other grieving parents and grandparents.

A year and a half after Chris died, our son Chuck married his sweetheart, Nora. It was a wonderful wedding, and it seemed we could be happy again. Things were changing, and life was moving on. But I was still hounding God because I couldn't let go of Chris. As I approached the third anniversary of his death, on the outside it appeared as if I was leading a normal life. However, in my heart I felt as though I had not healed at all.

I remember being at Mass the week before the third anniversary. I was talking to God and looking at the image of the Sacred Heart of Jesus, to whom I pray often. All of a sudden, in my prayers that day, I felt moved to say, "Okay, God, I'll let go of my son. You may have my Chris now, leg and all." Suddenly I was filled with joy! A strong, male inner voice spoke within and said, "He left your heart for My heart." I wanted to stand up and yell "Halleluiah!" I hurried home to tell all of my family and friends my wonderful news.

From that point on, although I still had sad days, I never went to that dark, empty place again. I now understand how depressed people feel, and I will always hold them in my prayers. I wish I could express how much joy I felt in my heart on the day that I heard those words: "He left your heart for My heart." I can only liken it to the birth of a child. The feeling was beyond happiness. Through all the pain and grief my family and I endured, I am still so happy to have had my son Chris. We still love our Chris, and we feel loved by him.

In 2000, my husband and I were blessed with our first grandchild, Julia, and three other grandchildren followed thereafter. Babies change everything. They bring such wonder, happiness, and love into our lives. All of our grandchildren have truly helped our family to heal.

Patricia Cerrutti and her husband, Pat, raised their three beautiful sons in Marblehead, Massachusetts. A retired town secretary who remains active in her church and the Penny Bear™ Company, Patricia enjoys caring for her four grandchildren and sharing Loving Consolation with grieving families.

MOMENTS OF GRACE

Betsy Walter

Miracles are happening all around us. I am not talking about the show-stopping, obvious miracles we sometimes hear about on the nightly news or morning talk shows. Rather, I am referring to the subtle experiences people often shrug off as mere coincidences or seemingly small events. Incidents that, when viewed in the right context and with a receptive mind, provide clarity and insight that enlighten our lives. I call these miracles *moments of grace.*

I became acutely aware of this type of miracle after the birth of our son, Vail. Our son was born with a terminal neurological disorder and lived for eighteen months. Although his life was short, his presence was tremendous, and he showered us with his wonder and glory every day of his life. This story describes three special moments of grace that my husband and I shared with our son. I refer to them as "Vail's ladybug explosion," "Vail's hot summer days in March," and "the pitter-patter of tiny feet."

From the moment Vail was born, my husband, Glen, and I instinctively realized he was different from the other babies in the nursery. I am not sure how we knew; we just did. The doctors initially and adamantly assured us that he was fine, ten toes and ten fingers, a healthy baby boy. Yet we just seemed to understand the truth, without really knowing it. The truth came three months later after receiving the results of a skin biopsy. Our precious baby Vail was born with GM1 gangliosidosis. The doctors predicted that he would live only a few years. He would suffer from seizures, blindness, and a long list of other complications. There would be no first step, no first day of kindergarten, no baseball tosses in the backyard with Dad, no first dance, and no happily ever after. It was a future that was difficult to comprehend.

However, armed with the love and support of family and friends, we learned to skillfully navigate around Vail's disorder and to concentrate our energy and attention on the beauty and grace of his life, truly celebrating each and every moment we shared together. As Dr. Crocker, one of Vail's specialists, poignantly explained at our first meeting, "This train is moving, and you can either choose to jump on and enjoy the ride or choose to stay behind and miss it." With his assistance and with the help of others, we wholeheartedly jumped aboard and never once looked back.

The first moment of grace we experienced is what I call Vail's ladybug explosion. It transpired on the day following his memorial service, yet the ladybugs (which I learned years later were actually Asian beetles) started arriving when our son was around ten months old. At that time, Vail's medical issues were becoming increasingly more complicated, and each day seemed to bring a new medical problem or ambulance ride to the hospital. After much consideration, my husband and I had reluctantly agreed to have twenty-one hours a day of home nursing care, a decision that was bittersweet. We desperately needed the help, and the nurses were wonderful, but their presence sometimes felt like an intrusion into what little peace we had with our son.

It was during this period in Vail's life that I started noticing the ladybugs in our upstairs bathroom. At first there were just a few, but later on, many more came. Oddly, the sight of the ladybugs gave me a degree of comfort and relief. Perhaps it was because I could faithfully rely on them to be there every morning at a time in my life when everything else felt unpredictable. As silly as it sounds, I looked forward to getting up in the morning and greeting the ladybugs that had claimed my bathroom for their home. I even began to watch over them, carefully cleaning around them and gently placing the dead ones in potted plants throughout the house.

The ladybugs graciously lived in our upstairs bathroom throughout Vail's life. Then, on the day following his memorial service, my husband and I had the immense pleasure of witnessing a ladybug explosion—Vail's ladybug explosion. I recall the moment so clearly. I walked outside and casually turned toward our house, and there it was: the ladybug explosion, with thousands and thousands of ladybugs adorning our house from top to bottom. At that instant I realized Vail was sending us a private message. He was communicating that he was okay—he was at peace. It was just as powerful as if he had walked right up to me, placed a tender kiss on my cheek, and said, "Mom, don't worry about me anymore. I am safe. I am free. No more struggling. No more pain."

Since then, I have learned that ladybug infestations are not uncommon and that most homeowners view this type of situation as a nuisance. Yet my husband and I experienced this moment as something grander, as something much more significant and compelling than just a ladybug infestation. That was twelve years ago, and I have never observed another ladybug infestation, and rarely do I notice ladybugs in my home anymore. If I do see them, they don't stick around for long.

I have also come to discover that many people deem ladybugs to symbolize protection and good luck. I like to believe that during Vail's life the ladybugs protected him and us; they shielded him from the scary battle waging in his small, fragile body and gave us the strength and courage to understand the splendor and magnitude of his life. Vail fought so hard and gave so much of himself. Although I can't deny the obviously tragic part of his story, we were also fortunate. Vail's life was a blessing and provided us with a type of wondrous joy that is nearly impossible to explain.

The second moment of grace, Vail's hot summer days in March, also occurred after he died. It revolved around an obsession I had developed when Vail was sixteen months old. At that juncture, he was physically very weak. He was heavily sedated with medication because it was the only way we could subdue the relentless seizures. He could no longer move his body by himself, and we turned him every four hours to prevent bedsores. He required constant oxygen to assist his labored breathing, and we performed chest physical therapy several times a day to prevent the onset of pneumonia. Vail could no longer manage to drink from a bottle, and we were tube feeding him. This was especially heartbreaking for me. Vail adored his bottles and feeding him brought both of us tremendous comfort. When I wasn't performing medically related tasks, I spent my time lying in bed with Vail, reading and singing to him and massaging his body.

It was during this difficult time that I became obsessed with wanting to take Vail outdoors. This idea consumed my thoughts for the last few months of his life. Before our son died, I desperately wanted him to feel a cool breeze against his checks, hear the playful sounds of nature, and feel the warmth of the sun shining on his face. Unfortunately, it was February in New England. The weather was especially cold and harsh, and Vail could not tolerate a visit outdoors. I began diligently hoping, wishing, and praying for warm weather.

As fate would have it, the weather did not cooperate, and Vail did not have the opportunity to go outside. In fact, we had a snowstorm the Sunday before he died. Vail passed away the following Tuesday, March 24, 1998. My husband and I were with our beautiful son when he died. Afterward, we carried his body to our bed and lay with him till morning, cradling and caressing him, repeatedly telling ourselves that he was in a better place.

Miraculously, we awoke to a brilliantly sunny and much warmer day. By the day of Vail's memorial service, it was a steamy ninety degrees. I know in my heart and soul that this was much more than a mere coincidence. My wish for Vail had been divinely answered. He was finally feeling the sun against his skin and loving it. Vail was truly dancing with the stars and skipping through the clouds on a hot summer day. I have never witnessed another ninety-degree day in March in New England.

The third moment of grace, the pitter-patter of tiny feet, occurred a few months later. Glen and I were lying in bed one night. It was late, and we were reading the local paper. Suddenly we heard the pitter-patter of tiny feet running up and down the hallway outside our bedroom. It was faint, but it was there. We looked at each other, confused and even a little frightened. I shot up from the bed and ran out to the hallway. No one was there. When I returned to our bedroom, both Glen and I were smiling, big triumphant smiles. We both *knew* it was Vail. There was no other explanation. Our son was watching over us and doing some of the things we had always wanted for him—being silly and running carefree and playfully in our hallway. I'm sure he was also checking in on his newborn baby brother, who lay sleeping in the crib next to our bed. I quietly laughed to myself. Do I tell him to slow down, that there is no running in the house? Not on your life.

As I reflect on this moment, I believe Vail was asking us to remember him as the playful and spirited boy he was, even though his body was not accommodating. He was asking us not to be sad for him, but rather to honor his life as one that brought happiness to many people. Above all, he was reminding us to cherish the precious moments we shared together and to carry his love with us, always and forever. I can't imagine how I would have endured that time in our lives twelve years ago without the loving support of my inspirational husband, our families, and all those who helped along the way.

We now have a second incredible son. His name is Cameron Vail. He was conceived when Vail was ten months old. My grand scheme was for Vail to meet his new sibling before he died. However, as I have come to discover, plans don't always unfold as we envision. Vail died a month before Cameron was born. I don't recall much regarding Cameron's birth, other than I could not feel my emotions. I remember lying on the birthing table conceptually understanding that I was excited about the birth of our second son and deeply saddened about the loss of Vail but actually feeling neither emotion; I was emotionally numb. It was a strange state of being.

Cameron was born kicking and screaming, and he has not let up yet. I mean that in a very loving and positive way. Although we didn't know it at the time, he was our savior, so to speak. He jumpstarted our healing process and never let it wander too far off course. I remember the first night in the hospital room after Cameron was born, listening to his endless crying and wondering if he would ever stop. My numbness quickly disappeared. My new job had arrived, and he was waiting. For sure, Cameron was letting us know that he was here and ready for life, with all its beauty and opportunities. He is still that way today, bigger than life in some ways, embracing it, always smiling and always eager to greet whatever is around the corner. Both of our sons, Vail and Cameron, have brought us tremendous joy!

Betsy Walter, Esq., and her husband, Glen, would like to offer their heartfelt gratitude to their parents, Betsy's brothers, Elissa Al-Chokhachy, Dr. Allen Crocker, and Dr. Harry Somers. She dedicates her story to the many remarkable people who participated in Vail's journey.

3

Smells

SMELLS TRANSPORT US THROUGH time and space to memories long gone by. In an instant, they are able to bring us right back to times once shared together. We associate certain smells with particular people, places, and events. Think about someone special in your life. Was there ever an aroma you associated with that person? For instance, the smell of baby shampoo may remind you of childhood memories of your children and grandchildren. The fragrance of a loved one's cologne or perfume may instantly bring back memories of that person. Perhaps your grandmother loved to bake cookies, and every time you inhale their delicious aroma, wherever you are, it reminds you of memorable family times together. Smells can serve as a meaningful connection between past and present—a bridge to times gone by.

Aromas are also linked to specific places. For instance, if you love the beach and often spent time there with someone, the smell of an ocean breeze could easily evoke those memories. But sometimes, after a loved one dies, bereaved family members are surprised when they unexpectedly smell a familiar scent associated with that loved one. There is no plausible explanation for how it got there, yet the clearly recognizable aroma is a gift. Not only does it bring back memories of their relationship, it lets them know they are never alone.

Within this chapter are five stories with examples of how smell is one of many vehicles used by spirit to reach out from beyond. Aromas have the ability to ignite emotional responses and memories. Through the gift of smell, those in spirit offer hope and reassurance that physical death can never separate the love that binds.

TOGETHER

Jeannette Lupoli

My husband, Nicholas Lupoli, was a large, independent, and proud Italian man. We had been married for thirty-nine years when he died in 2003 from complications following open-heart valve replacement surgery. I still miss Nicky a lot. Although spending time with our kids and grandkids is comforting, the thing that helps the most is the way my husband continues to let me know he is still nearby.

Nicky loved wearing all kinds of cologne. Although his favorite cologne was Jafra, I always purchased different brands for him to try whenever I went shopping. The week after he died, I packed up all of his colognes to give to our sons because I just couldn't have them in the house any longer. I stopped by my daughter-in-law Kati's home and left some Jafra in a bag on her couch. Then the two of us went out to lunch. When we returned, the house reeked of Jafra. It smelled as if someone had sprayed the entire bottle all over her home. I apologized, thinking perhaps a loose bottle cap had allowed the cologne to spill on her couch. But when we checked, all the bottles were tightly sealed. None of the cologne had leaked out, and nobody had been inside her home, since all of her kids were in school. We both knew it had to be Nicky letting us know he was there.

A week later, I had just walked out of our bedroom one morning when I saw my husband standing there in the hallway. He was wearing a beautiful brown suit, the same one he had worn at his goddaughter's college graduation a month before he died. I was ecstatic. I remember thinking, "Why is he wearing a brown suit? We buried him in a blue one." Nicky looked great! He was happy, healthy, and smiling. Without thinking, I said, "Oh, you're back. Do you want something to eat?" Nicky laughed and gave me a big smile. Then the vision faded, and in a moment he was gone. Although his visits are always brief, my husband has appeared to me several times since then.

Four years after Nicky died, our forty-five-year-old son, Jimmy, who had been living with chronic lymphocytic leukemia, became quite ill with a perforated bowel. Although he had surgery to correct the problem, he still had abdominal pain afterward. The doctors thought perhaps he might have gallstones, so they ordered a CAT scan. However, an allergic reaction to the dye resulted in Jimmy developing kidney failure and being placed on life support. After his father died, Jimmy had made me promise that I would "pull the plug" if he ever had to be hooked up to tubes to live. I told him I wasn't sure I could do that. He said, "Well then, Ma, just wake me up, and I'll pull my own plug." As difficult as it was, when the time came, I made that decision because I knew it was what Jimmy wanted; I knew he wouldn't want to live like that any longer.

The week after Jimmy died, I decided to return all of his leftover cologne to his girlfriend, Carol. Jimmy loved all kinds of cologne, and I thought Carol would like having them. I needed to return them just as I had with my husband's cologne to help me move through my grief. When I did, all of a sudden Carol and I both strongly smelled one of the colognes that Jimmy had worn. We quickly checked the bottles in the bag, but everything was closed and nothing had spilled. Just like his dad, Jimmy was letting us know he was there.

After that, Jimmy started visiting me at night. I would occasionally wake up to see him standing at the foot of my bed. At first he came alone, and boy, he looked great! Always dressed in black pants, a white open-collared shirt, and a black leather jacket, he would give me the biggest grin.

Nowadays, both Jimmy and his dad visit me together. I wake up in the night to see the two of them standing at the foot of my bed. Jimmy is always standing on the left in his black outfit, and his father, Nicky, is on the right in his brown suit. Although they never speak, they are always smiling. The last time I saw the two of them was about six months ago, after returning from an extended vacation in Hawaii. I had moved back to the old homestead where Nicky and I had raised our kids. Excitedly I said, "Hey, guys, how are you doing?" They just smiled and then disappeared.

Whenever I see the two of them, I'm happy in one way because I know they are well. They look healthy and happy, and they are together. In another way I'm sad because they are gone. But I know that if they can come to visit me here, then there has to be something else on the other side. That means all of us will be together again.

Jeannette Lupoli, a semi-retired credit manager, is the mother of six sons and seventeen grandchildren. Jeannette enjoys swimming, traveling, and crocheting, but mostly she loves spending time with her family.

Signs from Brandon

Kimberly Marino

For years, my husband and I had vacationed with my parents in their Florida condo where they spend the winter months. However, the week we spent with them in March of 1998 was quite a bit different. While we were there, Joe and I discovered that I was pregnant. All of us were so excited. We celebrated the news that our first child and my parents' first grandbaby was on the way.

I had a perfect pregnancy, with no morning sickness. Overall, I felt great and continued working full-time. Although my labor started two weeks late, everything seemed to be going along smoothly. When Joe and I finally arrived at the hospital, we were anxiously looking forward to becoming parents.

Other than an occasional dip in the baby's heart rate, labor seemed to be going pretty well. An epidural was effective. I wasn't feeling the contractions at all. As the hours went by, we became more and more excited. It was real. We were going to have a baby. Since we probably had a long night ahead of us, I encouraged Joe to go down to the cafeteria to get something to eat.

Fifteen minutes later, the obstetrician came into my room and ordered intravenous Pitocin to help speed up the contractions. At that time, the nurse reported that I had a fever. An antibiotic was given to treat a probable infection. Within minutes, I started vomiting. The nurse had trouble getting a good read on the baby's heart rate. Also, my body began to feel weak and limp. I felt as if I was drifting further and further away.

When Joe returned from dinner, he had no idea how sick I had become and that I was moving into a semiconscious state. At that point, Joe noticed that my body was covered with hives, and there was a red line going down the middle of my back. He ran to the nurses' station for help. The anesthesiologist arrived momentarily to administer Benadryl intravenously to treat an apparent allergic reaction. My blood pressure was 63/47 and dropping quickly.

An emergency Caesarean section was ordered. Joe was told that I was in critical condition. My vision was blurry, and I was losing consciousness. I had no control over my body. During the delivery, Joe held my hand; he never let it go. When our son was born at 6:08 PM on December 9, 1998, he wasn't breathing. Our baby never cried. He was put on life support and transferred to the neonatal intensive care unit (NICU). We hadn't even given him a name.

I believed that our son would be off the breathing machine in the morning and that everything would be all right, so I wouldn't let Joe disclose any of the details surrounding his birth. At 7:30 PM, my husband called my parents and told them, "Kim had a baby boy, and mom and baby are doing just fine." Neither of us had any idea how sick our son really was.

A few hours later when I first saw our baby in the NICU, he was in an incubator lying on lamb's wool. Even with the electrodes attached to his head, he looked so peaceful. Because he had so many tubes, I wasn't allowed to hold him, but I did touch him gently over and over. His skin was *so* soft. Our son was beautiful in *every* way!

When we got back to our room, it was midnight. Joe stayed with me and was able to sleep. I dozed lightly off and on. Around 4:00 AM, I was awake, pacing the floor and anxious. After checking with the NICU nurse, who reassured me that our son was resting peacefully, I returned to my room feeling relieved. Our baby was doing fine, and I had not unnecessarily worried my parents.

Sometime after that, our son took a turn for the worse. He began having seizures. Even though I was still in denial about the seriousness of what was going on, Joe insisted that I call my parents. When I did, my mom fainted. The news was too hard to take. I cried a lot. My body was in shock. Numb, I sat in the darkened hospital room and wept until my parents arrived. It was difficult for them to see their first grandchild on a respirator. Shortly thereafter, Joe and I named him Brandon Christopher.

Our families accompanied us to the quality-of-life meeting held at 4:00 PM. The chief physician of newborn medicine explained to us that our son was very sick as a result of not having enough oxygen due to the drop in my blood pressure during labor. Lack of oxygen caused the seizures. Because of the seizures, Brandon no longer had any brain activity or kidney function. For this reason, we came to a mutual decision that when the time came, life support would be removed.

At 5:00 PM, the nurse wheeled me back to my room. I was emotionally distraught and felt as if my whole world was falling apart. Joe was so angry with God. None of the hospital staff came to comfort us, even though they knew that our baby was critically ill. A well-meaning staff member had taped a note to my door that read, "Please do not come in." Longing to hold my baby, I felt so isolated and abandoned.

Once Brandon's condition worsened, the hospital chaplain baptized him. Shortly after that, Brandon was moved to his own special room so we could have privacy. With the assistance of the NICU staff and while Brandon was still on life support, Joe and I were able to give our newborn son a sponge bath. Following his bath, the nurse handed Brandon to me. Together, Joe and I held him and rocked him. Joe told Brandon how much we loved him. He would always be our son, and he should always listen for our voices. When our son's color worsened, he was taken off the breathing machine. Brandon took three little breaths, and he died in our arms. It was 8:00 AM on December 11.

We called our families to tell them that Brandon had passed away. Our parents came to the hospital to say their goodbyes. We all took turns holding Brandon, and we took lots of pictures. That day was the first and last time I held my son.

It was an overcast, gloomy, dreary day. I remember looking out the window to my right. The sun had just burst through the clouds, and it had started to snow. It was a brisk snow, fast and rapid, with numerous snowflakes, white and crisp. Even though it was snowing heavily, the sun continued to shine. I started to cry. I knew my son was being lifted up to heaven in that moment. I looked at Mom and said, "Brandon just went to heaven... because the angels just came and took him." Five minutes later, the snow stopped. It didn't snow any more that day. That was the first snow of the year.

Local support groups were helpful. I met a lot of wonderful parents who shared their stories with me in my time of sadness. We all cried together. It helped immensely to know that I was not the only mother in the world suffering from the loss of a child. Several months later, in May of 1999, Joe and I found out that I was expecting for the second time. Despite our joy, it was difficult being pregnant again.

On January 12, 2000, our second son, Robert, was delivered at a different hospital. The next morning, the first snowflakes of the year fell. It was the same crisp, white snow that fell for Brandon. It snowed and it snowed and it snowed. The more it snowed, the more reassured I felt that Brandon was with us on that day. With very few visitors, I was able to spend lots of time with my new little baby boy. Robert has been such a joy.

I have felt Brandon around me in several ways. Sometimes I feel his presence close to me. Initially I smelled him a lot, the same baby smell he had in the hospital. Over time, the smell faded away, but there have been lots of other signs that have let me know that Brandon is still in my life.

I had never owned a Beanie Baby, not even one. The month after Brandon died, I was at the shopping mall with Joe. I noticed an angel bear Beanie Baby. It was white, the color of snow. Even though the store was sold out of that particular bear, it reminded me of Brandon. If I wanted to own the angel bear Beanie Baby, I would need to return to the store on Monday morning and stand in line to purchase it. My friends and family thought I was crazy, but I didn't care. I woke up at 5:00 AM, showered, got dressed, and went outside. It was snowing! I knew Brandon was letting me know to go ahead and get the Beanie Baby, the white Beanie Baby, the same color as the snow. I was so excited to feel Brandon's presence! He was definitely there helping me on that day.

Brandon sends clear signs to let me know he's around, like when I sold my car. For twelve years I had owned a 1988 white Mercury Cougar, which was in mint condition. I placed an ad in the paper and easily sold it to a lady who responded to the ad. Over the phone, the lady told me that she was looking for an automobile for her sixteen-year-old son. He was getting his license and needed a car. They had been looking for some time, and for some reason, they couldn't seem to find the right car. When the lady came to look at my Cougar, she immediately said, "I know Brandon will just *love* this car." Even though Brandon is a popular name nowadays, it wasn't popular back then when she named her son. The lady bought the car on the spot. It made me so happy to know that "a Brandon" was going to be driving my car. She was the one and only person who answered my ad.

Signs from Brandon inevitably come on the days I need them the most. The last one happened after attending a birthday party with Robert. He came home with a large silver Mylar balloon with the words "Happy Birthday" printed on it. When we arrived home, Robert informed me that he wanted to send the balloon to his brother in heaven. It was dark and rainy, so I suggested that it would be much better to send the balloon in the morning. Six-year-old Robert was not going to take no for an answer. Not only did he want to send the balloon up to his brother that night, but he insisted that we send

Brandon his picture as well. I finally gave in after realizing that I was not going to win the argument.

We tied a photo of Robert onto the balloon and released it. Sure enough, as soon he let go of the string, the balloon flew right up into one of the trees and got stuck in our front yard! Disappointed, I explained that Brandon must have wanted it that way. Robert seemed satisfied with our efforts. The two of us went inside the house and off to bed shortly thereafter.

When Robert and I awoke the next morning, to our surprise the balloon was gone! It was nowhere in sight. We drove around the neighborhood, combed the streets, and looked everywhere without any success. Finally, I explained to Robert that the heavy rains and blistering winds must have taken his balloon up to heaven.

"Oh no, Mommy," Robert said. "I made a wish."

"What did you wish for, Robert?"

Very confidently he replied, "I told Brandon to send the balloon back to us when he's finished." I really didn't know what to say. Five days later, the two of us awoke to a bright, sunny day. I opened my kitchen blinds, and straight in front of me was Robert's balloon! It was wrapped up inside the tree in front of our house. I couldn't believe what I was seeing! There it was, still inflated, waving its Happy Birthday message from high up in the tree. Robert's picture was no longer attached, but I knew somehow Brandon was sending us a message.

As it happened, our house was on the market. On that same day, the day that Robert's balloon was returned to us, I received a deposit on our home, and it sold! Now I know the return of the balloon was Brandon's way of letting Robert and me know that it was okay for us to move on. He will always be with us wherever we go. Robert and I feel blessed to have Brandon in our lives.

It has been thirteen years since Brandon died. So much has happened in my life and in Robert's. I am now a single mom. My heart still aches for Brandon, but I am continuing to heal. I am so happy that my son continues to send Robert and me signs of hope, letting us know that he is near. Thank you, Brandon. We love you, too.

Kimberly Marino, mother of Brandon and Robert, is a certified radiologic technologist employed in a pediatric office providing services to children in need. Kim is grateful for the blessing of her wonderful sons and the loving support she receives from her family.

JUST BELIEVE

Andrea Godwin

My grandson Dylan James Manning was born on Thanksgiving Day of 2001. He was our first grandchild. My daughter, Sherri, her husband, Brian, and our whole family were so thankful for the blessing of Dylan. Because his parents had suffered three miscarriages, this beautiful brown-haired little boy with gorgeous blue eyes brought so much joy and healing to our family.

I am a daycare provider, and I come from a large family. I have always been around young children. Early on, I began noticing that Dylan, also known as DJ, did not seem to be hitting the developmental milestones for his age. Because he had arrived four weeks early, we all attributed his slower development to his premature birth. We worked extra hard with Dylan to see signs of improvement. But instead of progress, he began to regress. For instance, even though he was able to play patty cake, he started to slump over whenever he was sitting. His parents asked the doctor to order an MRI for further testing.

After many consultations with several pediatricians and specialists, Dylan was initially diagnosed with mild cerebral palsy, which is not a progressive disorder. It was heartbreaking news, but at least there was hope. We were told that by the time Dylan reached kindergarten, no one would realize that he struggled with developmental delays. Physical therapy was prescribed, and we enrolled my grandson in early intervention. Unfortunately, the exercise did not improve his strength; it only seemed to wear him out more.

Sherri noticed that Dylan was no longer making eye contact with her and was not interested in watching television like most other kids. He also didn't seem to be able to reach for his toys anymore. Sherri made an appointment to have Dylan's eyes checked with an

ophthalmologist, who immediately referred him to a retinal specialist for evaluation. The specialist told Sherri and Brian that it looked
like Tay-Sachs disease, a metabolic disorder that causes fatty deposits
on the brain. However, because of Dylan's heritage, the doctors were
uncertain if the diagnosis was accurate. Sherri and Brian requested
that the specialist write down the name of the disease for them, and
then they left with Dylan, relieved that their prayers for a diagnosis
had been answered. As far as they understood, their son lacked energy
and needed proper nourishment to move his muscles. All they had
to do was remove the fat storage around his brain. This made total
sense. At least they were finally making progress and getting answers.
Now all they needed to know was how to fix it.

Later that day while at my daycare, Sherri took time to research
online how she could help her son. Suddenly she began sobbing
uncontrollably, and I ran upstairs to help. Trembling and unable to
speak, my daughter pointed to the Tay-Sachs resource page on the
computer. Infantile Tay-Sachs disease is a terminal disorder that
causes deafness, blindness, paralysis, nonresponsiveness to the environment, and death before the age of five. There is no treatment and
no cure. I felt like someone had just stabbed me in the heart. But I
also knew that I had to remain strong in order to protect Sherri and
my grandchild. I assured her that we would find a way; this could not
be true. It felt like a bad dream.

My husband and I packed up a few things and spent the night
with Dylan and his parents. I began making phone calls to family
and friends to break the devastating news. Knowing Dylan's life was
now limited, we all began to live life a lot differently. Living one day
at a time, we cherished every second we had with him. One week
later, a blood test confirmed his diagnosis. Dylan had Tay-Sachs disease. He was only seventeen months old. Our world was falling apart.

I'm not sure how we made it through the initial shock of the news
and the difficult years that followed. My husband, Dylan's Pappy,

spent sleepless nights trying to contact doctors and scientists from around the world to help his grandson overcome this incurable disease. Our family and friends banded together to provide the love and support that was needed. Parents from my daycare quickly came to our aid by establishing a fund in Dylan's name; they wanted Sherri to be able to enjoy every minute with Dylan without having to worry about bills or go to work. That fund was the beginning of the nonprofit organization known as DJ's Foundation for Tay-Sachs Disease. It continues to this day. Our family can never begin to express our gratitude for the tireless efforts and ongoing generosity of so many.

I'll never forget the day the hospice nurse told us that Dylan would be leaving us in a few short weeks. It was important for us to tell him that he had our permission to let go. Even though we'd had three years to prepare for Dylan's death, how could *we* possibly let go of this precious child? When it was my turn to have special time alone with him, as hard as it was, I had to give my grandson permission to end his suffering. Even though I still wanted to hold him in my arms, I knew it wasn't right to want to keep Dylan here. Tearfully I said, "Go to God, Dylan, where you will be free of this icky disease and where you will finally be able to do all the things your short life has denied you. When you go, please send me a sign to let me know you are okay." I reassured Dylan that we would have the strength to go on without him, and I asked him for the sign of a yellow and black butterfly. I knew the butterfly would represent his life on earth and in heaven.

As I watched him battle for every breath, I struggled to make sense of it all. I related Dylan's life on earth to that of a butterfly. Just as the caterpillar moves very slowly, so did Dylan as he slipped further into the grips of this devastating disease. My grandson eventually became totally paralyzed, unable to move at all, similar to the caterpillar enclosed in the chrysalis. I knew that once he took his last breath, his outer shell would be gone. Yet Dylan would be transformed, just like the butterfly who escapes from the chrysalis with beautiful wings to fly.

On one of the last days of Dylan's life, I happened to be sitting outside on Sherri's front porch. While I was talking on the phone, a yellow and black butterfly flew right up to my face and fluttered around me in a circle. "Oh my gosh," I said jokingly, "I'm being attacked by a butterfly!" It was then that I realized Dylan was already letting go, and he wanted to give me a sign that he was going to a better place.

That same yellow and black butterfly seemed to hang around Dylan's yard that summer. One day, just as I walked out the back door, something large and black flew right past my head. At first I thought it was a bird that had almost touched me, but it was actually a big black butterfly. From then on until the time that Dylan died, the yellow and black butterfly would always be seen with the black one, floating around the yard. No matter how many times friends and relatives who came to visit Dylan tried to photograph these butterflies, the elusive duo were able to escape the photographic moment by flying away just in the nick of time.

Following a memorable sunrise walk with his mother, father, and his Pappy, Dylan passed away. His spirit was gone, and it was time to relinquish his body. I kissed my precious grandson one final time, and then I walked outside onto the back deck. When I did, a yellow and black butterfly flew right past Pappy and my son to the deck where I was sitting with my daughter-in-law. This time, the butterfly allowed me to walk up, get close to it, snap its picture, and even pick it up in my hands. When I asked my daughter-in-law to take a picture of me releasing the butterfly, it managed to fly away just before she snapped the picture. I told her not to worry—Dylan was letting us know that he just wanted to be free.

The butterfly signs continued. The following morning, my husband and I took our other grandson, Kenny, out for breakfast. Just before I walked into the restaurant, a yellow and black butterfly flew right up to me, touched my cheek, and then flew away. I knew it was a kiss sent from Dylan and that he had made it to heaven. My grandson always seemed to know when those butterfly kisses were needed most. Butterflies accompanied us as we entered the funeral home for his service and afterward at the cemetery. Even my two-year-old grandson Brady (Dylan's brother) said to me while sitting together in a church pew, "Look, Nanny...butterfly!" He pointed, but I couldn't see anything. Then, afterward, he asked sadly, "Where butterfly go, Nanny?" I knew Dylan was right there with us.

Four and a half months after Dylan passed away, my son, Ken, and his wife, Crystal, received the devastating news that the little baby boy they were expecting would be stillborn. As I sat in the waiting room during the delivery, I prayed to Dylan to please be there for his little cousin, Charles James. In an effort to pass the time, I picked up a book called *The Guidepost* from the table next to me. The book automatically opened to a postcard with a picture of two open hands releasing a butterfly. The words on the postcard read: "The Miracle of Healing." I knew it was a confirmation that God had heard my prayers; Dylan had received my message, and his little cousin would soon learn the ropes in heaven.

DJ's Foundation began to carry the motto "Just Believe...Just Believe in Life, Just Believe in Miracles, Just Believe in a Cure." Even though Dylan is gone, we *just believe* that he is in a better place, somewhere much more beautiful than we could ever have imagined. My daughter relates her life to that of the Pieta representation of the Blessed Mother holding her lifeless son in her arms. Even though a miracle was possible, God had other plans for her son.

Dylan had a very special five-year-old friend, Michaleigh, from my daycare, who absolutely adored him. Whenever Dylan visited Nanny's daycare, Michaleigh would lovingly care for my grandson. As his disease progressed and he was no longer able to go to Nanny's daycare, his little friend would visit him at his home. The last time Michaleigh visited Dylan, my friend Wanda was applying aromatherapy to his body. Using the raindrop technique, she utilized a combination of natural oils to relax his body. On that day, I invited Michaleigh to rub "Believe Oil" on Dylan's feet. With encouragement, Michaleigh reluctantly said, "You can go to heaven now, Dylan, but I will miss you." A few days later, my little grandson went to heaven.

Several days after Dylan's death, Michaleigh and her brother, Michael, were playing at their house. Suddenly they came running to their mother. They told her that Dylan had come to visit them, and he was in their bedroom. They all ran back to see. As soon as they entered the room, the strong and distinct aroma of Believe Oil filled the air! They knew the aroma was a sign from our little angel, Dylan, letting them know that he was watching over them. Also, just like I do, Michaleigh looks for butterflies from her friend, too.

Dylan was taken away from us far too soon, but we believe that he made a difference in the lives of so many and continues to do so through DJ's Foundation. His mission was completed far sooner than we ever would have imagined. Dylan took his last breath during a soothing tub bath while in his mommy's arms and with his daddy right beside them. As his parents gazed down with shock and anguish at his lifeless body, he gave them a smile that would last them an eternity. This is what allows them to go on, knowing he met God at that very moment. Right above Dylan was a photo of him in angel wings and a halo. On the opposite wall, a sign read: "Every time a bell rings, an angel gets their wings." Just then, the telephone rang. We *just believe* that our little angel is smiling down on us from heaven, sliding down rainbows and full of life again!

Andrea Godwin, wife, mother, and grandmother, is a daycare provider, which gives Andrea the opportunity to include her grandchildren. It's a joy beyond compare! Her love for children led her to become a nanny for a wonderful family with two boys.

The Light of My Life

Krysta O'Neill

When I first found out I was pregnant, I was excited, anxious, and stunned all at the same time. Although mostly thrilled, I was nervous about being able to give this little child the very best that life has to offer. My pregnancy went well, with its share of good days and bad days. However, a week before my due date, a routine ultrasound revealed that the amniotic fluid around my baby was low. My obstetrician hospitalized me that afternoon to induce labor. Shortly after the Pitocin started, my baby wasn't responding well, so I was prepped for an emergency Caesarean section. At 4:29 AM, they announced it was a boy. I was ecstatic!

All of a sudden, I realized I couldn't hear him crying. I called out, "Why isn't my baby crying? What's wrong?" No one answered. I suddenly felt nauseous, not knowing what was happening. Four doctors and nurses hovered over my son, working feverishly while I lay helpless. Brett was their primary concern, and rightly so. When they whisked him out of the room, I yelled to my husband and siblings repeatedly, "Go with him! Just go with him!" I had not yet seen my son.

As I anxiously waited to find out what was wrong, my sister and brother tried to reassure me. The neonatologist told me that Brett was very sick. I didn't know what that meant. Maybe he just had a bad cold. The nurse told me that my son had a pointy chin, cupped ears, rocker bottom feet, one ear bent a little, and a heart-shaped face. Then the doctor informed me that although the test results were still pending, Brett needed to be rushed by ambulance to Children's Hospital. "Then, please!" I pleaded. "I have to go with him!" I started removing my own IVs out of desperation. Fortunately, the doctor, sensing my intense despair, ordered another ambulance for me.

Just before I left, my obstetrician called. The consensus of all the doctors involved was that Brett probably had polycystic kidney disease, which was not compatible with life. I'll never forget those words: *not compatible with life!* How could my son have a terminal illness? He had had a perfectly normal ultrasound at twenty weeks. Yet the disease didn't manifest itself until thirty-two weeks. The doctor also said that Brett's belly was slightly enlarged, he had a hernia, and his heart was higher than it should have been. Sadly, my baby was dying.

As soon as my ambulance arrived at Children's Hospital, my stretcher was quickly wheeled to the pediatric intensive care unit to join my son. With my gurney positioned right next to his bed, I saw Brett and touched my son for the very first time. Brett was the most beautiful baby I had ever laid eyes on. Even with his respirator, my son was gorgeous! He was perfect. His bald head boasted a little blond peach fuzz. Brett weighed 8 pounds and 2 ounces.

I remember praying every second that I could. If there was one miracle I could have in my life, *please let this be it.* Even if I had to live in a cardboard box, *please just let him be here.* I would have gladly cut off my left leg if it would have helped. If only there was something I could have done to save my son.

The tubes prevented me from being able to cradle Brett in my arms, so I frequently touched him and caressed his hands and feet. Knowing I yearned to hold him, the nurses and doctors picked Brett up for a few minutes, tubes and all, and placed him on top of my chest while the doctor used the portable ambu bag to help him breathe.

Brett's Bimpy lay next to him along with a set of silver rosary beads from my sister-in-law, Kelli, which her grandmother had purchased in Portugal. I returned them to her after Brett died only to discover that nine months later, the silver color of the beads had miraculously changed to gold. The priest informed us that this was a sign from

God that our loved one was with Him. He went on to tell us that whoever owns the beads is very special, deeply religious, and must regularly recite the rosary, which Kelli did.

Father McCarthy led a formal baptism with our family and friends in the critical care unit. Afterward, he privately encouraged us to let Brett know that it was okay to go. Can you imagine telling your sweet little baby that it's okay to die? I did. But as his mother, I felt horribly guilty. It was the hardest thing I ever had to say. But I had to do it for Brett. He had no chance of survival.

Shortly thereafter, Brett passed away. He had lived for thirty-six hours. Brett was such a little fighter, and he tried so hard to stay. Once all the tubes were disconnected, the nurses offered me an opportunity to hold him. If I did, I knew in my heart I would grab Brett and run as far as I could; I would never let him go. As much as I desperately wanted to hold my son, giving him back one last time was something I just couldn't bear. Even though his father held him, I couldn't. I will never be confident that I made the right decision, but that was how I felt at the time.

Suddenly, after Brett's passing, I felt an urgency to get out of the hospital. The place that we had hoped would save my son now had become the place where he had died. Physically exhausted and emotionally in shock, my family and I left the hospital after home care had been arranged for me.

The next difficult task was planning Brett's funeral. Thanks to the incredible support from family members, all I needed to do was pick out his outfit and flowers. On the morning of his wake, I composed a poem for Brett in a matter of minutes. I am convinced my son helped me to write it. That poem is inscribed on his teddy-bear headstone at the cemetery.

Brett died from recessive autosomal polycystic kidney disease. I wrote to him almost every day in my journal, as I did while I was pregnant. Three months after he died, I awoke from the most detailed, vivid dream I have ever had. I jumped out of bed, pulled out my journal, and began writing so I could remember every piece of it.

Dear Brett,

I just awoke from the most fantastic dream only to learn that it was a complete nightmare. You were alive in the dream, but we knew you were sick and wouldn't be with us for very long. For some reason, you could talk, and you looked like an infant with the abilities of a three-year-old child. The vividness of this dream was so beautiful. Here's what I remember:

We were at Auntie Denise and Uncle Eric's house. I was holding you as I sat on the broken stool in the kitchen. Everyone was there. I went outside to take some pictures, because I knew we needed more pictures of you. I wish I had more pictures of you now. There was a beach, and we were in the water. I was snapping as many pictures of you as I could. Afterward, the water got wavy and splashed onto your face, which caused you to spit up. I took you out of the water and said, "Let's go brush your teeth since you just spit up." I could smell the spit-up so clearly, as if it were really there. We walked back to the house on the back deck, which now was our house. I sat down on the stairs and started singing "Rock-a-bye Baby." When I finished singing the song, you looked up and said, "Please don't sing anymore because you won't be able to sing to me again. Where I'm going to, you won't be able to sing to me, and it makes me sad."

I immediately woke up from the dream, which at that point was more like a nightmare. I was wailing. I just couldn't stop crying because I could *feel* you. I could *see* you. And I could *smell* you as if you were right there. It was just so quick and fluttering. I remember thinking all during that dream that as long as I didn't put you down to sleep, you'd be with me forever. When I woke up, it was like losing you all over again, except now, at least I have the memories of the dream. Brett, I wish I could hold you and rock you and sing to you. For the rest of my life, I would never put you down. My dear sweet, precious little boy, please watch over our family, and please help us to get to a place of peace and acceptance. I miss you more than you'll ever know.

With all my love for eternity,
Mom

The dream was spectacular. It was a few extra minutes that I had with my son. The feeling was just indescribable. Sitting on the back steps and rocking Brett was the most beautiful memory because I never got to cradle him next to my heart in the hospital, which was one of the hardest things of all.

I could smell Brett's baby smell for weeks after he died, and I can still tap into that smell today. The intense spit-up smell lasted for only a day or so. Even though the year after his death was tough, I am still so grateful for the memories I have. I know that Brett is helping me get through it all because I couldn't possibly do it without him.

I had one other dream of Brett while I was away on business about five months after his death. I don't remember the details clearly, but I do remember the strong feeling that we were together again. I awoke with a huge smile on my face knowing my Brett was with me. I called my family and told them I'd had another dream. Only this time, I was much more in a place of peace and acceptance. I had a warm feeling inside that everything was going to be okay. Best of all, I finally knew that my son was all right, which had always been my main concern.

Brett was the light of my life. In thirty-six hours, he made all my dreams come true simply because he was here. Brett was my first child. Although the marriage to his father did not survive, I was fortunate to marry again, this time to the love of my life. We have been blessed with a son, Shane, whose birthday is three days after Brett's. I will carry my beautiful son Brett in my heart and mind forever.

Krysta O'Neill is happily married to Stephen. She enjoys running, writing, business, and playing with her son and the many children in her family. Krysta is blessed to have the love and support of the most amazing family unit she knows.

Comforting Signs from Claudia

Julie Smith

Claudia was born on Friday, July 13. Her birth date worried me. Even though I was never really superstitious, my father and grandmother were. So I decided to reverse the superstition and just honor her day. Besides, what else could I do? Claudia was my third child. I already had two adorable children, Camden and Brittany. From the moment Claudia was born, I felt an intense need to enjoy every single moment we shared. I took her everywhere and even quit my part-time job in order to have more time together. Looking back, I must have known that Claudia would be here for only a short time.

Always smiling, my young daughter greeted everyone with her bright, bubbly personality. Claudia loved eating, drinking, laughing, and playing with everyone. She also loved the beach. We headed there whenever the weather was warm enough. Claudia would cruise around the sand and go from person to person, peeking inside their beach bags to see what food they had brought. One day, she crawled over to two older people sitting nearby. The next thing I knew, she was sitting in the woman's lap, resting her head on her shoulder. For ten minutes, Claudia sat in this woman's lap while the woman sang to her. When Claudia was ready, she crawled off her lap and back over to me. Later, the woman told me she was so thankful that Claudia had come over to her. She had been missing her own grandchildren, and Claudia had comforted her. Events like this happened all the time.

When Claudia had her first febrile seizure at eleven months old, everything changed. Although it lasted for only thirty seconds, intuitively I knew our lives would never be the same. The emergency room doctors told us that everything checked out fine. Claudia was laughing, playing with the doctors and nurses, and guzzling down every Pedialite bottle they gave her; meanwhile, I was freaking out.

When they discharged her, the doctors told us to expect another seizure, since most children experience a second febrile seizure within six months of the first.

We celebrated Claudia's first birthday, on July 13, with a big cookout at our home. All of her grandparents, aunts, uncles, and cousins were there. She had a great time opening her presents, stealing cake from her cousin's plate, and entertaining everyone with her bubbly personality. Her one-year-old checkup also turned out fine.

However, four weeks later, just as the doctors had predicted, Claudia had another seizure. I cuddled and calmed her, and in less than thirty seconds it was over. EMTs came to check her; her pediatrician's office reassured me this was common, but I still took her in to be evaluated. Nothing was out of the ordinary. They told me everything would be okay. We went home and tried to go about our day as normally as possible. Britt and I reluctantly put Claudia down for her nap. A short while later, Britt checked on Claudia, and she was blue. She had stopped breathing in her crib. Despite CPR by the EMTs and myself, we couldn't bring her back. I was in shock. We drove home from the hospital with an empty car seat and no Claudia. Friends and family had already gathered at our home to console us. I was numb; I had no feeling in my body. I couldn't believe this was happening to our family.

Somehow we got through the nightmare of planning a funeral for our baby. Our family and friends stepped up to the plate and amazingly pulled the entire event together. The minister read a story called "Waterbugs & Dragonflies" during her funeral. I remembered thinking how nicely that story explained Claudia's passing to Cam and Brittany. The next day, a few of us were sitting on our back porch. All of a sudden, dragonflies came swooping down on us from every angle. It was amazing! There were hundreds of dragonflies. They were everywhere, flying above and all around our heads. I had never seen so many dragonflies in one place, especially not in my backyard. Also, it was late in August, when most dragonflies have come and gone. I knew these dragonflies were sent from Claudia. They were the first of many comforting signs we received from our little angel.

Indescribable emptiness filled my heart and our home. As I stared at Claudia's picture, I worried that she was floating around in heaven somewhere, hungry, alone, and with a wet diaper. Only thirteen months old, she didn't know anybody in heaven. I wanted to be there to help her. When I told my husband, Ed, that I needed to go to her, he knew I was in a desperate place and wouldn't leave my side. Ed spent more time with me than he ever had before. He was so caring and strong for me. I saw a side of Ed that I had never seen before. Claudia's passing actually brought us closer together, not further apart, as I had feared.

The hours trickled by. All I wanted to do was sleep, since it was so difficult being awake without my baby to hold. At the same time, I didn't want to sleep, because when I woke up, more time would have passed without her. I tried traditional psychotherapy, but that didn't work for me. Finally, my friend Janet decided to offer her services. As an energy worker, Janet helps people heal their bodies through the movement of energy. She is also able to communicate with the spirit world.

My first session with Janet was nothing short of amazing. I lay down on her table, and she called in Claudia and my spiritual helpers. While lying there, all of a sudden I heard, *"Mommy, I love you."* It was Claudia! I knew it! Even though she wasn't verbal at the time of her passing, I knew in my heart it was her. I couldn't believe it. Tears poured out of my eyes. But I still wanted confirmation. I asked Janet to tell me if she had heard anything. Janet said, "I heard the most beautiful little voice say 'Mommy I love you.'" That put me on a new high. Claudia was with me! She had always been with me. She had never really left.

Our weekly sessions continued. Using Polarity and other forms of bodywork, Janet helped me to release the pain from my body. Although I didn't hear Claudia speak again, I knew she was there. Energy work is so powerful. It was just the right therapy for me. After a few weeks, Janet suggested that I see a therapist friend of hers named Garbis. He worked with EMDR (Eye Movement Desensitization and Reprocessing), a powerful technique to remove trauma from the body.

During our first appointment, Garbis explained that trauma, which is stored in the body, could eventually be worked out through dreams and subconscious thoughts. But we could also use the EMDR techniques of sound and motion to more quickly help me work through the traumatic aspects of Claudia's last day, moment by moment. Although our sessions were difficult and painful, afterward I felt calmer and elated for having moved that moment out of my body. Within nine weeks, we had completely worked through her last day, and I was feeling so much better. EMDR was one of the best things I could have done. I will always carry a deep sadness about Claudia's passing, but at least now I can revisit the moments of her last day without the heart-wrenching pain.

I continued doing energy work with Janet while working with Garbis. She also recommended that I take up yoga, which proved to be very helpful. It literally moved the deep pain out of my body. At times, for no apparent reason, while holding one position or another, I would sob or tears would just pour out of my eyes. Yoga helped me enormously during those dark days, and I have grown to love the release it continues to give me to this day.

Utilizing several modalities at the same time helped me move more quickly through my grief process. During the time I was working with Garbis and Janet, so many amazing things happened to my family and me, and they continue to happen to this day. From the books I read, I learned that younger children are more easily able to talk in the spirit world. I encouraged Brittany to keep talking to Claudia. One day, Brittany told me that she liked playing on her swing because *Claudia always visits her there*. I also read books to Cam about how spirits sometimes try to communicate with us using other energy sources, such as light and television. One day, Cam yelled out that *Claudia was playing with the TV and the lights*. He got it, too! Both children understood that life goes on, and Claudia was still with us.

Then, one night, I went to bed exhausted and sobbing, clinging to Claudia's blanket, missing her terribly. In the middle of the night, I awoke to a strong, fragrant scent of the ocean breeze in the bedroom. I could smell the seaweed, and I loved that smell. I got up to open the windows wider, but every window in my bedroom was closed. There was no ocean breeze in my room. Instantly I knew it was Claudia reaching out to me one more time! It brought me right back to all those memorable days we shared at the ocean. Claudia loved the beach, and we went there often. I felt so comforted.

I remember waking up another night and sitting straight up in bed. The hallway outside my bedroom door was filled with a huge spinning gold light! It was amazing! The light stretched from floor to ceiling. I was frozen, unable to blink or move, afraid that the light might go away. Again, Claudia was letting me know she was there.

On one particularly difficult night in November, I went to bed sobbing. I told Claudia that I couldn't do this anymore; I couldn't handle the heartache and the pain. The following morning, I awoke with a strong sense that Claudia wanted me to be intimate with Ed even though I had no energy for such things. My husband was sensing the same thing from Claudia. During that intimate time together orchestrated by Claudia, we conceived our daughter Annika, who was born five days before the first anniversary of Claudia's death.

I had a Vedic astrological birth chart done for Claudia by Janet's friend, Juliana. I hoped to find some answers, and the reading made a huge impact. Claudia's birth chart revealed that she was a powerful soul who would be here on earth for only a short time. Knowing this really helped me understand that we have little to do with the time we arrive and the time we leave. There is a higher plan.

Although so many things continue to happen, one other blessing occurred with a medium and author by the name of John Holland. I really liked his book and decided to try to schedule a reading with him. Of course, the only appointment he had available was on the 13th, the same day as Claudia's birthday. Clearly, Claudia had a hand in this, too. I never expected John would ever be able to satisfy me, and I almost didn't go. But I went with Janet, and we sat in a room with ten other people. John went from person to person, connecting each person to the spirit with whom they were hoping to communicate. My reading was amazing.

John began by telling me that I was supposed to be there on this particular day ... It was a day with a lot of meaning for me ... "This is a beautiful baby," he said. "I mean really beautiful. She looks like a little angel." John continued, saying that she loves the balloons, especially the white one. *Our family releases balloons to Claudia every year on her birthday with special notes inside. Last year, Ed sent her a white one.* Claudia loves the Christmas tree that we decorate and put up on her grave each year ... And our new home addition with all the windows—she likes to be in the new room with all of the sun. She loves how I always include her in our family discussions and how I act as if she were still here with us. *I always tell people I have four children, because I do.* Claudia likes this. She said there is a new baby in her crib, wearing her clothes and playing with her toys in her room. Claudia said I have her name on a bracelet, and that I have lockets of her hair and a locket with her picture in it. She also has an older "sporty" sister, a big brother, and a big, strong daddy.

John's reading went on and on ... It was more fulfilling than I ever could have imagined. This complete stranger affirmed everything that I knew was going on. It was so gratifying. I didn't care if I ever read another book, had another reading, or saw another medium; I didn't need anything anymore. Claudia was with me! It was confirmed, and I was thrilled!

Signs from Claudia are everywhere. Our connection continues. We talk to her daily. Claudia is and always will be a huge part of our family. She has surely deepened our spiritual awareness. She has taught us that death is not an ending, but is rather a transitional event to a much higher place. Claudia has awakened countless people in our hometown and beyond; she has helped so many people reach a deeper spiritual understanding. Our little angel has touched more lives than many do over the course of an entire lifetime. She is an amazing soul.

Julie Smith and her husband, Ed, are parents of four wonderful children: Camden, Brittany, Claudia, and Annika. Julie's greatest joy is her children. Thankful to Claudia for all that she continues to teach her, Julie's spirituality has deepened in ways she never dreamt possible.

4

Touch

Angels around us, angels beside us, angels within us.
Angels are watching over you when times are good or
stressed.
Their wings wrap gently around you, whispering you are
loved and blessed.

—ANGEL BLESSING

ONE OF THE WAYS we connect with those we love is through the gift of touch. We hold hands; we give hugs. We may snuggle up close with someone we love, hold each other in a warm embrace, and even exchange kisses. Through our nonverbal actions we demonstrate our affection, love, and caring for one another. Yet when someone we love dies, our heart aches for those physical expressions of love we once shared. We miss their tender touches, their hugs, and their physical presence in our lives.

Death is the ending of a physical relationship. Life will never be the same, as the relationship has been changed forever. Yet many bereaved individuals report feeling their deceased loved one's comforting touch even after the person has died.

Several widows have shared that they have felt their deceased husbands lying next to them in bed at night. They may have been awoken to a kiss on the cheek or lips, yet there was no one there that they could see. Even so, they describe the experience as a very physical one and quite similar to the one once shared. How then could this be possible, especially if we exist only in physical form? The only way would be if the soul survives physical death and is able to reach out from beyond.

Have you ever been hugged by your loved one in spirit? Or felt the gentle kiss of an angel on your cheek? Did you know that invisible hands sometimes pull people out of harm's way in order to save lives? This chapter contains five stories illustrating how loved ones in spirit reach out to touch and comfort the bereaved. Sometimes those who have passed on find creative ways to let us know they are still present. One of the ways is through the healing power of touch.

SIGNS FROM KIM

Cindy Taglini

My husband and I lost our daughter, Kim, four years ago to a drug overdose. She left behind a two-year-old son. The feelings of shock, loss, and grief were overwhelming. For a few weeks we attended a local grief support group for parents who had lost an adult child. When that ended, we decided to continue the group in our home. It helped so much to share our feelings with the other individuals in our group who had also lost an adult child. I believe our children live on, as we have received too many signs to believe otherwise.

One of the biggest signs from Kim came on Mother's Day in 2008. My husband had been pleading with her to please send us a sign. That day, my mother gifted me with the biggest snow globe I had ever seen, with an angel inside. She admitted she wasn't sure why she had bought it, as it wasn't a gift she would typically purchase. Yet our daughter had loved snow globes and had even collected them. I knew it was a sign from Kim letting us know she was fine.

Another sign comes every year over the holidays when I hang ornaments with my children's names on them on the Christmas tree. Every Christmas without fail since her death, Kim's ornaments, and only hers, end up on the floor. Also, one year a message came in our living room where I keep a stack of books on life hereafter. One of the books, all on its own, ended up on the floor. The name of the book was *Hello from Heaven*.

Many times, especially when I do yoga or meditate, I experience the feeling that someone is touching my hair. Sometimes I feel a slight tickling on the side of my face. Recently, my five-and-a-half-year-old grandson, Kim's son, told his father that he "got an angel kiss" from his mommy in heaven. I could go on and on with the stories of how Kim has made her presence known in our lives. These signs help us so much by giving us hope.

Cindy Taglini, wife, mother, and grandmother, runs her own housecleaning business. In her spare time, Cindy loves spending time with her grandson and taking her pug, Zoey, for walks. I love you, Kim. Life will never be the same.

A Life Saved

David Keith Lavoie

⌒

My life was changed forever when everyone in our last class was forced to stay after school because of the actions of one or two students. Perhaps if this had not happened, my little brother, Bryan Scott Lavoie, might still be alive today.

It was October 13, 1963, and I got off the late bus twenty minutes later than usual. Just as I did, several emergency vehicles with flashing lights and sirens went speeding by and stopped right in front of my house. I could hear my mother's voice from the backyard, screaming. I ran around to the back as fast as I could only to find a stranger desperately trying to get my four-year-old brother out of the pool. This man lived several houses away and had heard my mother's cries for help. Then the police officers and firefighters came running. Everyone tried to save Bryan. Despite all their best efforts, my little brother did not survive.

Apparently, Bryan had told our mother that he was going outside to wait for me to get off the bus. He must have gotten bored waiting and went around to the backyard. Our backyard had a fenced-in pool. Somehow Bryan must have either climbed the fence or figured out how to open the gate. When he did, Bryan fell into the swimming pool and drowned. He was only four years old. We were all in a state of shock, especially my mother.

Bryan was buried three days later. My mother's grief was so overwhelming that she couldn't even manage to care for herself, much less any of us. Dad and Mom's two older sisters had to feed her and help take care of her. Because the focus was on getting Mom better, nobody noticed that there were also three little boys at home who were suffering. Without even realizing it, I tucked away my pain over Bryan's loss so I could be strong for our family.

Then, on November 22, 1963, just a little over a month later, President John Fitzgerald Kennedy was assassinated. I remember sitting with my family members three days later in our home watching the president's state funeral on our black and white television. Surprisingly, when Mom saw three-year-old John F. Kennedy Jr. salute his father, she seemingly "woke up." She started saying, "That's Bryan! That's Bryan!" I have to admit that he looked a lot like my little brother. John-John was simply saying goodbye to his father with the salute. Yet somehow that salute snapped my mother out of the catatonic state she had been in. In her own way, Mom came to attention that day.

Bryan's tragic death should never have happened. Over the years, I have always felt that Mom blamed me for Bryan's death, which created distance in our relationship. Why couldn't she just understand that staying late after school that day really wasn't my fault? Fortunately, as a result of writing this story, I have finally been able to acknowledge and grieve my brother's loss, which has helped heal my relationship with Mom. We are now on better terms; I call her more frequently. In fact, I even call her now on Bryan's birthday.

One of the good things that happened because of this tragedy was that it raised awareness about the need for pool safety regulations. Even though our pool was fenced in, a legislative bill entitled the Lavoie Act was passed soon afterward in the neighboring state of Connecticut. Changes to local ordinances also started happening, mandating that every pool be enclosed and fenced in. As a result of Bryan losing his life, he is now saving the lives of many others.

My little brother Bryan was born on August 17, 1959. Each year on his birthday I think of him. I remember one birthday in particular that occurred in the mid-'80s, about twenty years or so after he died. On that day, I had an amazing encounter with my little brother. I work as a salesman, providing products to restaurants. I had just left the restaurant Cheers, in Boston, and was walking back to my car. I turned down Charles Street and was thinking about Bryan, his birthday, and the day he drowned. If he had still been alive, the two of us probably would have been celebrating his birthday together.

While walking down Charles Street, I came to the intersection where Mount Vernon Street and River Street converge with Charles. As I stepped off the curbside to cross the intersection, someone abruptly pulled me back onto the sidewalk just as a speeding car that was passing by almost hit me. It was such a close call! I immediately turned around to thank the person, but nobody was there. In fact, no one was even close enough to ask if they had seen what had just happened. Yet someone had pulled me back. I knew it because I had just felt the strength of their hands on my shoulders. That person saved my life. I am convinced to this day that it was Bryan.

On the day that my little brother pulled me out of the path of the speeding car, I went back to my car. I sat quietly inside for a few minutes as I tried to take in everything that had just happened. In that moment, I finally came to the realization that there really is someone out there. Most definitely, we are not alone. It's an awesome thing to know with absolute certainty that there's something better out there waiting for every single one of us. An experience like this surely would have made someone who didn't believe in religion believe in at least something. All in all, I find it incredibly reassuring to know that there is life after death.

Recently, I happened to return an empty, three-gallon water bottle to the store. I noticed that the bottle had the words "Born on August 17" printed on it. This was Bryan's birthday. It also happened to be the day on which he saved my life. I decided to keep the bottle as a reminder; my brother Bryan was letting me know one more time that he is still in my life.

Overall, I feel a lot better about things, thanks to my little brother. I'm glad he's still in my life. I'm grateful to know that life goes on. Even so, I still wish I could have been home earlier on the day he died. I wish I could have saved Bryan's life, but I am forever grateful that my little brother saved mine.

David Keith Lavoie is a retired Army major, restaurant manager, and product salesman. He and his wife, Pat, have three sons and two grandchildren. They love visiting their children and grandchildren and taking them to their lake house in Maine.

DREAM BABY

Martha W. Brandt

It was exciting but overwhelming news. "Congratulations!" my obstetrician said. "You're pregnant again." This was my fifth pregnancy.
My first had ended in a miscarriage in 1996. As a result, my husband and
I had waited five more years before conceiving David, then another
two and a half years for Karlsen, and another two and a half for Mary
Catharine. I was now approaching forty years old, and I was a little
hesitant to be excited, although I secretly wished for another girl.

After the initial shock of the news, I began basking in my body's
changes once again. All three of my live births had been uneventful
and truly divine, joyous gifts. However, our middle son, Karlsen, was
born with two holes in his heart that were detected at nine months of
age. His open-heart surgery at the age of three was a stressful, prayer-
ful time for our family. Fortunately, my strong faith allowed me to
completely entrust God with Karlsen's well-being. Although Karlsen
sailed through the surgery and has grown up to be a thriving, head-
strong pre-teen with no limitations, my husband and I worried about
the possibility of a recurrence in future pregnancies. Fortunately,
Mary Catharine was born without any signs of similar trauma, and
the two of us breathed a huge sigh of relief. We felt we were home
free.

As the fifth month of this new pregnancy approached, I was scheduled for an ultrasound to determine if there were any heart defects or
any other abnormalities in the baby's growth. Up to this point, I had
passed the precarious first trimester. I was well settled into the pregnancy and reveled in my radiance. Also, I thanked God each day for
the opportunity to give birth to another beautiful child. When my
husband and I saw our little baby moving around on the ultrasound

screen, we tenderly squeezed each other's hands; tears of joy filled my eyes. The news we received next came as a complete shock.

"I'm sorry to have to tell you this," stated the examining obstetrician in a flat, emotionless tone. "I strongly urge you to abort this pregnancy. The baby is in distress due to severe Down's syndrome and water on the brain. A full-term pregnancy is not possible. Even if this pregnancy was to go that far, the baby would not live long after birth."

My husband and I were speechless. There was a profound disconnect between seeing proof that the baby was moving and alive and receiving the news we couldn't accept. Upon seeing our distress, the obstetrician explained that we could seek a second opinion. I could barely walk out of the examination room. I collapsed against my husband with sobs that seemed to emanate from deep within my soul. I couldn't even call upon the Lord to help ease my pain. Our darling baby was another girl.

Our primary care obstetrician was much more sympathetic. He scheduled a second ultrasound two days later in a Catholic hospital just outside of Boston. The two days of waiting were filled with many emotions, including anger, dismay, denial, confusion, love, and impending loss. "Dear Lord," I sobbed each night, "I cannot bear this uncertainty. I trust you completely, but I can't let go. I cannot make this decision to abort the pregnancy. Please know that I am prepared to go through great sacrifice for my dear baby girl, Emma Sue."

When the day came for the appointment, I was amazingly calm and rested. I whispered a prayer in the examining room while waiting: "Dear Lord, please release me from making this decision of life and death. I trust in you completely. Amen."

When the examining doctor viewed the ultrasound screen and the baby, she spoke quietly: "I'm sorry. Your baby is no longer alive." Tears of relief flooded my being as I wept for our loss. At the same time, I found myself filled with gratitude for the decision I no longer had to make. On the day before I had the surgical procedure to remove my baby, I wrote my dear little Emma Sue a poem as a way of saying goodbye.

A few days after I had recovered from the surgery, I remember yearning for the promise of spring and new life. I began to realize that in order for me to find closure in my loss, I needed to turn my focus to my three beautiful children who, at this time, needed extra-special nurturing love and attention. By awakening to this understanding, I was able to transfer and transform my sorrow and loss into a deeper love for my family.

One week later, I was deeply grieving the loss of my precious Emma Sue when I had the most amazing dream. In the dream, I walked into my living room in the middle of the night and sat down in a chair next to a large bay window. I placed my head in my hands and began to sob uncontrollably. Sitting on the couch across from me was a young baby, approximately six months old, with beautiful thick, dark hair and wearing an adorable red sleeper suit. The baby was talking to me as I was crying so painfully. The baby said, "Mommy, *please* don't cry. I'm all right. Everything is going to be all right." I was so mad at myself in the dream; I would not go on the couch to hold, kiss, and cuddle that baby because I was grieving so desperately.

Once I woke up, I realized that the darling baby in my dream was my little angel, Emma Sue! This realization enabled me to forgive my "dream self" for not being able to comfort the baby. It also left me with a deep sense of relief and acceptance I had not felt prior to this incident. Being able to recall the events of that dream has been a tremendous source of strength and calm. It also blessed me with glimmers of hope, joy, and peace again, as I was deeply comforted to know that my vision was so much more than a dream. This new awareness allowed me to begin the important process of letting go.

Of course, the loss of Emma Sue was difficult for the whole family. My children were confused as to why their little baby sister wasn't coming home to live with us. They didn't understand why Mommy was so sad and even angry at times. It was such a help to be able to share the dream with David, Karlsen, and Mary Catharine and to be able to talk about little Emma Sue. I also sang them the following lullaby I wrote to help them with their grief:

Dream Baby

Twinkling stars and glittering snow,
Let Emma Sue know we love her so.
Church bells peal the heart song true
That selfless love touches just a few.
Born from God and Angels dear,
This child lost will always be near.
Tonight let her come to you three,
My beloved Dream Baby.

There were so many ways I felt the presence of little Emma Sue in my life. In addition to the dream experience with her, I remember strong scents of exotic flowers, both inside and outside my house as well as during the memorial service we held. Emma Sue would also make her presence known with the wind. For instance, I would be walking the dog when two particularly large spruce trees in the neighborhood would bow down suddenly from a strong gust of wind as I passed. During her outdoor memorial service, it was such a confirmation for my family and me when a huge gust of wind suddenly picked up and blew for several minutes on what had otherwise been a quiet, still day. Just knowing my dream baby was present filled me with an incredible sense of calm, peace, and understanding.

Seven years later, I can definitely still feel Emma Sue's presence, especially during times of duress. Sometimes I receive a warm "small hands" hug or feel a gentle nudging. I am amazed at how important Emma Sue still is in my life in a very good and positive way. Thankfully, my sorrow has gone; I have been able to come to accept that this was the type of relationship Emma Sue was meant to have with my family and me.

Although her loss deeply saddened us, our family was surely given a precious gift. Every day, Emma Sue helps us to love one another more deeply and to enjoy the wonderful gift of life we have been given. In addition, my precious dream baby has helped me to personally grow and to awaken to a whole new understanding of love.

Martha W. Brandt, quality engineer and award-winning poet, is passionate about writing children's stories, inspirational stories, and poetry. Marty enjoys running, raising funds for Children's Hospital Boston, singing, playing piano, crocheting prayer shawls, and volunteering with the Great Danes Service Dog Project.

My Body Is in Heaven

Gwen Burns

⌒

My son, Brandon, was a very special little boy who wore his heart on his sleeve. He often asked about God and Jesus. Brandon would ask if Jesus was everywhere and if He knew all the time what we were doing. I would reply affirmatively. Yet my young son would upset me whenever he said things like, "When I die . . ." What a scary thing for a six-year-old to say.

I remember lying with Brandon on his bed about four months before he died. I was running my fingers through his hair when, all of a sudden, I started to cry. All I could say was, "God, I know you are going to take him, but please don't!" I never told anyone this because I didn't want them to think I was just another paranoid mom.

The day before our car crashed, Brandon was running alongside my nephew and me, and I could swear my son *glowed*. I said to myself, "I hope I keep this image in my memory forever." The next evening, a drunk driver hit our car, and Brandon was killed. That most horrific day of my entire life changed me forever.

Two months later, I was driving down the road with my two-year-old daughter, K'Dawn. She looked at me, raised her left hand in the air, and said, "Body [because she couldn't say Brandon], holdee my hand," as she opened and closed her fingers. A month later, I heard K'Dawn talking on her play phone and having a conversation with her "Body" and with Jesus.

On the one-year anniversary of the crash, I was crying and having a really hard time. K'Dawn walked up to me with her hands on her hips and said, "I toldee you, Mom. My Body is in heaven, and Jesus is holding my Body!" Because she said it so matter-of-factly and with such a look of peace on her face, there was no doubt in my mind that her big brother was right there beside her. He still watches over his little sister from heaven.

I have been blessed with several experiences of seeing Brandon. I even woke up from a deep sleep one time to feel his presence in the bedroom; I knew with all of my heart that he was there.

I miss my son, and I will until the day I die. During those first few years after his death, my little girl, K'Dawn, gave me more peace than anyone because in her mind and soul, it was all black and white— Jesus was watching over my son. I know that Brandon watches over us every single day; he will always remain alive in my heart. I also know that I will always and forever be his mother. Even for the little time we shared together, I feel so blessed to have had Brandon here on earth as my son.

Gwen Burns, RN and mother, works as a labor and delivery room and nursery nurse. She has learned that there are three Fs to help with the grief journey: faith, family, and friends. Gwen cherishes and continues to use all three.

Our Christmas Angel

Laurette A. Potter

—⁓—

I first connected with my son, Marshall, eleven weeks after he was conceived. Two days earlier, his heartbeat had been inaudible on the Doppler heart rate monitor. Waves of relief swept over me the instant I saw his little heart beating on the ultrasound monitor. Just over an inch long, my son appeared so incredibly small. Little did I know how big he would become to me and to all who would grow to love him.

Marshall Daniel Mo Potter arrived twelve days early on August 16, 2002. His daddy and I were thrilled to be blessed with a healthy baby boy. Our incredibly content son had the quietest cry I had ever heard. He rarely cried, and when he did, it was so soft and sweet. Unbeknownst to us, his body was progressively losing muscle tone, which would eventually impede his ability to swallow and breathe.

When Marshall was only four weeks old, I remember picking up my best friend's son, Gage, who was just a few weeks older. I couldn't believe the difference in muscle strength between the two boys. When my girlfriend picked up Marshall, she confirmed what I had been thinking. My son was significantly weaker than hers. The following week, the pediatrician remarked that Marshall's muscle tone was abnormally low. Since it was probably nothing, he recommended we wait two weeks and then return for reevaluation.

Two agonizing weeks of worry slowly crept by. Our son seemed to be moving his arms and legs less and less, and he eventually stopped moving them altogether. Whatever sounds he had been making were also weaker. During his checkup, the pediatrician recommended a neurological evaluation as soon as possible. My husband, Mark, and I became increasingly concerned that something was wrong with Marshall, yet never once did we think our little baby boy could be dying.

During a second early intervention home visit, the nurse urged us to seek immediate medical attention for our eight-week-old son because of the amount of effort it was taking for him to breathe. Mark and I rushed Marshall to the local hospital, where labored breathing and absent reflexes were confirmed. He was transferred quickly by ambulance to the University of Massachusetts Memorial Hospital, where numerous tests were performed.

The following day, Marshall's neurologist, a team of nurses, and a social worker met with us to explain that our son had a rare genetic disorder called spinal muscular atrophy (SMA). Even though we had never heard of the disease, we were horrified just knowing that our son's illness had a name. We were completely unprepared to hear what the neurologist said next: "There is no cure. Your baby will likely die before his first birthday." Millions of feelings began rushing through my body. I suddenly felt very weak and sick to my stomach. Weeping, my husband and I gripped each other as we learned that our baby was dying. Through devastation and tears, we vowed to be strong for Marshall and to remain together. We couldn't possibly bear losing our relationship in addition to losing our precious son. Our family immediately surrounded us with love and support, assuring us that we would get through this challenge together. I wasn't so sure, as I seriously doubted my ability to care for a dying infant.

My husband provided the most incredible comfort and support of all. I don't know how I could have possibly gotten through it without him. On the ride home from the hospital, we renewed our promise to remain strong for our son, and we decided to establish some ground rules. No crying in front of Marshall. He would sleep with us from then on, and we would take as many pictures as possible. We are so glad now that we did, since we look at the photos daily. Mark and I brought Marshall everywhere so our son could experience as much in his short time with us as possible. We took him to church, to the zoo, to the beach, and to a tree farm to cut down his first and only Christmas tree.

Marshall even got to sit in the driver's seat of a Mustang Cobra. We shared our son with all who loved him, encouraging them to spend as much time with him as possible. We appreciated every moment we had together. Without even knowing it, Marshall had started his important life work, and our lessons had begun. He had so many things to teach.

Over the course of Marshall's illness, the most important thing he taught me was how to love. I showered my son with every ounce of love possible. I also knew that I would love and appreciate every child in this world so much more as a direct result of having loved my son. Thanks to Marshall, I now live every day fully, as if it were my last. A smiling child and the feeling of wet, gentle baby kisses on my nose have taken on a new meaning. Marshall taught me the importance of simple things, such as a warm breeze on my face, sunshine in my eyes, and pushing my son around the neighborhood in his stroller. I wanted to hold on to those moments forever. I am proud to say that Marshall has been my greatest teacher. Although he never spoke a word, my son became my hero in his brief stay here on earth.

In addition to everything Marshall was teaching me, I began educating myself about spinal muscular atrophy. I spent endless hours researching everything about SMA. I found websites with the names and faces of other children and families whose lives had been affected by the disease. I read stories written by parents of affected children, some alive and others who had passed on. I learned about the irreversible progression of the disease and the difficult decisions we would need to make—decisions no parent should ever have to make regarding feeding tubes, breathing machines, intubation, and resuscitation. My husband and I formulated a plan of action for every possible scenario even though we knew our son would eventually lose his life no matter what decisions we might make. I was angry, hurt, devastated, and terrified all at the same time. Finally, Mark and I made the decision to treat Marshall exactly how we would want to be treated if faced with the same situation. We decided to make the best yet most heart-wrenching decision that we possibly could for our son: when the time came, we would let our baby go.

Our son was able to remain at home throughout the entire course of his illness supported by hospice services and the loving dedication of his nurse, Nancy. Yet saying goodbye to someone so loved was nothing less than heartbreaking. Because Mark and I were aware that Marshall's time on earth was drawing to a close, we often said to him, "Send us a sign so we will always know that you are still with us." Cradled in the arms of his daddy and in the presence of many who loved him, Marshall was lovingly returned to heaven on December 22, 2002. At just four months and six days old, Marshall traded in his earthly body for his very own set of angel wings.

Within a few hours, my husband and I started to take apart Marshall's nursery, something we needed to do to begin to heal. I sent my husband downstairs to retrieve an empty plastic bin so we could start folding Marshall's tiny clothes to pack away. When Mark returned with the bin, he had a huge smile on his face and was laughing. I was irritated, for it was hardly a time to be joyous. Mark reached into the empty bin and pulled out a lonely Christmas ornament—an angel, of course! It was a tiny, two-inch, clear-plastic angel with a golden halo. Instantly, I knew it was not just a coincidence, and I began to smile along with my husband. Our son had found a way to let us know he was now our little angel. What incredible comfort and joy we felt to know our baby was still with us.

Then, just three days after he had left us, Marshall returned once again. Mark and I had gone to my Tante (the French word for aunt) Celia's house for Christmas dinner. Blizzard-like conditions cut our visit short, so my husband, sister, brother-in-law, and I headed to our home. When we arrived, the back door, which I had left locked, was wide open, with snow and water covering the kitchen floor. While our husbands worked on parking the car, my sister and I frantically ran throughout the house to see if any valuables had been stolen. Everything, including our two dogs and cat, was safe and sound. Relieved, I wandered into the living room only to discover Marshall's Christmas card picture lying in the middle of the living room floor, some twenty feet away from where I had left it. In astonishment, I yelled to my sister to come quickly.

My sister rushed in to find me peering down at the photo on the floor of Marshall dressed in his angel wings and diaper with his big blue eyes laughing precociously. Amazed, Caroline and I stared at the picture and then started to giggle. It had to be Marshall. The photo had somehow moved twenty feet off the mantel, and the locked back door had been found wide open. If it had been an intruder, why had nothing ~~had~~ been taken from our home? I happily picked up the picture, returned it to the mantel where I had placed it several weeks prior, and thanked Marshall for coming, as I always do. Our son had made his presence known on our first Christmas night without him in the silly way only a child would do.

From time to time, our young son still makes his presence known. Recently I was sitting at my computer when I felt something touch my cheek. I reached up to find nothing there. My cheek continued to tingle for the longest time when all of a sudden I realized it had to be Marshall! I begged him to do it again. The tingling happened three more times. I was so moved by his presence, I began to cry. Then chills started going up and down my spine. Finally, I asked Marshall to repeat the sensation somewhere else on my body, because I still needed confirmation. Incredibly, my scalp started to tingle. I was amazed and grateful all at the same time. I thanked my sweet little son for coming, and I begged him to please keep coming back. It makes my heart happy to know whenever Marshall is near.

Whether it is the sparkle of a star at night, the presence of a rainbow in the sky, or even something as subtle as the glimmer of the sun on a blanket of freshly fallen snow, Mark and I are continually reminded of Marshall and our newfound ability to appreciate the life we have so graciously been given. We still miss our son, and we love him endlessly.

My life will never be the same. But I have accepted that, and I have done my best to move on. Thank you, our sweet little Marshall, for warming our hearts, blessing our lives, and surrounding us with your love!

Laurette A. Potter, wife, mother, and occupational therapy assistant, passionately raises funds for Marshall's Miles. She and her wonderful husband, Mark, have been blessed with two more beautiful children, Murphy and Anders. Their angel, Marshall, will remain a special part of their lives always.

5

A Sense of Presence

*A shiver runs down your spine when you realize it is not
our imagination.
Something is watching us out there.*

—SOPHY BURNHAM, *A Book of Angels*

HAVE YOU EVER HAD the feeling that someone was in the room with
you, but when you looked around, nobody was there? Have you ever
felt watched over by a loved one who has died? Physical death does
not have to mean the end of a loving relationship. Those we love in
spirit are still able to be close to us, and sometimes we can sense their
physical presence. I remember one woman who told me that after her
husband died, she searched for him upstairs, downstairs, in the attic,
in the basement, and even in all of the closets. She said, "I knew he
was dead. But I could *feel* his presence!"

Another widow told me that when her car was spinning out of control, she knew she would be all right because she could feel her husband's presence next to her in the car. Fortunately, both she and the car were left unharmed, as were the two other cars and their drivers that were spinning out of control, too. Have you ever felt protected or guided by someone you loved? Have you ever felt a sense of presence?

Our loved ones in spirit come close in times of need. Whenever we are sad or lonely, they can easily come to comfort us. As spiritual beings, they are no longer limited by time or space or earthly human form. They can be with us in a split second if we need them or call out their names. If you ever sense your loved one's presence, just know it is a blessing. And be sure to thank them for coming.

This chapter contains six stories describing an experience of a sense of presence after a loved one has died. How wonderful to have an awareness that your loved one is still present in your life. If you have lost someone special, perhaps look for new ways to stay connected as you move through the pain of loss and grief. Truly, your loved ones in spirit live on, and so do your loving relationships.

BIRTHDAY WISHES

Gina Fimbel

⌒

I feel my son's presence all the time. Andrew's spirit has been so comforting to me and such a light in my world. Since he died, I miss his
physical presence. Yet I am so grateful for the way his spirit lives on in
my life and in the lives of our family.

The number three holds special significance for the two of us.
Andrew was born at 3:43 in the afternoon; six months later, he passed
away at 3:33 in the afternoon. Soon after his death, I started to notice
the numbers 333 showing up in my life at just the right times. When
I needed to feel him, when I was heavy with grief or even when I was
recalling happy memories of him, the numbers 333 seemed to magi-
cally appear. Whenever this happens now, I know Andrew is near.

I remember one dreary, rainy birthday in particular. The day did
not feel special at all. Even though my husband called several times
to check in on me, it was my first birthday following our son's death,
and I couldn't stop thinking of Andrew. Since I was new at my job,
no one knew it was my birthday. I went through all the motions of
returning phone calls, attending meetings, and so forth. But I was
feeling especially sad and lonely, thinking that the best birthday present in the world would have been to hold my precious baby who had
been taken away from me so suddenly.

As soon as I finished work, I headed out to battle the DC metro area
traffic. Feeling sorry for myself, I wanted to quickly get home, crawl
into bed, and cry my eyes out. As usual, the traffic was stop and go.
I noticed a car right beside me that seemed to be purposely driving
parallel to me, and I wondered what his problem was. Suddenly the car
abruptly moved right in front of my car, almost cutting me off. Before
I could beep my horn, I noticed the license plate: "HPYBDAY." Wow!
How very cool. I felt as though the universe were wishing me a happy

birthday, and it felt great. Smiling to myself, I wondered if it could be my son wishing his mama a happy birthday. Still thinking that it was just a coincidence but feeling grateful for the sign, I kept driving when yet another car swerved in front of me with 333 as the last three numbers on the license plate! With tears in my eyes and gratitude overflowing from every inch of my body, I thanked God and my son for thinking of me. My little angel had just wished me a happy birthday. But it was way more than that. It was confirmation that Andrew loved me and missed me, too, and most of all that he was okay.

That was the first time I felt in my soul that Andrew's spirit was still on a journey and that he was okay. Now I believe that my son is safe in God's hands. Because of Andrew, I am a better person, wife, and mother; I will be eternally grateful for his continued presence in my life. Don't get me wrong. I miss being able to physically touch and hold my child. I still have many days when I feel sad, angry, or bitter, wondering how such a precious soul could be taken so quickly. Yet I am extremely grateful for my son Andrew. Every day, his life is a gift that keeps on giving. Thank you, little man, thank you.

Gina Fimbel, MSW, lives in Wilmington, North Carolina, with her husband and twin boys, Brayden and Luke. Before having the boys, she worked at a homeless shelter for women and children and in foster care. Gina currently serves as a court-appointed special advocate.

Hope from Beyond

Elissa Bishop-Becker

My husband, Randy, and I said goodbye to our lives on Long Island and drove south. As the highway unwound between my daughter, Ericka, and me, I let the excitement of the journey anesthetize my sense of a wrenching pull poised to snap, like an umbilical cord stretched to its limit. Two weeks later, she visited us at our new home in Williamsburg.

"Hey guys, I love you, but I gotta go," she said as she prepared to go out for the evening. It was Saturday, and Ericka planned to leave on Monday, happily anticipating her return to Yale and the beginning of her junior year as a leader of Freshperson Conference. She looked forward to welcoming the incoming freshmen and spending a week orienting them to their new home.

That night, Ericka went out with her Yale friend Kat. However, I was still feeling anxious and disoriented from what had happened the day before. Kat was supposed to be away on vacation with her family, but we had suddenly come face to face with them in a mall parking lot. I felt a shock go through me, and, from that moment on, I felt as if something was off balance. I asked Ericka to please stay home that night, but she refused, smiling indulgently at her overprotective mom. I tried to convince myself that she would be okay.

At 2:00 AM, Ericka called to tell us she was going to Kat's house to spend the night. At 3:00 AM, the phone rang again. Kat's mother said they hadn't arrived yet, and she was worried. At 4:00 AM, Kat's mother called back. She and her husband were on their way to Riverside Hospital, where Kat was getting her face stitched up. There had been an accident.

The police met us outside the emergency entrance door. One of the officers took us down the hall and into a private room. He looked at me sorrowfully and shook his head. "She didn't make it," he said. I screamed, "NO! NO! NO!" and kicked the metal hospital bed frame as hard as I could, as if that would ground me or make the world make sense again.

The next few days were a blur of tears, grief, and sedatives. I remember the warmth of friends who surrounded and supported us with hugs, sympathy, and an endless parade of casseroles. They answered phones, cleaned, picked up family and friends at airports, and picked me up when I fell down in despair and agony. I remember sitting alone in a room with my child in her coffin, singing the song I sang to her at bedtime when she was little. It was an old French song called "Dessous Ma Fenêtre." "Sing your song, Mommy," she would say. So I sang it to my Eri-Moo one last time. Afterward, I slipped my ruby and diamond ring on her finger. It was the ring I had planned to give her for her twenty-first birthday the following May. Then I took her plain silver band and put it on my finger.

There were hundreds of shattered and grief-stricken faces at her funeral. Many spoke of their love and sorrow. I read aloud Ericka's autobiographical essay written only seventeen days before she died. The last paragraph sounded eerily prophetic:

> In my world, friends have been seasons, and I have lived as treely as a tree can. Shedding, shedding, always shedding friendly, aimless leaves. I want, more than anything, to be granted wings and move with the sun and to be able to hold you all close to me. So sing around me and dance and cry. Yell about frustration and throw things at me. Think about life and touch me and know me. And, maybe if I stand really still, and wish really hard for the summer to stay, it won't. But maybe you will.

It felt impossible to face a future without my daughter. I felt her energy around me like a hug. The warm, loving, tingly feeling stayed wrapped around me for days. With absolute certainty, I knew my daughter wanted me to find a way to communicate with her. I remembered I had bought a Ouija board many years earlier, even though I had never used it. Randy and I took it to Memorial Park, sat down on lawn chairs next to her grave, and hoped we'd be able to connect with Ericka. We asked the board questions, and surprisingly, messages were relayed back to us. The first two messages came from someone on the other side who said they knew Ericka; they would let her know we were trying to reach her. On the third day, we finally connected! This is what Randy and I remember from our first two conversations with Ericka. After that, we recorded them:

"I love you," I said.

"I love you, too," she said.

"Do you miss us?"

"Yes. Don't cry."

"Is there anything you'd like us to tell people here?"

"Tell them 'I love you.'"

There was some playfulness. Ericka called one of my comments "lame." The easy familiarity of her words filled me with joy and wonder. I asked how she was feeling, and she said "happy and good."

"Was the accident painful or frightening?"

"No."

"Were you at your funeral?"

"Yes. It was nice."

"Do you approve of my idea for a book about you?"

"Wow. That's something. Good. Published." She said her great-grandfather was there with her, that she had another friend there as well, and that she had been dancing. She told me to go see Kat in the hospital. I said "I love you" again, and we said goodbye. Randy and I were amazed and relieved. She was gone, but she was there! We were joyful, but we were grieving. It was a potent, fruitful, agonizing, and healing mix of feelings.

During our third conversation, Ericka said she was tired and had been resting. She said that we would be together again, and that she was a guide. I asked, "Do you regret having such a short life?" She replied, "To everything there is a season."

"What season is it?" I asked.

"Now."

"Do you have another name there?"

"Rikkity."

"Do you miss Yale?"

"Yes. Friends. Brian. Rich."

"Is there anything you'd like us to say to them?"

"I love you."

"Is there anything we could have done?"

"No."

"Is there anything we can do?"

"Live. Enjoy."

Randy and I looked at each other, our eyes filled with tears yet wide with amazement and hope. And that was the beginning of our communications that continue to this day, which Rikkity calls Spiritual Persistence. Our daughter has shown us a perspective on grief, loss, physical reality, and spirituality that we never could have dreamt of before she reached out from her side and we reached back from ours. When she died, we thought our lives were over. And indeed, our lives, as we had known them, were over. But our new lives had just begun.

Elissa Bishop-Becker, MEd, LPC, NCC, wife of Rev. Dr. Randolph Becker and mother of Ericka (Rikkity), is a licensed professional counselor living in Key West, Florida. She enjoys the sun and sea, and is continuously learning from ongoing communications with spirit.

Checking Things Out

Judith Kong

⸻

When I was six months pregnant, my obstetrician told me that my unborn baby might be too sick to survive his birth. Travis was born with osteogenesis imperfecta, a rare genetic bone disorder characterized by brittle bones. With most of his bones crumpled at birth, my new baby was given a three-month prognosis. He lived almost twenty years. Though he often endured severe pain, Travis loved deeply, had a dry sense of humor, and touched everyone he met with his courage. He enjoyed hanging out with his friends. He especially liked to hang out with athletes, because Travis had the heart of an athlete even though his body was small, weak, and fragile.

On the day I found Travis dead in his dorm room, I fell to pieces. I just never expected his death to come so abruptly. I couldn't breathe. I couldn't imagine how I would go on without him. That night, the college Travis attended held a memorial service for him followed by a reception in his dorm. Grief-stricken, we all emerged from the church together, headed over to the reception, and found ourselves right in the middle of a full lunar eclipse. As the moon disappeared in the sky, it felt like a sign that Travis was finally on a journey to a better place.

One of Travis's biggest joys was his nephew, Dawson, who was a year old when Travis died. The spring after his death, my husband and I built a play area in the backyard for Dawson, complete with playhouse. A few days later, the strangest thing happened. A flock of turkeys, which I had never seen before and have not seen since, landed in our backyard. One of the turkeys actually paraded inside the playhouse *checking things out* while his proud buddies looked on. That would have been just like Travis. He always wanted to be sure things were just right for his nephew. In my heart, I knew it was Travis still wanting to be a part of Dawson's life.

A few days later, another strange thing happened. Teased by a squirrel, my Australian shepherd chased it up the pine tree next to our home. Then the dog started barking frantically at the ground. I walked over to discover a newborn squirrel, no bigger than a walnut, lying on the grass. With the sandbox shovel, I gently picked up the baby squirrel and placed it in the tree in the same loving way I had nurtured and protected Travis. When I checked later on, the baby squirrel was gone, hopefully reunited with its mother. The whole baby squirrel incident felt so profound. Maybe it means I need to let go. Trav, I'm trying, but it is so hard. Even though you're in a better place, I need to trust that you are being well cared for, too.

Two years after Travis's death, his sister gave birth to her second child, whom she named Owen Travis. Owen came out smiling ear to ear. I believe his Uncle Travis was probably right there with him, whispering in his ear and making sure that everything was all set for his new nephew.

My son, Travis, is always with me. I can sense his presence wherever I go. I am grateful for the gentle reminders that he brings. I just hope that he keeps checking things out. Oh yeah, Trav, I'm glad you have wings, even if they are the wings of a turkey.

Judy Kong, RN, CHPN, hospice nurse, has been married for twenty-five years and is the mother of three and grandmother of two. Her family has always been most important. She especially loves spending time with her grandsons, Dawson and Owen.

Signs from Beyond

Darlene Goodwin

My brother Robert committed suicide when I was thirteen years old. Unsure of what suicide meant, I thought he was just missing. So whenever people asked how I was doing, I told them I was fine. After all, my big brother was coming back. I'll never forget the night Robert let me know otherwise. At the time, I shared a daybed with my little sister. I had just pulled the trundle bed out halfway and looked down the hall. Then I lay down. I remember turning over and then back again in my bed. When I did, I saw Robert sitting in a chair right in front of me! I knew it was my brother because of his dark, curly brown hair and the way his hands cradled his face. I asked, "Robert, what did you do?"

He looked right at me, crying, and all he could say was, "I'm sorry. I'm so sorry ..." And then he was gone. I knew then that my brother was gone for good. I immediately ran into the kitchen and dialed his phone number. My stepmother saw me and ran after me. Afterward, she brought me into her bedroom. I explained what had happened and that I had seen Robert. She told me that was ridiculous, and that I was making it up. She also warned me not to tell my father since it would make him even more upset. I remember feeling like I wanted to throw up. I cried the whole night, knowing that I had just seen my big brother and that I would never see him again.

The next morning, I couldn't wait to see my other brother to tell him that I had seen Robert. He, too, thought I was just making it up. It was so frustrating because no one would believe me. Yet I had seen Robert with my very own eyes. That night, my brother had come to say goodbye and to help me understand he was not coming back. I still think about it to this day.

A few years later, my Nanny died from cancer. That Christmas, I slept overnight at my mother's apartment. We stayed up late talking for a while, and then it was time for bed. Since I was the last one to leave the living room, Mom asked me to unplug the Christmas tree lights, which I did. While we were lying in bed and chatting, the Christmas lights suddenly flashed on and off. My mother said, "I thought you unplugged them." I assured her that I had. I went to the living room to check, and sure enough, they were unplugged, just as I had left them. I went back to bed, and ten minutes later the lights went on again. This time, we both really freaked out. I was shaking, fearful that someone might be in the apartment with us. We walked into the living room together only to find the Christmas tree plug lying on the floor—unplugged. "I guess it must be Nanny or Robert saying hi," I surmised out loud. Mom looked right at me. She said, "That's silly," and we went back to bed. I had the feeling of butterflies in my stomach, excitedly *knowing* that it was them.

Then, all of a sudden, my mother's cassette answering machine started clicking on and off. At that point my mother really started freaking out. She jumped out of bed, looking as white as our sheets. I was confused. Why hadn't she been more spooked about the Christmas lights? Mom grabbed my hand, and we walked slowly into her kitchen. By then, I was giggling. Mom went over to her answering machine and picked it up, and it was unplugged, too! In fact, the cord was wrapped around the machine! My giggling turned into a feeling of *holy moly!* Again, I looked at Mom and said, "They're just trying to say hi!" That was the end of the conversation. Now, whenever I ask Mom if she still remembers the night Nanny and Robert were messing with us, she replies, "I sure do! They scared the heck out of us!"

On September 11, 2001, I was twenty-four years old and living on Long Island. That morning I woke up with a horrible foreboding feeling. Although none of my family members were hurt by the events of that day, that eerie feeling would not go away. Then, ten days later, my father called and asked me to come over to the house as soon as possible. My older brother, Jimmy, was gone. Jimmy had died from an accidental drug overdose, and he had died in the same house in which Robert had taken his life many years earlier. I just couldn't believe this was happening. Jimmy was my best friend, and I still miss him so much. I often think about how different my life would be if he were still here. But I do feel him sometimes. When I get upset or scared, I can feel his arm around me. And, of course, I could never forget his jovial laugh.

Four years later, my husband and I moved off the island into a suburban, five-bedroom home. Right from the start, I could feel Jimmy there with me. Whenever I washed the dishes, I could feel his presence behind me, yet when I turned around, no one would be there. Other times, when no one was home, I could hear someone walking around upstairs. Then, on the anniversary of his death, I happened to be sitting at the kitchen table with my son and daughter writing down the date. I said, "Oh, today's September 27th. Uncle Jimmy has been gone for seven years today." Just then, the lid of the kitchen garbage can swung back and forth right in front of our eyes! We all looked around the room. No one was near the garbage can, and we all saw it move. The whole thing gave me chills, and it made me smile knowing Jimmy was there.

Finally, on Jimmy's birthday, I was sitting on the couch with my kids looking at pictures of him when we heard a loud bang in the kitchen. When I went to see what had happened, I found that the case of water bottles had somehow tipped onto the floor, and the microwave was inexplicably running, too. It made me happy to know that Jimmy was right there with us.

I can't possibly explain how much I still miss my best friend and big brother. Even though Jimmy has been gone for ten years, it hasn't gotten any easier. But I take comfort in the little things he does for me to let me know he is near.

Believe it or not, I am a skeptic. I believe only what I see. These are things I have seen with my own eyes. It's very hard to share the things I've seen and heard with my family members and friends without them thinking I'm a little crazy. Nowadays, I don't care what anyone thinks or says. I'm glad I've had these experiences. They are mine, and I will always cherish them. And I look forward to having more some day.

Darlene Goodwin is married to her best friend, Dave. Employed in the medical field, Darlene loves the ocean, collecting seashells and listening to the waves breaking. The mother of three, she and her family have started a new life adventure by moving to Florida.

MIRACLES OF HEALING

Richard Fuller

The phone call from my daughter, Annette, in January of 1997 changed my life. She told me to rush to the hospital in Silver Spring, Maryland, because her sister, Karen, was dying. All I remember is that I panicked and the next seventy-two hours were a blur. I don't know how I managed to catch a plane and make it to my daughter, Karen, in time for when they disconnected her life support, as well as for her death and the services that followed. Karen had been diagnosed nine years earlier with stage-three metastatic breast cancer. Somehow, through the miracles of modern medicine, including chemotherapy, radiation, special diets, and a T-cell transplant, my daughter lived another nine fruitful but painful years. During that time, Karen pursued her career as a television news producer, and before she died at age thirty-six, she was employed as a full-time producer by NBC News in Washington, DC. However, Karen's extended life, professional accomplishments, and healing were not the only miracles we witnessed. My insightful and caring daughter helped her agnostic dad at the age of sixty to find God.

At the time, I had been attending a Catholic church as a visitor for almost a year, accompanying someone else. Because my father had been a runaway Catholic and my mother a runaway Jew, no religion had been observed in our home. I was very angry with God about my sister dying at fifteen and my mother at fifty-nine, plus World War II and every hurricane, forest fire, and tornado. However, when I returned from Karen's funeral in Maryland, I had this inexplicable desire to go to church. From the moment my hand touched the church's glass front door, I began weeping. I did not stop until I left Mass. For the first time in my life, I felt the love and comfort of God in my life. Somehow, through the heart-wrenching loss of my daughter, I had been able to find God. I took RCIA classes, and on Easter

Vigil in 1998, I was baptized into the Catholic Church. I have never been more content. So that phone call in January of 1997 signaled a new beginning of all kinds of miracles. I learned that Karen and I were neither the first recipients of God's love nor the last. His love is there for all of us. Over time, I have also learned that sadness and grief are necessary human qualities, but that those we have lost are in a better place.

Another incredible miracle has been the blessing of being able to feel Karen in my life every single day since she died. Now, my daughter watches over me, smiles, and perhaps even laughs out loud at the silly things I often do. For all I know, Karen is that bright star that twinkles down at me each night whenever I look up to the heavens. There is not a day that goes by that I don't feel her presence. Karen seems to sit on my shoulder comforting me. I can *feel* her saying all the loving things she said when she was alive. Furthermore, in times of stress, I sense her presence even more. If I just focus on Karen, the trials begin to diminish; she seems to be able to put things into perspective for me. Indeed, I talk to Karen every day, as well as to my mom and dad, who are with her in spirit. I don't always get answers, but I can sense their unquestionable presence, love, and total support. My appreciation for them all has soared.

Here is the greatest news of all. After feeling pain, loneliness, anger, unbearable sorrow, and grief that seems endless, it is possible to find peace. I have. And so can you.

Richard Fuller, husband and father, is mostly retired, having had careers in advertising, sales, and publicity.

Holding On to Hope and Love

Michele A. Harris

My beloved sister, Mara, was a lover and a believer. Petite in stature, with long, beautiful dark hair, her smile could light up the world; and for many people, she did just that. As the baby in our family, she was honest, sometimes to a fault, and always gave love and acceptance to others. Mara believed that anything was possible. She believed in God and the saints, the power of prayer, love, and even magic. She felt a deep connection to the universe and shared it with all of those around her, especially her children, Mercey and Mason. She loved them endlessly, and the time she devoted to them was special.

Mara and I had the same father but different mothers. Even though we grew up in separate homes, we were extremely close. Because her early years had been filled with turmoil, my sister knew firsthand that some of life's experiences have the ability to rob people of their hope, yet she never let go of hers. Mara lost her mother at a very young age and found comfort by reading a letter, over and over, that her mother had written to her. Years later, she inspired her friends and family to write letters to their daughters and even developed a website as a means to share encouragement and hope. There, she wrote a letter to her own daughter, Mercey. That letter eventually became her eulogy, which I read at her funeral. I often wonder if she knew how profound the letter would be in its impact on her daughter and so many others.

Her sudden, tragic death at the age of thirty-nine caused the kind of pain that most people can't possibly even imagine. Not only did we lose Mara, but we also lost her four-year-old son, Mason. Fortunately, her bright, intuitive, and lively seven-year-old daughter survived the ordeal. But Mercey had been left traumatized by the horrific loss of her entire family, and she went to live with our sister, Maxine.

The next several months were extraordinarily difficult for all of us. However, throughout the pain and suffering, we were met with many blessings—the kind that can be explained only by the fact that we had two angels in our midst leading and guiding the way. On the day that Mara and Mason were taken from this world, my daughter felt comforted by a strong feeling of presence from her aunt, with whom she shared a special bond.

While we have had many encounters, there is one in particular that stands out the most. Last fall, we needed to find a new school for Mercey. Throughout the search, Maxine felt led by our sister, Mara, to keep looking until she finally found a Catholic school willing to take her. On the first day at her new school, Mercey nervously walked up the stairs of the old Victorian-style building, once an orphanage, where she met her new principal, a nun.

Mesmerized by the statue of Mary and baby Jesus straight ahead, she dropped her school bags, began to cry, and exclaimed, "This is where I belong! My mom wants me here. I can *feel* her. This is where Mommy and Mason are and where I will learn about heaven and God." Mercey stood in amazement and began twirling around, later described by the principal "as if she was in Disneyland for the first time." She felt her mother's warm embrace, and she felt her younger brother's playful spirit alive there, too.

When I spoke with my niece that afternoon, her voice was full of joy and peace. Mercey explained that she didn't want the school day to end; she never wanted to leave. She believed that, although her mother's body was no longer here, her spirit and soul were alive and would never leave her. She would always be comforted by her mother's love. And in this place of love, she found hope.

Michele A. Harris, MEd, proud mother of Jarad and Michaela, has worked as a counselor in higher education for over fourteen years. Devoted to helping empower others through awareness and education, Michele believes that everyone has a special life purpose—some people just need guidance in discovering it.

6

Signs

Pay attention to all the leaves, the flowers, the birds and the dewdrops. If you can stop and look deeply, you will be able to recognize your beloved one manifesting again and again in different forms. You will again embrace the joy of life.

—THICH NHAT HANH

THIS WORLD IS FILLED with God's love and is divinely orchestrated. Once we realize the interconnectedness of all things, we discover gifts from spirit at every turn. Synchronistic events are interwoven throughout the fabric of life. Have you ever received a sign from a deceased loved one? Has nature ever sent you a message of love?

Those who have passed on from this world send signs of hope to let us know they are near. Sometimes beautiful rainbows appear at poignant moments in the grief journey. Butterflies repeatedly hover nearby as symbols of transformation. They gently remind us that our loved ones have not died; they have simply changed form. Perhaps a heart-shaped leaf will mysteriously appear on the ground on a particularly difficult day. Some people frequently find pennies, nickels, dimes, and quarters. These are all hope-filled messages that whisper, "I am with you. You are not alone."

Animals sometimes serve as messengers. If a hawk or eagle connection previously existed with the loved one in spirit, that feathered creature may often be seen soaring overhead. For others with a similar connection, the gift might come in the form of feathers. Some bereaved individuals experience baffling power outages during their grief journeys. Lights may flash off and on, or meaningful songs may inexplicably play on their cell phones. Others notice number sequences repeating or uplifting messages on license plates when they need them most. Still others report voicemail messages mysteriously showing up on answering machines after their loved one has died.

This chapter contains nineteen stories describing signs sent from loved ones in spirit. While some signs were subtle, others were more dramatic. Yet each was unique, personal, and significant to the contributor. These signs and gifts from spirit offer hope that life is eternal and love is immortal. The world is filled with mystery and magic from above. It is up to us to recognize the messages of love.

RAINBOW BLESSING

Joanne Hadley

⌐⌐⌐

I'll never forget the day the most spectacular rainbow I had ever seen appeared over Myrtle Beach. People driving by pulled over and got out to marvel at this incredible rainbow spanning the entire length of the beach; I joined them. The colors were vivid and brighter than anything I had ever seen. We all agreed that something extraordinary was happening right there in front of us. This was no ordinary rainbow. Very otherworldly, it completely filled the sky.

A few hours later, my husband mentioned that the mother of the Smith family in town had given birth to a baby boy earlier that day. He was born with a fatal heart defect. Although his older brother had survived a similar defect with numerous surgeries, this baby died shortly after he was born. Moments after the baby passed, while his father was holding him, a miraculous rainbow appeared outside—a memorable gift from a special little baby to his parents. Amazingly, at that same time many of us from town found ourselves unexpectedly gathered together on Myrtle Beach in awe of one of the most beautiful rainbows we could recall.

Joanne Hadley, mother of two, has been happily married for thirty years. An artist by trade, Joanne especially appreciates the exquisite moments in life that reveal to her the world is far grander than ever imagined.

Messages from Meghan

Nancy Kuhn

———

Our beautiful daughter, Meghan Rae Kuhn, celebrated her twenty-first birthday at the Shannon Airport on her way home from a dream trip to Ireland to visit one of her college classmates. Five weeks later, on May 5, 2007, she died peacefully in her sleep from a virus in her heart that no one knew was there. We were heartbroken. It felt as though we were living in a numbing fog. Yet "coincidences" were occurring all around us. It was those coincidences and connections with Meghan that helped us navigate through our grief.

Our family's experience on Memorial Day three weeks later really made me sit up and take notice. My husband, three children, and I took a Red Sox flag, a butterfly ornament, and our beach chairs to the cemetery to be closer to Meg. As I sat staring aimlessly at all the plants and mementos left on her grave, my eyes paused briefly on a peace lily plant that had been left there by some of her closest friends. What drew my attention to the plant were the unusual brown markings on one of the large white flowers. They literally spelled out the word "hi," and I didn't dare believe my eyes. Could this be a message from Meghan? I called out to my kids and my rational husband, who I knew would set me straight. After closely examining the flower, even my husband concluded that the marks were natural! We excitedly took pictures of the plant, but I hesitated to show them to anyone. It just seemed too paranormal. Nevertheless, the experience felt comforting. Now I realize how important it is to share these messages in whatever form they take. With God, all things are possible.

From then on, I started to keep a journal. There were so many things to write about as I reflected on the prior weeks. I found solace in this new way of staying connected to my daughter. Then came the day when I was driving by the cemetery and crying out loud,

"Meghan, where are you? Are you okay? What can I do for you?" Immediately I heard a strong, steady drum beat coming from my car radio. I turned up the volume and heard the song "Like a Prayer," with Madonna singing about how hearing a voice can feel like home. Later that evening when I wrote about it in my journal, it occurred to me that Madonna's song playing at that moment had not been random. I had called out to Meghan with questions, and she had found a way to answer me. I needed to do my part.

To mark the first anniversary of Meghan's passing, I decided I wanted to watch the sunrise on Plymouth Beach. I asked our friends and family to just think of Meg on that morning. Yet, when my husband, kids, and I arrived at the beach, it felt as though we had been transported into the movie *Field of Dreams*. Car after car pulled into the darkened beach parking lot with their headlights beaming brightly. Over eighty people came to hug us and to celebrate Meg's life. Meghan loved to bring people together, and she had done it in a big way. Through our tears, we celebrated. And even though we couldn't actually see the sun shining through the clouds that morning, we all knew it was there.

Despite the subtle messages I had been receiving, I longed to communicate more directly with Meg. Therefore, I decided to contact a reputable spiritual medium. I found myself disappointed because the communication was not as direct as I had hoped. Several times the medium mentioned Hoops and Yoyo during the session. This made no sense to me at all. Ten days later in a Hallmark store, I came across a display of little pink and green cartoon characters. At eye level I noticed two bobble-headed statues—one was a pink kitty named Hoops and the other was a green bunny named Yoyo. The message written on Hoops was "I've found my happy place," and the message on Yoyo was "I'm in my worry-free zone." Not only were these words comforting to me, but I later learned that Meghan loved these little Hallmark characters. She had even sent Hoops and Yoyo e-cards to her friends. Messages come in interesting ways.

Colby College very generously invited our family to the May 2008 graduation ceremony. That was the year Meghan would have graduated. We decided to attend the event in her honor. Even though it was difficult to be there without our daughter graduating, I could strongly feel Meg's presence with us that day. Also, a picture taken of my husband and me with her friends that day captured what appeared to be a white flame of light over my heart. The flame was right next to the locket I wear with Meg's picture and lock of hair. Wow! Once again, my lovely daughter had found a way to let us know she was there.

We all love Meghan and miss her physical presence every day. As her mom, these messages and the many others that I've received help me to feel that Meghan is okay, happy, and worry-free. Until the day I join her and experience where she is, I know our relationship will continue. For that, I am eternally grateful.

Nancy Kuhn lives and works in the extraordinary community of Plymouth, Massachusetts. She is thankful to God, her family, and her friends for their love and support.

HEAVEN ON EARTH: IT'S A CAMP THING

Ali Lerner Doyle

For many children with a severe or terminal illness, the Double "H" Hole in the Woods Ranch Summer Camp is heaven on earth. The focus of the camp is life, not death; laughter, not tears; and being who you are. Double H is a place where laughter defeats pain, dreams override fear, and life is to be celebrated. During the summer of 2000, when I was nineteen years old, I had the honor of being a counselor at Double H, a camp sponsored by the Paul Newman Foundation. I shared an incredible experience with these children as well as the group of counselors, nurses, doctors, and volunteers. I would often explain to the campers that they were the true teachers, not us, an idea they found as silly as our mashed potato–eating contests.

For many of the kids I befriended, camp was a break from the hospital routine and an opportunity to have a normal childhood experience. Our weekly activities included a trip to Six Flags amusement park, a carnival, a dance, a talent show, cabin night, fishing, ropes, swimming, food fights, and much more. During the fifth session of camp, I was a "Foxy Lady" counselor for the Fox Cabin, which was made up of ten to fourteen-year-old girls. Kelly, a twelve-year-old living with cancer, was one of my campers. Our friendship formed from the immediate discovery of our love for tie-dye shirts, and it blossomed as we made friendship bracelets on the first day in the Fox Cabin. As the week progressed, we became the best of buds. We were dates to the dance together, decked out in our favorite tie-dye shirts and green bandanas. During the talent show, we performed Britney Spears' summer hit "Oops!...I Did It Again." Nightly, Kelly would refuse to go to sleep until I tucked her in.

On carnival night, Kelly was hanging out with another counselor, Katy, with whom she also shared a special bond. As Kelly wheeled herself into the carnival with Katy's assistance, a bright yellow sunflower doll caught her eye. Kelly's smile exactly matched the doll's ear-to-ear grin, and she became determined to win that doll as her prize. After much persistence, Kelly finally won her doll and beamed with pride as she hugged the doll close to her chest. Until the end of camp, the sunflower doll remained right next to Kelly in her bed each night. And, as Kelly's mom drove her away from camp at the end of that summer session, the doll sat on Kelly's lap, the two of them smiling ear to ear.

Two weeks later, I received word that Kelly's health was failing. I happened to meet one of Kelly's old roommates from the hospital at the beginning of the eighth and final camp session. She mentioned that Kelly wasn't doing so well, but she was still raving about the fun she'd had at camp. Worried, I sent a letter with pictures and decided to visit Kelly in the hospital. She was being treated at a medical center a little over an hour away from camp. I gave her mom a phone call on Monday, only to hear that she didn't expect Kelly to live past the end of the week. I made plans to visit her on Wednesday. Kelly passed away before I arrived that morning, which meant I never made it to the hospital to see her one last time.

Kelly's funeral service was on Friday morning. Katy and I, along with other people from camp, went to the service. Her family had set aside a table with some of Kelly's stuffed animals for people to take home so they could have something physical to remember her by. On that table sat Kelly's doll from camp, the ear-to-ear grin still shining from its bright sunflower face. That familiar smile struck a nerve for both Katy and me as we remembered how much Kelly loved it. Katy took the doll they'd both worked so hard to earn; she left the service hugging the doll tightly to her chest, just as Kelly had repeatedly done.

After a rather abrupt and sad ending to the summer, camp officially ended less than a day after Kelly's service, and I was on an airplane back to Washington, DC, for the start of my junior year at American University. Arriving there, I waited in vain all Saturday afternoon and evening for the trusty storage company to deliver my belongings. They were nowhere to be seen. Early Sunday morning, I decided to search the package room for a letter from my parents that contained all my storage company receipts. As luck would have it, that package was missing as well. However, much to my surprise, there was another package there sent to me by my grandparents.

Disappointed that neither my belongings nor the letter had arrived, I walked slowly back to my room with the small cardboard package in hand from my grandparents. I sat on my bed and began to tear apart the nicely bound brown container. As I flipped open the cardboard flaps, I instantly dropped the box and began to cry. Inside was a bright yellow sunflower stuffed doll. It was exactly the same doll that Kelly had won at the carnival. Some might call it coincidence, but I believe it was a sign from heaven and a gift from Kelly. A mere day and a half after the funeral, there was no way my grandparents could have known about Kelly or her doll. It wasn't until several weeks later that I actually told them about the situation and the people involved.

I do believe that Kelly somehow sent me a message through two people I love and treasure here on earth. I believe everything happens for a reason, and it was Kelly's way of telling me that she is okay and she is watching over me from heaven. It is truly amazing to watch God's work in action. After a summer at Double H, I know that miracles happen every day. We just need to keep our minds open and listen with all our hearts.

Ali Lerner Doyle, MD, is from Omaha, Nebraska. She met her wonderful husband, Mark, at the Double H Ranch. As graduates of Ross University School of Medicine, they are completing their residency programs at Upstate Medical University, Ali in OB/GYN and Mark in Family Medicine.

April Snow Squall

Regis McDuffee

In the spring of 2002, I felt as if I was the luckiest father in the world; I had three wonderful sons. Brendan was a junior in high school in Peterborough, New Hampshire. Dylan was a sophomore at Assumption College in Worcester, Massachusetts. And my oldest son, Morgan, who had transferred from Ohio Wesleyan a year and a half earlier, was completing his senior year at Bates College in Lewiston, Maine. Although their mother, Lisa, and I had been divorced for more than six years, the two of us had always gotten along when it came to the well-being of our boys. I was proud of each son. With Morgan ready to graduate and embark upon his adult life, I was not taking any of this pride for granted.

During the early morning hours of March 3, 2002, my world changed. My son Morgan was fatally stabbed while coming to the aid of three classmates. The tragic incident occurred in downtown Lewiston as a result of friends engaging in an argument with a group of local teens. The argument escalated into a brawl. Just moments before the escalation, Morgan happened to walk by, accompanied by his fiancée, Suzi, and his younger brother Dylan. He noticed the quarrel and requested that his younger classmates, who were also Bates lacrosse teammates, break up the argument and go home. Morgan thought his suggestion had been followed, but within minutes, a fight broke out, and his teammates were on the ground being kicked. Morgan intervened and lost his life.

My entire family and community of friends have been devastated since that morning. Morgan was as perfect a son as any parent could ask for. It is only when Morgan's friends relate wonderful stories about him that I ever get any sense of relief from this senseless act of brutality. On that morning, every member of our family and Suzi's had to dig very deep not to fall apart from the tragedy. I am sure we all must have tapped into Morgan's emotional and spiritual strength to help carry us through the endless heartache and despair that followed.

I had always known Morgan was special, but there were times when my thoughts and pride about him might just have been the thoughts of any father who feels an uncompromising love for his son. In the months and years that followed, right up until this day, I can say with certainty that many people, some close to our family and others I have never met, felt the same way about Morgan. Always warm, engaging, passionate, and respectful, he made friends easily. A big, strong, athletic, handsome young man, Morgan had a positive aura about him. Anyone who knew him could never forget his constant and contagious smile.

Morgan was also a worrier. He was always concerned about the well-being of his younger brothers, Dylan and Brendan. Prior to the start of their lacrosse camp each year, Morgan always made arrangements with his coaches to voluntarily coach just so his younger brothers could attend for free. He also made sure to telephone Dylan and Brendan from college, instructing them on what high school courses would be best for them to take in order to get into a good college. "Hey, Morgan," I would say to him. "That's the parent's job!" But my son had to put in his own two cents. He cared that much. All of us feel such a void.

During his junior year at Bates, Morgan was elected a tri-captain of the lacrosse team after only one season of playing with them. That honor is generally reserved for seniors. In addition, his teammates thought so much of his leadership abilities and contributions that they selected Morgan as their sole captain of the lacrosse team during his senior year. According to his lacrosse coach, Peter Lasagna, "Morgan glowed. He was the man you wanted as your best friend, your son, your brother, your captain, and your son-in-law. He lived to serve the needs of all." Morgan was also passionate about his school-work, which included his senior thesis. His early completion of the thesis allowed my conscientious and industrious son to be honored with the first posthumous bachelor's degree in Bates history.

On the night he died, his mother and I had dinner with Morgan, along with a few of the players and their families, to celebrate the lacrosse team's first victory of the year. All of us sat together at a long table in a Lewiston restaurant near the Bates campus. I remember feeling this terrific sense of pride as I observed Morgan speaking with one of the parents. I overheard that the man was planning a trip to Australia, and Morgan was anxious to tell him about the wonderful trip he had just taken there with his fiancée, Suzi, a couple of months prior. The parent was fixed on every word that Morgan spoke. It really moved me at just how graceful Morgan was during this exchange of ideas. Morgan had fully grown up, and the world somehow belonged to him. I remember thinking about Morgan's future, and I had no doubt about his success. After the bill was paid, Morgan hugged me in his usual manner and said, "I love you." He did the same for his mom. I drove back to Newburyport, Massachusetts, and his mother headed back to New Hampshire. Within hours, we were both driving back to Maine after hearing the news that Morgan had been stabbed. The wonderful future that I had envisioned for my son a few hours earlier had been forever shattered.

After five lengthy, arduous years involving more than one trial, the court presented Morgan's murderer with a guilty verdict. The judge asked family members and my son's closest friends to write impact statements as a part of the process to help determine a suitable sentence for the guilty party. When I read over the many impact statements that were presented, I was struck by how many people considered Morgan to be their best friend. Always there for his friends, my son made each one feel as though he or she were the most important person in the world. Morgan was so sincere, and his friendships meant the world to him.

A month after Morgan's death, an extraordinary event occurred. On an unusually warm and sunny day in April, I was visiting my friend, Lise, in New Hampshire. Despite the beautiful day, I remained indoors. I was missing my son. While sitting quietly alone, I was reflecting and listening to music when Andrea Bocelli's song "Con Te Partiro" came on the stereo. The first two times I heard the song it was snowing outside; the snow seemed to fall in perfect cadence with the music. I love when it snows, and I love that song. I walked over to Lise's room and said, "Whenever I hear that song, I always wish that it would snow..."

Just then, Lise motioned for me to come quickly and look out her window. From the warm, sunny day outside, the weather had changed dramatically. Through her window, the two of us witnessed a snow squall that quickly covered the ground in only two or three minutes! The snow was the very thing I had wished for, and it lasted maybe half a minute or so longer than the song. Then, just as quickly as before, the weather reverted to the warm, sunny day we had been enjoying. The snow squall was surely an unexpected gift. It didn't occur to me until later in the evening that perhaps Morgan had something to do with the squall. I telephoned Lise from my home to tell her what I suspected. After I shared my thoughts, Lise agreed that it was obviously a gift from Morgan. At the time, I was so grateful that Lise "got it," too.

The snow squall left me with a nice feeling that lasted for days. However, it was not until later, when I had a long telephone conversation with a woman I had never met, that I was truly amazed. Morgan's fiancée, Suzi, had telephoned to tell me about a wonderful conversation she'd just had with a woman from Colorado named Anrahyah. My ex-wife's friend had told Suzi that she needed to contact Anrahyah, because Anrahyah had wonderful intuitive insights to share about Morgan. When Suzi called me, she was so excited because the two of them had talked for over two hours. Anrahyah gave Suzi so much information about Morgan's being, including details about privately shared moments with him that no one else could have known. Suzi strongly encouraged me to contact this woman and gave me her telephone number.

I tried calling Anrahyah in Colorado for more than a week before we finally connected. When we did, the two of us spoke for at least two hours. One of the things Anrahyah shared with me had to do with a conversation I'd had with Morgan before he died. Not one other person knew the information that Morgan and I had discussed. She also told me that Morgan was in a really good place. Somehow, he was able to communicate to us through Anrahyah. Plenty of details and private information were given to convince me that everything she was sharing was true. As we concluded our telephone conversation with thank yous and goodbyes, Anrahyah ended the discussion with one final thought: "Morgan wants to let you know that he is so happy that you got it…"

"What exactly do you mean, Anrahyah?"

"You know, the snow squall." I was blown away! The snow squall was indeed a gift from Morgan after all! I was instantly transported back to that warm, spring day in New Hampshire…listening to Andrea Bocelli's "Con Te Partiro"…when it had snowed! I'd had a strong sense that the snow squall was from Morgan, so it was such an incredible confirmation to hear it from Anrahyah. What was interesting about the song and that rare moment has to do with the song title. The Italian title "Con Te Partiro" stranslates to "Time to Say Goodbye." Perhaps the snow squall was Morgan's way of saying goodbye to me for now, and Anrahyah's gift was to confirm that Morgan lives on.

One of my most cherished possessions is a postcard that Morgan and Suzi sent me from Australia a few months before he died. Morgan and Suzi were halfway around the world and in love; this was a perfect time for the two of them. Morgan described their travels, and he talked about a sailing trip to the Whitsunday Islands. The postcard read: "It's the best sailing in the world…On my early morning run to the top of the mountain, you can see the coral reef extend for miles. Dad, you would love to be on this run."

On the same trip, Morgan called collect from Thailand on the day of the World Trade Center bombing. They were in a remote area where no one spoke English. People were glued to their television sets. Morgan thought they were watching some disaster movie. As soon as he realized what had happened, he telephoned immediately. Morgan had worked at Moran's Restaurant at the World Trade Center the previous two summers. A family friend owned it, and Morgan knew a lot of people, including cousins and uncles, who worked in the area. He was concerned about everyone, and he gave me a long list of friends to follow up with. Morgan's thoughtful concern for others had always made me so proud of my son.

As the years have passed and after speaking with so many people who knew and loved Morgan, it has become very clear to me how senseless his murder was—it was senseless because his killer had no idea who he stabbed. My son was just one of his random victims in the night. If the killer had known Morgan even for just a few moments, it would have been impossible to take the life of this remarkable young man. Morgan made friends with everyone and was admired by people from all walks of life. If he had only been given the chance, I am convinced that he would have won over his killer with his friendship and his smile.

Hundreds of people attended Morgan's wake, funeral, and the memorial service that was held at Bates to pay tribute. We displayed pictures of him from the time he was a baby all the way throughout his college career. I don't think there was one photo among the bunch that didn't show his radiant personality and exuberant smile.

So many words were shared about such an extraordinary, loyal, and vibrant young man who truly left his mark on the world. Even the president of Bates College spoke at his service. President Harward said: "Morgan was a leader and a peacemaker...What Morgan did was to try to help his friends. Wouldn't we all like to think we would act so selflessly?"

I still miss Morgan. Whenever I find myself missing him, I try to remember the many wonderful moments we shared, as well as Anrahyah's uplifting messages. And, I will never forget Morgan's snow squall on that warm New Hampshire day in the middle of Andrea Bocelli singing "Con Te Partiro," and how much comfort it brought me for the longest time. Now, whenever it snows, I listen to "Con Te Partiro" and reflect on that special time I spent with my son.

Regis McDuffee works in the office furniture business. Regis skis, sails, and kayaks with his sons, Dylan and Brendan, every chance he gets. They all have vivid memories of doing the same with Morgan.

Sean's Surprise Visit

Bonnie O'Neil

My twenty-one-year-old son, Sean, took his own life on May 30, 2000. From the time he was a teenager, he struggled with depression and tried to numb his personal pain using drugs. Our family was devastated by his loss. The pain felt unbearable to all of us. Besides me, Sean left his father, three sisters, wife, and six-month-old daughter, Ciara. However, he started leaving subtle messages from the grave not long after. The most profound experience occurred shortly after his passing.

Sean loved all kinds of vehicles, from Volkswagen Beetles to Ford trucks. Eleven days prior to his death, he had purchased a brand-new white truck, which he stored in my garage. He kept his other new work truck at his home. About a year after he died, I was upstairs reading in my bedroom one evening when I heard the sound of my garage door repeatedly going up and down. I thought perhaps my older daughter had decided to go out to the store. But she hadn't mentioned it, and all of us were already in bed. So I went downstairs to find out what was going on. My daughter looked as pale as could be in her bedroom. "Mom!" she exclaimed. "I was lying in bed when all of a sudden the garage door kept going up and down about three or four times. So I tried to open the door that leads to the garage, but for some unknown reason it wouldn't open!"

At that point, we decided to try opening the garage door together. The doorknob turned easily. We entered the garage, and no one was inside. Sean's truck was still there, and the overhead door was shut in the same position in which I had left it. We looked around for a bit, but nothing in the garage looked disturbed. We were in shock. Something had definitely happened that night that we couldn't explain. It just didn't make sense. The erratic garage door activity has never happened again since. I wonder … maybe Sean was in the garage that night checking on his truck, and he didn't want his sister to see him. Also, I found a light inexplicably turned on inside my china cabinet that same night when it had been shut off earlier.

After getting over the wonderment of what happened that evening, I've come to the conclusion that Sean wanted to stop by for one last visit. He didn't mean for it to be frightening or scary. Sean just wanted us to know that he was still around, and that he is still looking out for his family. Since that time, one of my younger daughters has had several experiences with her brother, including dream visitations, hearing the sound of his work boots going up the stairs, and feeling his presence in the car with her. Even years later Sean's daughter had a dream of her dad picking her up and introducing her to the whole family.

Even though I can no longer physically hold my only son, I know that he is still around. I can feel him every day, and his love is what keeps me going. People sometimes ask me if I believe in life after death. I never ponder my answer. I don't need to. I know that my son is living on, and that Sean is watching over us.

Bonnie O'Neil is a single mother of four children. Born in Chicago, Illinois, she raised her children in Arizona. Bonnie enjoys cooking, genealogy, reading, animals, and her three adorable grandchildren, Ciara, Liam, and Mary Grace.

KRISTEN'S BUTTERFLIES

Laura Ouellette Lauria

Kristen Ann Montanari was my best friend. We did everything together. We went on double dates together, got our first jobs together, went to the high school prom together, and even went to college together. Though we sometimes fought, Kristen and I truly loved one another. And, when push came to shove, we were there for each other, even through Kristen's devastating diagnosis of non-Hodgkin's lymphoma at the young age of twenty-three.

Everyone loved to be around Kristen because she was always ready to have fun. She was a beautiful young woman, inside and out, with long brown hair, dark brown eyes, and long dark eyelashes. Kristen's enthusiasm, laughter, and smile were contagious. It was hard to be down whenever she was around, even while visiting her in the hospital when she was sick with cancer.

Kristen had a way of making people feel special just by being in her presence. Such a wonderful friend to so many, she was always ready to lend a hand and to listen or offer any advice that could help. In fact, I never made an important decision without consulting her. Whether it was writing an essay for our high school English class or going on a date with someone new, I always talked it over with Kristen first. Always honest, she gave me the solid advice I was looking for, without judgment. I learned so much about love and friendship from Kristen.

On July 18, 1993, seven months after being diagnosed, Kristen lost her battle with cancer. I was devastated. I never believed it would happen, perhaps because I couldn't fathom the thought of being on this earth without her. Kristen was so much a part of me; I didn't know how I could possibly continue on without her constant love, support, and friendship.

For many weeks, I painfully grieved the loss of my beloved friend, feeling as though she had left me all alone. I had a tough time sleeping at night, as well as keeping my mind occupied. It was so difficult to feel anything but great sorrow and loneliness. I spent lots of time with her mom, dad, family, and friends. I desperately longed for a sign from Kristen to let me know she was okay and that she really wasn't gone. I would pray for it to happen. That very first sign took several months, but when it happened, it was incredible. I had a dream, and Kristen came to visit me in the dream.

Having just completed my master's degree, I had finally been hired for my first job as an elementary school guidance counselor when the dream occurred. I found myself in my childhood home walking toward the kitchen. The front door of our split-entry home was wide open when the doorbell rang. I quickly turned to look at the doorway, and there stood Kristen with a gorgeous suntan and wearing sunglasses! She was radiant. I gasped with excitement. "I thought you were dead! Everyone thinks you're dead. *Where have you been?!*" I asked as I cried. I was elated at the mere sight of her. She was finally with me again, looking even more beautiful than I had remembered.

"Oh," Kristen said, so matter-of-factly, "I needed a vacation."

I hugged my best friend as she entered my home and we started to walk up the stairs together. "Kristen, you need to call your house!" I suddenly exclaimed. "Everyone thinks you're gone."

She walked over to my kitchen wall phone and nonchalantly picked up the receiver. As she did, Kristen turned to me and said, "Oh, I heard you got a job. It's about f*&^ing time! Oh, hello, Mom?" As crude as her words were, I *knew* this was truly a message from Kristen, as those were the exact words she would have spoken to me in exactly that same way. I awoke from the dream so excited, believing that Kristen was still alive. When I remembered it wasn't true, I felt saddened and disappointed. But within minutes, I realized that perhaps this was Kristen's way of letting me know she was all right. It was the sign I had been waiting for.

I had another dream about my best friend a few months later. In this dream, Kristen was alive, and her mother was dead. We were sitting on the curb next to a maple tree near her house. The two of us were talking about her mother (whom I have always called Mrs. M) and how truly wonderful she was. I told Kristen how much I loved Mrs. M, and how I had often felt she was my *other* mother. I also mentioned to Kristen how good her mother had been to her when she was sick.

Kristen fired back, "You don't know the half of it. My mother did so much for me, Laura, you have no idea. She was the best! I am so grateful that I had her by my side." Kristen paused and then asked, "Now what?" I woke up from the dream feeling strongly that Kristen wanted me to relay this important message to her mom. So I did. Mrs. M cried and thanked me. I think Mrs. M was truly touched by the dream. It was clear to me that Kristen was conveying her deep love and appreciation for her mother.

Shortly after Kristen's death, I gathered all the letters, cards, and memorabilia I had received from her and carefully placed them in a special memory file. I didn't want to lose anything. I liked the idea of having everything in one place to easily access whenever I felt the need to reminisce or feel closer to Kristen. A few years after her death, I happened to be home all alone on Valentine's Day with no Valentine in my life. I was feeling pretty lonely. In prior years with Kristen, there had been several Valentine's Days when I was alone and Kristen wasn't. Somehow, my best friend was always able to make me feel okay about it. This time, I didn't have Kristen to help me through the day. I decided to clean my apartment in hopes that seeing it clean would help me feel better.

When I moved my bed to the side to vacuum underneath it, I noticed a card stuck between the box spring and mattress. I picked up the card and immediately recognized it. I began to cry. It was an old birthday card from Kristen that she had accidentally given me two years in a row, which, of course, we laughed about at the time. I wondered how it had gotten there. I had kept all her cards neatly tucked away in my memory file. I proceeded to open the card and read the handwritten words by Kristen declaring our friendship and wishing me well in the coming year. After seeing her familiar flowery handwriting, the feelings of loneliness began to subside. Amazingly, almost eight years after her death, she was still making me feel okay.

Eight years after Kristen's death, a wonderful man, Mike, came into my life. In November of 2002, we were engaged. I had always thought I would be calling Kristen to tell her my exciting news at whatever hour of the day. I felt such a sense of sorrow that I couldn't share it with her. So Mike and I visited her parents and shared our good news with them.

Because I worked for the public school system, my fiancé and I decided on a summer wedding. When we went to book the hall for the reception, we discovered that there were very few dates available in the summer. In fact, there were only two dates open, one of which was July 19, 2003, the day following the ten-year anniversary of Kristen's death. What a difficult day that would be, especially without Kristen as my maid of honor. After a great deal of thought, Mike and I chose that day with the conscious decision to honor Kristen at our wedding; we would release butterflies after the wedding in her memory.

I searched for butterfly farms in the area, and I finally found one that would ship them to my home. However, because monarch butterflies are a difficult species to breed, they were limited in number and quite expensive. I ordered a few monarchs along with several painted lady butterflies for the wedding.

Because brides traditionally wear something borrowed on their wedding day for good luck, I asked Mrs. M if I could borrow something of Kristen's for my wedding. In my mind, I'd hoped that she would lend me the angel pin that was on Kristen's purse when she died. I also decided to write Kristen a letter a few days before the wedding. At the rehearsal dinner, Mrs. M presented me with an anklet and Kristen's angel pin. I handed Mrs. M my letter. I told her she could read it if she wanted to. In the letter, I had secretly written to Kristen, telling her that I hoped one of the butterflies would somehow stand out to let me know she was there with me at my wedding.

Immediately following the wedding ceremony, my husband and I went outside the front of the church, along with the wedding party and all the guests, to release the butterflies in memory of Kristen. As we did, most of the butterflies clung to the white netting in the box. Mike and I laughed as we coaxed them out of the white box in order to set them free. I looked up at Mrs. M, who was standing on the church steps. By the expression on her face, I could tell she had read my letter to Kristen. Then, we both simultaneously looked down at my dress. There was one lone butterfly that had landed next to the ivory bow and remained with me for quite some time. Mrs. M and I locked eyes and smiled. Kristen was really with me. Her mother and I both knew it.

The butterfly signs kept coming. At critical points in my life after my wedding day, it seemed that monarch butterflies would miraculously appear. Whether it was to give me hope while my husband was undergoing surgery or to help me close an old relationship, it was Kristen's way of letting me know she was still with me. One time, I telephoned Mr. and Mrs. M on Kristen's birthday, as I do each year. It was a sunny, crisp autumn day with the leaves brightly colored. I told them how the day seemed so much like Kristen, and then shared all my experiences with the butterflies. That evening, Mr. M called me to tell me that *The Boston Globe* was featuring an article that day on monarch butterflies in their North Weekly section. Wow, a monarch butterfly article on Kristen's birthday! What a great birthday present for Kristen and what amazing synchronicity once again!

That same day, I remember my young son Nicholas playing with a plaque that my mother had given me a few years earlier in honor of Kristen. The plaque was a music box that played Kristen's funeral song, "Wind Beneath My Wings." A few days prior, I had wound up the music box to let Nicholas hear the song. But on that day, on Kristen's birthday, I hadn't picked it up or wound it up at all. Spontaneously, Nicholas picked up the box, and when he did, Kristen's funeral song began to play. Tears filled my eyes as I sat on the floor with my son. I decided to wind it up one more time. With an impish little grin, Nicholas looked up at me, stuck his tongue out and smiled, just like Kristen. I am thankful for all the little ways that Kristen lets me know she is still close by. Kristen, thank you for being my best friend. Thank you for the butterflies. And most of all, thank you for always being there for me and for continuing to be the wind beneath my wings.

Laura Ouellette Lauria, MEd, worked as an elementary guidance counselor for twelve years prior to deciding to stay home with her kids. Laura loves writing, golfing, and spending time with family. She and her husband, Mike, live in the Boston area with their two boys.

Miss Mischief

Elissa Davey

People ask me, "How can you bury a baby? It's got to be the hardest thing to do!" My answer is always, "How can I not?" As the founder of the Garden of Innocence, a nonprofit organization that provides dignified burials for abandoned children, I have been taking care of these children since 1995. I have learned so much from them. The babies have taught me that even though they may be gone from our sight, they still know everything that is going on. They can also still help us and guide us, since they are fully aware of what we are doing for them.

I would like to share one such story about a little girl who was found off Sunrise Highway in San Diego County. Wrapped in a handmade blanket, with her dated hospital tag still on her leg, this newborn had been lying there for two years. No animals or bugs had touched her little body, which had been mummified by the cold winter weather. As soon as the Garden of Innocence learned of her, we touched her as she surely touched all of us. We named her Michaela, and made plans for her burial.

I was leaving to meet the driver scheduled to transport Michaela when I received a call from him informing me that his truck was full; I would have to transport her in my car from the morgue to the mortuary. I had never driven with a body in my car, so I wondered what I should do. I decided to sing every nursery rhyme I could think of to let Michaela know that someone loved her. I was still singing to her when we arrived at the mortuary, so I slowed my car down to finish the last song. Then I told her that she would be going inside the mortuary refrigerator for just a bit longer, and afterward she would have the most wonderful service. Also, I apologized for disturbing her, but I let her know that she would soon be going home. I carried her inside, removed her from the handmade little casket she had been riding in, wrapped her in a handmade blanket, and lovingly placed Michaela in the hands of the mortuary personnel.

The following morning, I had just sat down in the passenger seat of my car when the car door locked before my husband had a chance to get in. My husband gave me a quick questioning look. I responded, "I didn't touch the lock." Interestingly, my husband used to play this same prank on me, locking the door whenever I would try to get inside the car. He would laugh at me at the time, thinking it was funny. I never found it funny at all. In fact, I found it rather mean-spirited.

But on this particular day, the car door locked after I had gotten in, with him on the outside this time. I unlocked the door, and before he could open it, it locked again. My husband looked at me, making a rude hand gesture. I told him again that I hadn't touched the lock. I unlocked the door again, and once again, it locked before he could get in. I unlocked it a fourth time, and this time when he tried to get in, the car door lock went up and down, lock, unlock, lock, unlock, lock. Finally I said, "Michaela, if you are in this car, knock it off!"

Instantly the locking stopped, and it never happened again, ever! I smiled as I realized that Michaela was right there with me, playing tricks on my husband and giving him a good dose of his own medicine. Just as I had loved and respected her, Michaela had shown me in her own playful way that she was right there helping me, too. I love Michaela, and I speak of her as my little imp. I bet if she had lived, she would have been a fun-loving stinker.

Elissa Davey, mother, grandmother, and realtor, is the founder of the nonprofit Garden of Innocence National, which currently has gardens in five states and in Poland. Elissa hopes to expand their work to all fifty states and abroad through the loving generosity and kindness of others.

Angel Whispers on the Wings of a Dragonfly

Angela Rodriguez

My husband and I were sitting in the living room talking about our precious son when the clock struck midnight on August 2, 2009. Pain immediately pierced our hearts and tears began to flow from our eyes. It was the one-year anniversary of Francisco Jr.'s death. Spinal muscular atrophy had taken our baby boy from us on his seven-month birthday. The two of us longed to see the smile that had brought us so much joy. How we wished we could look into those gorgeous, big brown eyes and run our fingers through his long, curly hair once again.

I picked up Francisco's stuffed doggie, grabbed my husband by the hand, and opened the front door. We headed outside to look at the stars and weep. When I opened the door, a beautiful baby dragonfly sitting on the door's overhang brace greeted us. It was the most beautiful dragonfly I had ever seen. Almost instantly, our tears stopped flowing and our hearts filled with peace. Francisco was right there with us, and we could feel it all over. This was a sign from our amazing baby.

I let the dragonfly crawl onto my hands and then sat on the floor to take in the moment. I held that dragonfly for a good five minutes as I repeatedly thanked our son for sending such an amazing gift on one of the hardest days of all. We even captured the moment on our camera phone. It wasn't the first time that Francisco had sent us a dragonfly, but it was the first time that we actually got pictures of it. That night, my husband and I spent a few hours outside talking to Francisco and reminding him how much he was loved. We didn't shed another tear on that day. No matter how much we wanted to cry, we just couldn't. It was a different kind of feeling than we normally felt. There was a strange sense of peace in the air.

In the past, every time my husband and I visited Francisco Jr.'s garden grave, dragonflies were there to greet us. One time we even visited his grave during a thunderstorm. While on our knees yelling, crying, asking God why He had taken our son and begging Him to give him back to us, a huge dragonfly flew right up to our faces in the pouring rain, stayed a few moments, and flew away. Without fail, whenever we are at our lowest, Francisco always sends a sign to lift our spirits. Angels are real. They let us know they are near us all the time. Sometimes we just have to open our eyes and hearts to feel their presence.

We are truly blessed for every moment we have had with our beautiful son. Rest peacefully in heaven, Panchito. One day, Mommy and Papi will be there to hold you in our arms once again. We look forward to that day. Until then, we are taking one day at a time. We love and miss you more than ever!

Angela Rodriguez is married to her wonderful husband, Francisco Sr. Being a mommy to Francisco Jr. was a dream come true. Those seven months were the best days of her life. The small things in life are what matter most.

OUR ETERNAL BOND

Barbara Desclos

⸻

"If ever a day goes by that I don't say that I love you, know *always* that I do." These words, along with two long-stemmed roses and a butterfly gently fluttering over them, are etched on a glass plaque given to me by my son, Matthew, on Mother's Day in 1999. Matthew was very proud of this gift; it was the first Mother's Day gift he had purchased with money earned from his first job as a bag boy at a local grocery store.

Matthew was my only child. My handsome, six-foot-tall, brown-haired and beautiful, blue-eyed son was taken from me shortly after his sixteenth birthday in an automobile accident. Matthew died on a hot summer Sunday afternoon only two blocks from our home. My son had previously told me that he wasn't afraid of dying. When it was his time, he would go, but he also reassured me that he would always be with me. I know that Matthew is with me every day and everywhere I go.

Shortly before his death, Matthew had gone swimming with a group of friends. Two Tupac Shakur songs, "Life Goes On" and "I Ain't Mad at Cha," came on the radio. Matthew told his friends that he wanted both of these songs to be played at his funeral. Unfortunately, his friends didn't relay this information to me until several weeks after the funeral. I wondered how a healthy young teenager could have had such insight into his own life and death. How did Matthew know that his time on this earth would be short?

Since his passing, my son has let me know in several ways that he's okay. The first time had to do with the donation of his corneas to an organ bank. Matthew and I had previously discussed the subject of organ donation. In fact, my son had planned to sign up to be an organ donor the day he got his driver's license, something he never had the opportunity to do. Since hospitals are now mandated to ask family members about donating their deceased loved one's organs, in a sense Matthew had already made the decision for me. Both of Matthew's corneas were donated to a local organ bank, as I knew this was exactly what he would have wanted. I also requested that if either of the recipients wanted to correspond with me, I would certainly welcome hearing from them.

A few days before my first Christmas without Matthew, I found myself alone at the cemetery, crying and talking to him as I often did. I was here on this earth without him, and he was out there somewhere without me. I needed to know that my son was safe and at peace. I asked Matthew to please let me know in any way he could that he was all right.

The very next day, I received a letter in the mail from the organ bank. Inside the envelope was a letter written by a gentleman thanking me for the gift of Matthew's cornea. Because of my decision to donate my son's corneas, this man was now able to see. Matthew had indeed come through for me. And as hard as that first Christmas was without him, just knowing that a part of Matthew was still here on this earth helped me make it through that difficult holiday.

Months went by and before I knew it, Mother's Day was approaching. It would be my first Mother's Day in seventeen years without my son. How would I survive the day? The feelings were overwhelming. It was Mother's Day. But was I still a mother? Everywhere I turned I saw mothers with their children. All I could think was, *Where is my son?* I just couldn't believe this was happening to me.

The day before Mother's Day, I walked out to my mailbox and found another envelope from the organ bank. I took the envelope inside and opened it. I found another letter, this time from the recipient of my son's other cornea. The gentleman who had written the letter told me that receiving Matthew's cornea had made it possible for him to keep his job. Now he would be able to finish putting his daughters through college and to watch his young grandchildren grow up. I cried and cried. Again, I was so proud of my son. Yet my heart ached for him. I missed him so.

As much as I miss Matthew every single day, the holidays are always the most difficult. During Christmastime of 2002, I was visiting my parents when I noticed a five-by-seven framed photograph of Matthew in their dining room. It was one I had never seen before. Their best friends had taken the picture at my brother and sister-in-law's wedding reception in 1996. The couple had framed the photograph and given it to my parents as a Christmas gift. I asked Mother if I could borrow the framed picture in order to make a copy. When I arrived home, I took apart the frame and found not one, but two pictures inside. The first was the original picture that I had asked to borrow. Underneath was a second picture taken of Matthew and me at the wedding reception. I had never seen this picture, nor did my parents know it was there. What an incredible Christmas gift from my son! Once again, Matthew had found a way to let me know that he was okay, and we would always be together.

It has now been over seven years since Matthew's death. He continues to take care of me, helping me find the strength and faith to go on without him. In November of 2005, my mother died following her courageous battle with pancreatic cancer. On my way to care for her during her last days, I would often stop by the cemetery where Matthew was buried. I would plead with my son to please help me find the strength to face losing another person whom I loved so dearly. I know my son, Matthew, heard me. While caring for my mother a short while later, I happened to walk into her room and overheard her talking to someone. I looked around the room and saw no one there. Then I heard Mom call out my son's name, Matthew. Instantly, I knew Matthew was there, helping my mother prepare for the long journey on which she was about to embark.

During our last conversation on the afternoon of her passing, I asked my mother to please take care of Matthew as soon as they were together again. Mom promised that she would. That conversation has brought me so much peace. Matthew and his grandmother are together now. It comforts me to know that my son is no longer alone. He is with his favorite person in the world, his Grammy.

Matthew may not be with me physically, but the emotional bond we share is just as alive as ever. I am comforted to know that my son is watching over me and protecting me. I still talk to him, and I know in my heart that Matthew hears me. Matthew will always love me just as much as I love him; our bond is forever.

Barbara Desclos lives in New Hampshire with her husband and four stepchildren, along with their two dogs and seven cats. Barbara works as a licensed nursing assistant at a local nursing home and as a hospice volunteer.

LIFE IS GOOD

Donna Craig

Life was good. I remember holding my baby, Robby, while crossing a busy street; my two-year-old son, Hunter, was holding on to my left hand, and I was telling my five-year-old daughter, Allison, to hold on to Robby's foot, to look both ways, and to walk fast. I often think back to this memorable time when my children were little, safe, and happy, and to that time when I felt safe and happy, too.

In the fall of 1999, our daughter, Allison, was just starting her final year at Colby Sawyer College. Hunter was a freshman at New England College just thirty minutes away from Allison. Our youngest son, Robby, was a junior at Marblehead High School, and my husband and I were busy working at our hardware store in the next town over. All of us were fulfilling our own dreams and goals.

When Hunter was accepted into New England College, we were all thrilled. Hunter was a wonderful athlete and was so excited that he would be playing on NEC's lacrosse team. Hunter had scored the second highest number of points in lacrosse in the state of Massachusetts that year, and the newspapers referred to him as "Goodwill Hunter." His younger brother, Robby, had assisted on almost every one of Hunter's goals. Twenty-two months apart in age, they were an awesome duo. Sports were always important to us as a family.

As captain of the Marblehead High School hockey and lacrosse teams, Hunter received the Coaches Award for Leadership. I think Hunter intuitively knew what each team member needed. Our son played hard and put everything he had into whatever he was doing. Hunter was vibrant, mischievous, fun, and popular in his class. This blond, blue-eyed, handsome young man would often be seen wearing a yellow "Life is good" baseball cap. He was a kind, thoughtful friend who wasn't afraid to speak his mind when any of his friends needed direction or help.

Hunter attended New England College for only six weeks. He died in a tragic accident in a car driven by one of his best friends on October 19, 1999. Mike and Scott were in the front seat of the car. Hunter and his friend Amanda were in the back seat trying to get their seat belts on, but their seat belts were jammed. They knew Mike was driving too fast and yelled at him to slow down.

When Mike dropped Amanda off, she begged him again to please slow down. He didn't. A few minutes later, their car hit a tree at eighty miles per hour. Mike and Hunter were thrown from the car. Mike was in a coma for a month due to head injuries. Scott had had his seatbelt on and was released from the hospital the next day. Hunter was the only one who died.

When my son died, I wasn't thinking about whether I would have a connection with him from the other side. For me, it was about re-membering that life was good. I needed to carry on and go forward. I also needed to let teenagers know that you need to be responsible, and your consequences for your actions are yours. It wasn't about Hunter's death. It was about Hunter's life and the many people he had touched.

Hunter's nineteenth birthday was on November 15, 1999, three weeks after he died. As a reminder, I had fifty yellow "Life is good" pins made up and handed them out to his high school friends. I have now given out over 8,000 pins, mostly to high school students after talks I have given to them on safe, responsible decision-making and behavior.

On the first Christmas after Hunter died, Allison gave a close friend a Penny Bear wearing a yellow, hand-knit sweater with a "Life is good" pin on it; it was named the "Hunter Bear" in honor of my son. Every year, we give out at least a hundred Hunter Bears to new Marblehead and Swampscott drivers as a reminder that life is too good to waste—please drive safely and responsibly and buckle up.

Two years after Hunter died and many coincidences later, my good friend Gail gifted me with a reading from a local psychic for my fiftieth birthday. Gail said, "Let's just both go, have some fun, and see what happens." The psychic's name was George. In just thirty minutes, I could tell that he definitely knew my son, but most of all, that Hunter was all right. George shared things that only I would know, and described to me some of the things that would be happening in the future. He also told me that Hunter's job on the other side now was to help people cross over.

I usually visit George around Hunter's birthday. During one reading, George asked if I had noticed any unusual electrical signs from Hunter. I had seen streetlights going on and off, blinking repeatedly. Sometimes my old car radio would turn on and off, and my car's brake lights would stay on after the car had already been parked and turned off. Also, the clock would often read twenty-one past the hour whenever I was thinking of Hunter, which still happens to this day. Hunter's hockey number was twenty-one, and Robby's lacrosse number was also twenty-one. Even when I'm rushing out the door with many other things on my mind, I will look up at the clock as I'm leaving. It almost always seems to read twenty-one past the hour. Now I just say, "Good morning, Hunter."

The number connection also happens with my husband, Hunter Sr. Recently he received a hat from our daughter and her husband that they had purchased on their honeymoon in Ireland. Inadvertently, he left the Irish hat in a Costco shopping cart. Halfway home, my husband realized that he had left it a nd immediately called Costco, asking them to please hold on to the hat if they found it. The next evening, he went back to Costco. As he drove into the parking lot, my husband thought, "Wow, I got here really quickly." He looked down at the car clock, and it read 5:21 PM. In acknowledgment he said, "Thank you, Hunter." My husband drove to the area where he had parked the previous day, and there was his Irish hat, right on top of all the shopping carts! Things like that happen to us all the time.

Another time, George asked me to tell him about *the tree*. I explained that Hunter had died because the car had hit a tree. George said, "Not that tree, the *other* tree." When I suggested that maybe he was referring to the kids' tree fort from when they were little, he said, "No. I see Hunter sitting under a tree. Maybe it's a time you don't know about, but he is telling you about a tree." One month later, our family received a lovely letter from New England College. They were planting a tree in Hunter's memory. It was the year Hunter would have graduated, 2003. I know our son was so proud and wanted to share this honor with all of us. During my occasional visits to psychics, I find that the information they provide simply validates what I already know to be true.

One time, as I was leaving the house for work, I looked up at the clock, and it was 9:21. I walked to my car and found a penny next to it. Perhaps it was a penny from heaven. I looked down at my Wheaten Terrier, Paddy, and asked, "What does all this mean?" Paddy just looked at me and tilted his cute head, and in that moment a black crow flew right down the middle of the street over our heads. I examined the penny closer and found that the penny was made in 1980, the year that Hunter was born. What did all this mean? I smiled, so grateful my son was letting me know one more time that he was with me. Thank you, Hunter. I love and miss you so much, too!

Donna Craig, mother of three wonderful children and two grandchildren, has been married to her high school sweetheart for thirty-five years. Having sold their hardware store and gift shop, she is now focused on being a grandmother, the next exciting chapter. Life is so good!

Confirmation from Mom

Mary Beth Sweet

My husband and I debated all the way to the hospital whether we wanted to know if I was having a baby boy or girl; even at the start of the ultrasound, we hadn't yet made the decision. But the odd look that came over the technician's face as she quickly excused herself from the room for a moment derailed all thoughts of pink and blue blankets. Thirty-two weeks into my otherwise healthy pregnancy, the world seemed to come to a standstill in that moment. The next two weeks seemed like a numb blur of tests, specialists, and sleepless nights, all to the same end. The baby girl that I was carrying inside of me was not likely to survive the rest of the pregnancy, let alone the delivery. Our little girl had a rare syndrome not detectable with the usual prenatal genetic markers. To this day, we've only ever had a "best match" diagnosis. The second-level ultrasound confirmed that only the base of her brain had developed, and she had little chance of surviving the delivery. Our world was shattered.

It had been less than two and a half years since I had lost my mother, my best friend, to a courageous battle with cancer. I never dreamt that I would be facing the pain of such a deep loss so soon again. It had already been tough not being able to share my pregnancy with Mom. Although she had known her first three grandchildren before she died, Mom had been a grandmother for only twenty-four months. As her health declined, her greatest regret was missing out on watching her grandchildren grow.

As the reality of our unborn daughter's fate settled in, we made plans for her. She was to be baptized as soon as she was delivered. Then she would be buried alongside my mom in a private service. With my baby still kicking inside of me, we were making plans for her final resting place even though she hadn't even drawn her first breath.

The circumstances of her condition made the final weeks of the pregnancy mentally and physically unbearable. On the night before I was to be induced, my labor started on its own. Twelve hours later, I was blessed with the sound of the sweetest cry; my daughter had survived the delivery! I was so happy to be able to meet my baby girl and let her know how much she was loved. My husband and I named her Lauren. We knew our moments together would be few. A short time after delivery, a minister visited us in the neonatal intensive care unit. Lauren was fussy and seemed pained until the minister laid a hand on her in prayer; an immediate peace came over her. The fussing stopped and a sense of calm came over all of us. The moments became hours, the hours became a day, the day became a week…

After ten days of spending every possible minute with Lauren and worrying that we would miss her final moments if we were not there with her, the hospital staff asked if we would like to take her home. This was a question that we never expected to hear. Lauren had surpassed all expectations. Even when her feeding tube was removed, she was able to learn how to drink from a special soft bottle, from which we squeezed milk to her in between breaths. My husband and I began the preparations to bring her home. She needed a special car bed to help support her head, something that is normally a special-order item. Yet, remarkably, we found one at the first store we visited. We arranged daily appointments with a wonderful visiting nurse. Knowing we were bringing Lauren home for her final hours, we also made arrangements with the local police and EMTs. This included formalizing a "do not resuscitate" order, the most difficult document I have ever signed.

During the weeks that followed—yes, weeks—we ran the whole gamut of emotions. Those weeks were incredible, exhilarating, exhausting, and stressful. We made every effort to give Lauren the life that every baby deserves. She was part of the family, and she was involved in our everyday activities. This included mundane trips to the grocery store, daycare pickups for her older sister, and family dinner gatherings for St. Patrick's Day and Easter. She even had a sidewalk seat along the Boston Marathon route to cheer on the runners. Lauren remained a constant source of joy and peace. Every person who came to visit with her remarked that there was something so peaceful about this child.

One unusually warm, seventy-five-degree day in April, I sat alone with Lauren on the deck, feeding her a bottle. That afternoon, the birds were particularly cheerful, singing so beautifully and loudly that I had to move into the house so I could hear Lauren's sweet breaths. As I readjusted both of us, I realized that I was not hearing her breathe. I laid her on the floor and put my ear to her chest, but I still did not hear anything. She had passed. In need of support and reassurance, I contacted our nurse and called my husband home from work.

At one point, the police and EMTs were telephoned according to the protocol necessary for when a death occurs at home. They arrived quietly and respectfully, and they waited with us for the funeral director. I recounted the afternoon to no one in particular, just to anyone present, which included my husband, my sister, a girlfriend, our nurse, and many other emergency respondents. I recapped the peacefulness of the day, with the sun shining, the warm breeze blowing, and the birds singing. Lauren's death was a calm and gentle passing. I looked down at my precious girl and then up at my sister. "Do you think she's with Mom? I wish I could be sure she's there with Mom."

A moment later, the light bulb in the lamp right next to me blew out. The funny thing was, Mom knew I never liked that lamp. I looked up with tears in my eyes and a smile so wide. Feeling so uplifted, I announced, "Mom has her! She is there!" For me, this was a confirmation that my mom finally had the grandbaby she was missing!

Mary Beth Sweet, training specialist, is married to Paul. They have three earthly angels, Lindsay, Leah, and Landon, and one baby angel, Lauren, in heaven. Mary Beth's angels never cease to amuse, amaze, and inspire her every day.

LUCAS, A.K.A. TURTLE

Nance Welles

My grandson, Lucas Daniel Giaconelli, was killed in a hit-and-run accident while trying to get to the safer side of the street on his skateboard. He was only fifteen years old at the time. Everyone called him Turtle because of his long neck and gigantic brown eyes.

A few weeks after my grandson passed away, I found myself visiting local cemeteries to find a suitable resting place for his ashes. One particular spot at the Eternal Hills Cemetery in Oceanside seemed promising. There was a statue of Mary, and under the statue was a marble slab that contained individual plaques with ashes behind them. In front of the statue was another statue of a male admirer kneeling and looking up at Mary adoringly. I decided to bring Turtle's sister, Andrea, to see what she thought.

When we got to the area, Andrea didn't seem to care for the location. I found myself disappointed even though I tried not to show it. As I stood there next to the admiring statue, I noticed something on his outstretched left arm. Since my vision was not that good, I called out to my granddaughter to come closer. "Andrea, what is that?" I questioned.

"Nana, it's a turtle," she replied. At first, Andrea believed that I might have planted it there to help her in her grief. Of course, I did not. Sure enough, it was a small, crudely carved wooden turtle right there on the statue's arm. I believe it was a gift from Lucas, a.k.a Turtle, letting us know that he was in a better place. So, we happily took the turtle home with us. Lucas had meant everything to Andrea. Her only sibling was the rock of our family and her light at the end of the tunnel. Andrea now keeps her turtle with her wherever she goes.

Thank you, Lucas, for sending us that message of love and reassurance. We all love and miss you very much. Not a day goes by without you on our minds and in our hearts.

Nance Welles is an avid volunteer who works for the Trauma Intervention Team of North County. Nance and her granddaughter, Andrea, are committed to raising funds for the Vista Skatepark Coalition to rebuild a skatepark in Vista, California, in honor of Lucas.

GLITTER GIRL

Nancy Cincotta

⌒

In thirty-five years working as a social worker, I have helped many children facing life-threatening illnesses. Several hundred of the children I have worked with have died. As a result, I have heard many interesting stories from their parents, family members, and friends. These experiences have forced me to broaden my thinking about life, death, and the possibility of after-death communication with grieving family members following the death of a child. It has become apparent to me that not everything that happens in this world can be understood or explained.

Bereaved parents often describe connections, signs, and experiences suggesting that their children are sending them messages. Most of the time these experiences are quite comforting, although occasionally some find them unnerving. Regardless, parents generally crave contact from their children in any form. Although some parents do not receive signs during the day, they report sensing their child's presence in dreams.

I had the privilege of working with one young girl, Alice, who always seemed wiser than her years. Even at the age of ten, Alice seemed more like a teenager, relating easily to children of all ages. Many groups of children, young and old, and parents readily accepted her. Alice held a deep religious conviction; she believed that she had been put here on the earth with a purpose. This extraordinary young woman served as a source of inspiration for many other children and families affected by Fanconi anemia (FA), a genetic disorder by which she had been challenged her entire life. Although she needed blood transfusions frequently, Alice never thought of this as a burden; rather, it was just another thing that gave her life purpose and defined her. This upbeat child had a way of making everything seem okay, regardless of what was going on.

Over the years, I was fortunate to speak with Alice on a fairly regular basis. I often asked her to mentor other children and teens with Fanconi anemia and to offer encouragement to their parents. In addition to our professional relationship, we also had a whimsical way of connecting. Alice was fun-loving, creative, and always a pleasure to be around. She would happily engage in any of our arts and crafts projects and group sessions, and she would also be the first to lead a song or join a dance routine. Alice was a talker, and she wanted the world to know about her journey with Fanconi anemia.

One afternoon, I arrived home from work and discovered glitter strewn all over my kitchen floor. I was perplexed. How could this have happened? No one had been in my apartment since I had left that morning, and I typically kept the glitter stored away in another room. When I checked my office messages, I heard a message from Alice's mother. She sounded stressed, so I called her back immediately. As soon as I reached her, I learned that Alice had died; she had died during the same period of time that I had been away from my apartment. After much detective work, I could only surmise that Alice, with her fun-loving spirit, had been responsible for the glitter.

Alice was on everyone's mind at the Fanconi anemia family meeting later that year. The FA group typically releases balloons each time they are together in honor of all the children who have died. When they released the balloons that day, a lovely rainbow emerged, which served as a powerful sign of hope to all in attendance.

It has been five years since Alice died. While attending the Fanconi anemia annual meeting this year, special memories of Alice once again filled my mind. Afterward, when all the participants released balloons for the children who had died, a bird appeared and followed the balloons until they were out of sight. Alice was so committed to her friends and cohorts with FA. Whenever I attend these meetings, she is always in my thoughts. She remains an inspiration.

Nancy Cincotta, MSW, MPhil, is the Director of Psychosocial Services at Camp Sunshine at Sebago Lake in Casco, Maine. With a career dedicated to children with life-threatening illnesses and their families, her recent research interests have focused on hope and the resilience of families facing challenging situations.

Butterfly Effect

Pamela Healey

Butterflies—fleeting, enchanting, miraculously springing from cater-pillars—are symbols of transformation, resurrection, and the loved ones who have left our arms. Our son, Conor, who was born with Trisomy 18, a life-limiting genetic disorder, died within hours of ar-riving home from the hospital. Since then, numerous butterflies, tiny flying jewels, have appeared to my family members and me, giving us tremendous assurance that his spirit remains with us here.

Whenever our two children, adopted later, spot either a monarch or a swallowtail butterfly, they always alert me; other butterflies have found us. One example of this occurred on the sixth anniversary of Conor's death. As I wheeled my daughter's carriage along the wind-ing boardwalk of a nature path, a beautiful iridescent butterfly sud-denly emerged from the swamp. The butterfly found its way inside the bonnet of the baby carriage. My daughter laughed and reached out as she tried to catch her silent visitor before it traveled skyward.

A few years later, our children decided that we needed to light a fire in the fireplace to celebrate my early December birthday. My hus-band lugged in an armful of wood and placed it near the fireplace. As we sat together enjoying our fireside cake and ice cream, a large blue-black butterfly began to circle above our heads. I smiled, pleased that Conor had found a way to join in the family festivities. Because it was freezing outdoors, I kept the butterfly inside, until a science teacher, who had also lost an infant son, later assured me that it would survive. She explained that it was a mourning cloak butterfly, which typically winters inside rock crevices and, she surmised, wood-piles, too. We had heated our house with wood for ten years and spo-radically used wood for twenty more, but only once had a butterfly ever emerged from the logs. On that evening, I had two children at my feet and also one in my heart, who had brought a meaningful sign of hope for my birthday.

My family had another butterfly encounter immediately following a five-day SOFT conference to support families of affected children with rare trisomies. Some members of SOFT shared their experiences of rainbows and butterflies, which they believed to be signs from the children they were grieving. I had just been asked to write an article about "coincidences," or occurrences not rationally explained, that seemed to be angel-directed. I was jotting down some ideas on a pad of paper as we drove out of Rochester along the New York Thruway. I began thinking about Conor and another child, Jillian, also born with Trisomy 18, who had lived for nine years. Both of these children had been born on the same day, April 2, 1986; Conor had been born in Boston and Jillian in Germany, where her father was stationed. As I reflected on the first SOFT conference that I had attended many years earlier, I remembered that the first child I had seen when I entered the hotel lobby was six-year-old Jillian; her mother lovingly handed her to me. I contemplated whether two children born with the same disorder on the same day was a coincidence or just a statistical probability. All of a sudden, two monarch butterflies simultaneously landed on the passenger side of the car windshield. They stayed there long enough for all of us to see them and then slid off seemingly unharmed. Even though our car was traveling at sixty miles per hour, the two butterflies did not separate from one another, nor did the wind squish them. Their timely appearance certainly qualified as a coincidence.

Butterflies visit us wherever we go, whether it is the beach, a road race, or a soccer game. One butterfly greeted me, my husband, and our two children as we emerged from the tree line to begin the bare-faced ascent of Mount Monadnock. When we make that climb, now an annual family event, we are always accompanied by butterflies. Without fail, butterflies surprise, delight, and comfort our family.

Not only has Conor visited us through butterfly encounters, but he has also surprised us in other ways. One Christmas morning, I awakened early to fill the stockings, placing flowers in Conor's red-and-white-trimmed stocking and toys and treats in the others. I spotted a red-and-white-striped bow and decided to use it to decorate the white owl cookie jar where I keep my receipts. Because the owl head was too large for the tied ribbon to slide over, I lifted it off, slipped the ribbon and bow around the neck, and replaced the head. It was then that I noticed a slim strip of paper with pink-and-green markings lying on the ribbon, like a butterfly resting on a flower. It read: "A balloon has been released in memory of Conor Michael Healey…." This acknowledgment, given at a SOFT conference years before, had come from deep inside the cookie jar. Its migration cannot logically be explained other than by a Christmas morning visit from our son.

Pamela Healey, PhD, spends time supporting families changed by trisomy after more than forty years working as a special educator. Pam writes, takes photographs, looks for sea glass on beach walks, travels with her family, and always waits for butterflies.

Love from Matthew

James Troland

My first grandchild, Matthew James Troland, was born on January 5, 2007. It was the happiest day of my life. I remember visiting him at the hospital only three hours after his birth. As I walked proudly down the hallway toward his room, I could hear Matthew crying very loudly. The love I already felt in my heart for him was greater than any love I had ever experienced. There was something so profound about seeing my own child—the child his mother and I had raised together—have a child of his own.

Six weeks later, my joy turned into sorrow and sadness. My young grandson had been diagnosed with spinal muscular atrophy, a genetic disease similar to ALS in adults. His doctor told me that Matthew wouldn't live to see his first birthday. I left the hospital in anger, sadness, and total disbelief.

For the first five months of his life, Matthew did very well. He was the happiest child I had ever seen, and he had the best parents ever. They did so much for him in the short time he was with us. Often, they brought Matthew to one of their favorite places, the Southwick Zoo. In one section, where the wild deer roam freely, the deer would come up close to my grandson and take a good look.

Right after Father's Day, Matthew became very ill and needed to be airlifted to Children's Hospital in Boston for treatment. After a week of intensive efforts to stabilize him medically, he was discharged home with hospice. Sadly, he died there in his parents' arms on June 27th. Our hearts were broken into a million little pieces. I still miss him so much.

Three days after Matthew's funeral, I happened to look at the azalea bush growing in my front yard, which typically flowers in late April and early May. Among all the dead blossoms, I discovered one small, pink flower fully in bloom. As soon as I saw it, I became very emotional. I felt excited, happy, sad, and overjoyed. For me, it was a sign that the love my grandson and I shared for a brief time was still alive. Matthew's love would always be with me, even after his death. Later that autumn, a solitary purple flower bloomed on my rhododendron, too.

Our family held a small celebration on what would have been Matthew's first birthday. To honor Matthew, we released balloons at dusk in the backyard. Just as we let them go, a herd of eight deer quietly joined us about thirty yards away. We all stood in amazement. I had never seen that many deer together at one time nor have I since. The deer had come to wish my grandson a happy first birthday.

James Troland, husband, father, and grandfather, has three grown children. A retired factory worker, he and his wife, Mary, live in Bellingham, Massachusetts, and on Cape Cod. They enjoy traveling and doing outdoor activities together.

And the Curtain Gently Fluttered

R. Jill Biller

⌒

Sometimes a person enters your life for only a brief time, yet changes your life forever. Michael was one of those people. This young man had been diagnosed with HIV/AIDS during the '80s at a time when very little was known about the virus. The general public was terrified. No one knew how it was spread, and people likened it to the plague. But the worst part was the prejudice, the prejudice against the first group to be identified with the illness—the gay community. HIV/AIDS was initially called GRID, or gay-related immunodeficiency disease. Those infected with the disease were called PWAs, or people with AIDS. Some believed that PWAs should be put in camps and kept away from the rest of us. Others felt certain that God's wrath was punishing their homosexual behavior. Scores and scores of people, including family members, loved ones, friends, and medical professionals, abandoned these individuals for fear they would catch the disease. It was a horrible time.

At the time, I was the head of a nonprofit organization funded by the federal government to provide AIDS education in northern Indiana. My job was to educate schools, churches, hospitals, and anyone interested in the virus about its transmission and the atrocities of how people were being treated. I ran support groups and spent time with those individuals infected with the virus, as well as their family members and friends, in their homes, at hospitals, and at funeral homes. I spent lots of time with those who feared and hated as well as those who had the illness. I met many wonderful people who had contracted this dreaded disease, and one of them was Michael.

I first met Michael in a hospital setting. He was in a coma and fighting cytomegalovirus, or CMV, with his HIV/AIDS-depressed immune system. With Michael's death appearing imminent, I visited him often and spent time with his aging parents, who faced their own health challenges. They feared the loss of their only child, Michael, a former pastor, who had been abandoned by his church and his friends when he was diagnosed with AIDS. Then something strange happened. Inexplicably, Michael came out of the coma. He was released home almost immediately into the care of his elderly parents with a Hickman shunt placed under his skin on his upper chest. The shunt enabled easier venous access for his medications and blood work with fewer needle sticks, but it also required strict monitoring and care to prevent infection. His loving parents were diligent in their role as his caregivers, feeding him, keeping the shunt area clean, and making sure their son got all the rest he needed.

A few days later, I received a call from Michael's mom. The shunt site appeared red, hot, and swollen. I told her I would come over, but Michael needed to call his doctor right away. Shortly after I got there, the telephone rang, and Michael spoke with his physician. Afterward, he hung up the phone, stunned. "The doctor didn't want to see me again," Michael said in a muffled voice. "He told me that I have to find someone else to look at me. He said that I deserved what I had, and that he didn't care what happened to me." My heart stopped, and so did my breath. I couldn't believe that a doctor could say such a thing. Then, the fire and rage came up inside of me that I had felt so many times before from having worked with this community over the years. These young people were dying and suffering, and yet they were being treated with such inhumanity.

I offered to advocate for Michael and to do whatever needed to be done. Michael just sat there as if he had just been kicked in the face. After what seemed like an eternity, he finally spoke. He told me that he needed to rest, and he needed time to think about it; he would get back to me in a day or so. "Michael, this is serious. You know that these infections can get worse so quickly. Are you sure?" Despite my intense desire to call a doctor, our attorneys, or anyone for help, I could not sway Michael. Afterward, I encouraged his parents to please call if they needed me, and I drove home in tears of sadness and anger over the hatred, injustice, and abject cruelty. My heart broke over and over and over again.

Two days later, Michael's mother called to tell me that Michael had a raging fever, but he refused to call the doctor; would I please come? As soon as I got there, his grieving father escorted me into Michael's bedroom, where he was lying on a single bed in the corner of the room. I sat down in the chair next to him. "Michael, let me call the doctor. You need to be seen and probably put on some heavy-duty antibiotics. You're really sick, and you can't wait."

But Michael wasn't waiting. He had no intention of calling the doctor, nor did he want me to call one either. He was tired of being treated the way the doctor had treated him. Everyone, including the hospital staff, friends, and even his church, had pushed him away once they had found out about his diagnosis. "I'm a good person," he said. "Not a great person, but a good person. I don't deserve this. No one does, and I don't have to be treated this way anymore. My parents can't care for me; they can barely take care of themselves with their serious medical conditions.

"What you don't know is that I have faith, and I always have. I am a man of God, and I gave myself to His service many years ago. I know that the place I will go to will be a place without the hatred and the fear I have felt since I first was diagnosed. I don't want to be treated that way anymore, and I have the right to choose whether I have medical treatment or not. I know you don't understand, and I'm sorry that this hurts you, and I know how angry you are with all of those treating me so inhumanely."

"Michael, it's not me or my hurt that you need to think of. What about your poor parents? What about their pain?"

"They know I am dying, whether it is now or next month. I see the pain they endure every day that I am here. They don't deserve this either. They can't even tell the friends they have known forever that their son has AIDS. This is not just about me and my pain; it's about them and their pain. They don't deserve this. They don't, and I don't. I can't do this anymore."

I sat there without any words, but only feelings of deep sadness for this wonderful man. I felt helpless and hopeless; there was nothing I could do. His parents, standing outside the doorway, had heard everything. I could not fathom their pain. Michael had made his decision out of love for them. I thought about them as I silently drove home.

Two days later, Michael's mother called, urging me to come; Michael was dying. As soon as I got there, his parents, with reddened eyes from crying, led me to Michael's bedroom. I touched his burning forehead. When I did, Michael's eyes opened. I sat down on the chair and reached out to hold his hand. I fought back tears of deep sadness and raging anger; the anger faded when Michael looked at me and spoke. "Are you okay?" he asked. All I could do was nod my head. "I want you to know that I will be okay," he said. "This part doesn't frighten me. He's taking me home now. I will be okay."

His voice was like a whisper, and then he closed his eyes. The tears came; I couldn't hold them back. I just sat there for what seemed like a long time, holding his hand, while the sun shone in through the open window. Then, all of a sudden, he took a breath, a very shallow breath, with his body too weak to do any more, and he was gone. I witnessed a faint shimmer, just a shimmer, appear to slip from him with that last breath. Then the curtain panel nearest to Michael gently fluttered; it seemed as if a gentle breeze had touched it, yet I felt no breeze in the room. I got up and went into the other room to let his parents know that Michael had passed. Allowing them private time together, I went to the door and let myself out, knowing they would call if they needed me.

Michael is still with me. I can see his room, the bed, and the night-stand with the lamp, the open window, and the white curtains. I can still see his face, his peaceful face, caring for me into his death, worrying about whether I would be all right, even as he was dying. I thought that I had Michael's hand in mine, when in reality, Michael took my hand in his. He shared with me a profound faith, and in that unexpected moment that was his death, he changed the way I saw the world forever.

R. Jill Biller, LMT, worked in AIDS education during the '80s; after the federal funding was taken away from rural areas, she found another healing profession. Jill is a massage therapist and an educator, having had her own healing practice for over twenty-one years.

I Love You to the Moon and Back

Fran Sawdei

———

The loss of my thirty-year-old son and only child, Tom, has been the most tragic, unimaginable, and incomprehensible event of my life. In February of 2009, my dear son died from the trauma of a near-fatal bicycle/car accident coupled with the disease of drug addiction to anesthetize his pain. Knowing I will never again experience his vibrant personality, see his incredible smile, or share my everyday life with him has been so, so tough.

Eight months after his death, I found myself at a very low point. Even though my faith had helped me to entrust God with the pain and sadness that I had experienced on my grief journey, I still needed to know that my son was okay. I was struggling with life and consumed with grief when I experienced an extraordinary dream visit that gave me such a boost. Only after sharing the experience with a friend did I learn that such things were possible. Tom looked so good in the dream, and he kept telling me how happy he was. He also gave me a wonderful hug, the strength of which I can still feel to this day. Looking back, that dream visit gave me the confidence to relax my grief, thus allowing me to feel my son with me in spirit.

Being able to move forward spiritually and symbolically with Tom has helped me live life instead of living death. Gradually, as I experienced a variety of strong connections with him, I could sense him guiding me throughout the day. I felt him reaching out to me in spirit, proud and gloriously happy, watching over his father and me from above. Amazingly, Tom has helped me learn how to laugh again and how to celebrate his life. I now realize that grief isn't the only expression of my love; Tom is helping me find joy in life once again. Sharing these spiritual connections has helped my husband, too. He now feels our dear son with him in so many ways.

Nature has provided me with the strongest connection of all to Tom. After his death, I remember begging and pleading for a sign from him that he was okay. Then a beautiful rainbow appeared right in front of my husband and me. I recall watching its brightness grow, but my acute and early grief blinded me from seeing it as a sign from Tom. Recently, when I opened my eyes one morning, the first thing I saw was the most beautiful rainbow. This time I became excited because I realized it was a glorious sign from my son; what a wonderful way to start my day with him close by. Also, Tom and I shared a connection with red-tailed hawks, as well as with dolphins. Whenever the red-tailed hawk soars freely over our home and above my car as I drive, I feel uplifted because I know my son is near. I also sense his loving presence when I walk along the beach and see the playful dolphins swimming close to shore.

Four months before Tom died, we moved into a home appropriately called La Bella Luna, since the beautiful moon sits right over our front door. Some nights, my husband and I are awakened by the brightness of the full moon shining into our bedroom. It reminds us of Tom's ongoing presence in our lives and his favorite saying years before: "I love you to the moon and back." I also sense Tom close by when I discover flowers blooming out of season, birds singing and peering in my window, and butterflies fluttering so close. I love when I see personalized license plates with meaningful messages at times when I need them most. Sometimes cloud formations will appear, such as a heart on the anniversary of his death or a cloud kiss in the form of an X when I was pleading for a sign that all was well. All of these things bring joy to my heart, and I make sure to thank Tom with an inner "hello" and "I love you" whenever they occur. My son has also sent many earthly angels who provide hope, guidance, comfort, and encouragement through my grief. In my heart, I know Tom is sending these signs and messages to ease my pain. My dear son is bringing light into my life to shine above the darkness.

I feel so happy and blessed to be able to experience my beloved son on such a regular basis. Through the devastation and loss, I have been reborn with a new, heightened awareness of life. Instead of living life going forward "after Tom," I now live my life fully because of him. Even in death, my son shines brightly and influences every decision I make. He has proven to me that love can never die. My dear Tom, I will love you forever. May my laugh always reach you in heaven, and may your love, light, and encouragement always reach me on earth.

Fran Sawdei, retired teacher, has been married to her wonderful husband, Mike, for forty-one years. She enjoys reading, long walks, family, and friends. Her ninety-five-year-old mother, who has Alzheimer's, adds so much love to Fran's life.

A Shooting Star

Maria Cleary

My twins, Michael and MaKenzie, were born three and a half months early. Although Michael's prospects for survival were poor due to immature lungs, MaKenzie seemed more stable. Extraordinary medical efforts were made to stabilize Michael's critical condition. However, things changed unexpectedly when the hospital called to inform us that it was MaKenzie, not Michael, who had taken a turn for the worse. My husband and I rushed to the hospital. Less than four hours later, our MaKenzie died. She was twelve days old.

Amidst the loss of our daughter, we were fortunate that her twin, Michael, fully recovered within days. We felt so blessed to be able to bring him home and have him grow up to be our happy, healthy, talkative little boy. About a year after MaKenzie's death, we started trying to have another baby. I remember driving home from work one night around 11:00. As always, I was talking to MaKenzie during this private time together. I had been aware for some time that MaKenzie was somehow able to help the members of our family through the challenges and difficulties of life. She was watching out for us. On this night, I needed her help. After talking to her for quite a while, I asked MaKenzie to give me a sign to let me know she had heard me. She did just that. A minute later, a shooting star came down in the night sky directly in front of me. I knew MaKenzie had heard me. Shortly after, I found out that I was pregnant.

During my pregnancy, I was convinced that I was having a girl. Three weeks after I had an amniocentesis, the nurse called me with the results. She asked if I wanted to know if I was having a girl or a boy. I replied, "You can tell me if you want, but I already *know* I'm having a girl." I was right. Our beautiful daughter, Brooke, was born on September 4, 1998, exactly two years to the day that Michael and

MaKenzie were due to be born. MaKenzie, thank you for your help. We want you to know that we all love you!

Maria Cleary, hairdresser, enjoys providing customers with a new look. Being a mom is the most important thing in the world to her. Maria loves spending time with family and friends and especially going to the beach with Mike and Brooke.

GIFTS FROM MY BOY

Terry Lathan

I had just started working on the dinner dishes when a knock on the front door changed our lives forever. It was Thursday, August 14, 2008. My wife, Anne, opened the door to find a chaplain from the King County sheriff's office. Immediately I knew something was wrong, and I went out to see who was there. He asked, "Are you the parents of Cameron Lathan?" From that point on, life became a blur. The chaplain informed us that our twenty-year-old son and only child had died early that morning in his sleep.

At the tender age of three, Cameron had been diagnosed with epilepsy. We frequently took him to see specialists who altered medications and treatments often. It soon became apparent that our young son would battle epilepsy his entire life. Although most of the seizure activity happened during sleep, he sometimes had seizures strong enough to take him down to the ground and even break bones.

Cameron didn't let his epilepsy define him, though. As a youth, he participated in soccer, baseball, and basketball. He flourished in Cub Scouts and even went on to become an Eagle Scout. During those years, Cam belonged to a scouting honor society called the Order of the Arrow. Cam's love for feathers, raven feathers in particular, started in this Native American service group. The raven played an important role in the story of the world. As members of the OA ceremony team, Cam and his fellow scouts would dress up in Native American regalia and perform all kinds of ceremonies.

In May of 2008, Cameron left home for a job opportunity in Alaska. There, he began working at the Mt. McKinley Lodge, owned and operated by Princess Tours, where thousands of people vacationed each summer. Cameron worked in their employee dining hall. He learned not only about the food business, but also how to make friends quickly. Early that summer, my wife and I flew to Alaska to visit our son. We stayed at the lodge with him and even took Cam for a weekend of family fun in Anchorage. Little did we know that if we had waited to go later that summer, as we had considered, we never would have had that precious time together.

The first few days after we received the news of Cam's death are still a blur. Even now, I have to ask others to help me remember that time. My wife, my mother-in-law, and I traveled to Alaska the next day to bring Cameron's ashes home. When he was little, I always carried him on my lap whenever we traveled. It was odd that on this last time we traveled together, there he was on my lap once again.

It took almost a week for arrangements to be finalized before we were able to bring his ashes home. While we waited, the three of us took day trips around the Anchorage area to help occupy our minds and pass the time. Although it felt like we were living a nightmare, in retrospect that time was very healing. We took car rides, sometimes heading off in no particular direction. We had an opportunity to grieve without any possible distractions from others being around.

Cameron's employer was incredible throughout the whole ordeal. They provided us with travel and lodging where Cameron worked, and in Anchorage, too. They also hosted us for a lovely dinner at the lodge on the night we arrived. There, we were able to meet Cameron's friends and coworkers. Although the evening started out a bit uncomfortable, it ended up being a wonderful way to meet those who had been an important part of our son's life. It was also an evening of closure for the staff as they said goodbye to a friend.

While we were gathering Cam's belongings from his room, we noticed that he had purchased a few items. It was no surprise to us at all to have found a raven's head carved out of moose antler among his things. That raven's head currently hangs on the wall near our "shrine" for Cameron. Over the next few months, I began experiencing something that I cannot explain using logic. I started seeing crows, blackbirds, and ravens everywhere I went. At first, I thought I was seeing the birds because I wanted to see them, in the same way I might repeatedly see a car I was thinking about purchasing wherever I drove. Even at church on Sundays, outside the windows there would be blackbirds on trees, and not just a few. There would be at least thirty or forty birds on the trees at one time.

I also started finding bird feathers everywhere I went. Initially, it started off with an occasional feather that almost seemed insignificant. However, once I realized that the feathers were not just a coincidence, they started arriving in bunches. One day, I actually discovered six separate feathers on my walk.

The most amazing feather appeared to me in such a bizarre way. I had just driven home from work and parked my car in the driveway. After being in the house for a minute, I realized I had forgotten to pick up the mail. I walked out to the mailbox right past my car and retrieved it. When I was almost back to the front door, I realized I had also forgotten my cell phone in the car. I turned around, and as I approached the car, I noticed something quite unusual. There, on the windshield, was a medium-sized black feather. It wasn't just sitting on the window, either. It was stuck there. I had to lift up the wiper blade to take the feather off the windshield, as it had been trapped there with about a half-inch stuck under the blade. That feather was not there while I was driving home, and it wasn't there when I walked past the car to get the mail. And even if it had been there, how could a feather have gotten underneath the windshield wiper blade all by itself?

That experience made me a believer that my son was sending me little clues and messages. Cameron was letting me know that he was around me. Once I allowed myself to think in this manner, I began to feel more comfortable and at ease. I still often see feathers. Last November, I attended the middle school's final football game of the year. It was held at a stadium where Cameron always videotaped the games for our team. On that particular day, I was sad for the season to end; watching games on that field had brought back special memories with my son. During warm-ups before the game, I noticed the opposing coach walking toward me, so I headed his way. After about thirty paces, I had to stop for a few seconds to tie my left shoe. As I stooped over and knelt down, I couldn't believe my eyes! There was a feather sticking out from beneath my shoe, right in the middle of the football field! A huge smile ran across my face. I finished tying my shoe and stood up just as the other coach approached me. He asked if the grin on my face was any indication of how I felt my team was going to do that day. I just chuckled, knowing that with Cameron on my side, it didn't matter what the outcome would be.

So, do I believe that our loved ones can still make a connection with us once they are gone? Even though I didn't believe before, I do now. It is not just my wanting to see them. I now have proof that it is so much more. And even if I am wrong, I still feel all warm inside whenever I look down for no reason only to see a little gift from my boy.

Terry Lathan and his wife of twenty-six years, Anne, enjoy living on Star Lake, just south of Seattle, Washington. Terry is a middle school teacher and coach. He continues to be involved with Scouts and has an amazing collection of feathers.

7

Dreams

DREAMTIME OFFERS AN UNUSUAL opportunity for healing. Did you know that bereaved individuals commonly see deceased loved ones in their dreams? Almost always, they appear happy, healthy, and with bodies that are completely healed. Wearing ordinary clothes or robes of white, they may even be bathed in light. Also, the colors in the dreamlike experience may be brighter than ever seen before; the senses may be heightened, and emotions may be amplified as well. Usually, in order to remember dreams, we have to write them down as soon as we awaken. Yet, intensely memorable dream visitations don't need to be written down; they can be recalled perfectly even years later.

Although not everyone remembers their dreams, some do, and the experience can be transformative. Dreams are the place where we work on our subconscious thoughts, worries, and concerns. Although many dreams are ordinary and fleeting, there are others in which we are clearly working through our loss and grief. An example of this occurred for me after the death of my birth mother, from whom I had been estranged for most of my life. In every dream, I would find myself chasing her down corridors. She was always out of reach, and I would awaken just as I was about to catch her. As frustrating as it was, those dreams were a metaphor for our relationship. Finally, I was gifted with a dream of resolution. We were both lying on stretchers, and my blood was being transfused directly into her. Even though I knew she would die, I still wanted to give her one more chance at life. Then her soul sat up from her body, spoke to me, and told me that she had been misunderstood her whole life. She had to go; she had no choice. That visit brought me peace. Although I have not seen her in my dreams since, she does send rainbows, especially in times of need, to let me know she is near.

Amazingly, healing can happen in our dreams just by spending time together with those we love. Having an opportunity to receive guidance and support or even to say goodbye can make such a difference for the bereaved. This chapter contains ten stories describing significant dream visitations. The love shared and messages received offer hope and reassurance that our loved ones in spirit live on.

Dancing with David

Melissa Critchley

David and I were very close. He was exactly one thousand days older than I, which we both thought was magical. It seemed to explain the interesting bond and psychic connection the two of us shared. We dated for nineteen months in high school, and despite his cheating on me, we remained close family friends, as my family had adopted him as one of their own. My mother even taught David how to drive.

When I moved away to college, David went into the Marines, and he married soon after that. Because his wife wasn't fond of the idea of David staying in touch with an old girlfriend, our contact with one another ended. Two years later, I decided to send him an e-mail. My phone rang a half hour later, and it was David. I said, "You must have gotten my e-mail..."

"What e-mail?" he asked. I thought he was joking, but after further probing, I discovered he really had not received my e-mail. What an uncanny connection. Even with two years of no contact, each of us felt the need to reach out to the other at that same moment in time.

With limited communication over the next few years, I was saddened to learn that David had died in a car accident. Apparently, his car pulled out in front of a large truck, and he was killed instantly. Unable to attend his funeral due to work responsibilities out of state, I grieved his loss all alone.

A few nights later, David visited me in a dream. Holding my hand, David led me down a dirt path that felt familiar to both of us. I sensed we were near a military base, but I was unsure of the location. I noticed an open wooden gate up ahead. It was a bright, sunny, dusty day, and although it seemed as though it should have been hot, I didn't feel any heat. Then we approached a large group of happy people, mostly adults, who were barbecuing.

I looked around and realized we were in the backyard of my mother's house. While upbeat music played, the barbecue continued. Then the two of us began to dance—a warm, evenly paced, rhythmic dance between two good friends. No words were spoken, but the joy I felt dancing with David was the most joy I have ever experienced, either awake or asleep. I blissfully danced and danced with him until I awoke, and when I did, I instantly knew that David was all right.

After reflecting on the experience for the next few days, I suddenly remembered a pact I had made with him years earlier when we were dating. If one of us died, we promised to give the other person a sign to let them know we were all right. We also made the promise not to scare the crap out of the other person when we did. How miraculous that despite all the years apart, limited contact, and my forgetting the pact we made, David had remembered.

I hadn't told too many people about my experience with him until a couple of years ago when David's name came up in a conversation with my mother. I offhandedly mentioned the dream to Mom when she started to cry. "Why didn't you tell me sooner?" she asked. Apparently, Mom had blamed herself all these years for David's death because she had been the one who had taught him how to drive. She recalled how he often drove too quickly. Maybe if she had reminded David to slow down a few more times, he might have been a better driver. Personally, I don't think anything would have made a difference. David was who he was—fast and upbeat. Also, perhaps the location of the barbecue in Mom's backyard was David's way of asking me to let Mom know that he was all right. I don't know for sure. But one thing I do know is that the vision I shared with David unquestionably helped my mother and me cope with his passing.

Melissa Critchley is a Minnesota artist and a travel and event coordinator for the University of Minnesota. In her graduate work, Melissa is studying the use of techniques from shamanism to prevent and reduce workplace stress.

JELL-O WRESTLING

Sherri H. Epstein

⎯⎯⎯

During my junior year at Bryant College in Smithfield, Rhode Island, I was having the time of my life learning about friendships, love, and life. Then the phone call came. My grandmother, Bertha, had suffered a heart attack. Her condition was stable, but Nana's heart was severely damaged. The doctor's were not sure how long she would live. I immediately drove home to see her and visited her daily in the hospital. During the last two weeks of her life, my grandmother told me the most amazing stories. I had never heard those stories before, such as how she used to love to ride the horse and buggy with her nine brothers and sisters when she was a little girl growing up. She also told me what it was like to have inventions such as radios, automobiles, and home computers change the world in which she lived.

Throughout her eighty-four years, Nana enjoyed life to the fullest. She knew all of my secrets and was the greatest grandmother ever. Nana wasn't wealthy, but she was surely rich with love. When she died in May of 1988, she was the first person close to me that I had lost.

After Nana's funeral and the week of sitting shiva, I returned to college. I attempted to prepare for finals with only a few weeks left to study, but for some reason I just couldn't concentrate. I couldn't stop thinking about Nana. How could she have left me? With whom would I share my secrets now? Would Nana still hear me? With the dates for final exams approaching fast, I found myself incapable of studying. I just couldn't bring myself to open a book.

Then one night I had a vivid dream. I was walking alone in a wooded area and came upon a clearing with a picnic table in it. There, sitting at the picnic table, was my grandmother, looking happy, healthy, and about ten years younger. Awestruck and without the slightest bit of fear, I asked, "What are you doing here? You're dead!"

Nana smiled and said, "I can see how upset you are, but it's really important that you study for your tests. You are about to graduate and start a brand-new chapter of your life. The *only* way to move on is to study."

I told her how much I missed her. Nana replied, "I will always be here to listen to your secrets." Reassuringly she went on to say, "Don't worry about me. I'm having a great time. We're about to go Jell-O wrestling, so I have to go." Then she got up and walked off. I thought, *Hmm…Jell-O wrestling. How strange!* Somehow, I just couldn't imagine my plump, eighty-four-year-old Jewish grandmother, Bertha, getting up from the table to go Jell-O wrestling. It seemed extremely strange.

Amazingly, when I woke up, I found myself much more at ease. I was finally able to sit down and begin studying. Thanks to Nana, I passed all my finals and graduated the following May.

In April of 1990, I happened to be at work in my cubicle when I received several distressing calls from my sorority sisters. Our sorority sister Kristin had been hit by a drunk driver while jogging and died. Kristin was such an amazing kid. We had affectionately nicknamed her Gizmo after the movie character in *Gremlins* who jumps out of the box and yells, "Bright lights!" Wherever she went, Kristin was a bright light to everyone. Gizmo was a junior at Bryant at the time of her death.

I packed my bags and drove to Rhode Island to be with my sorority sisters during this sad time. I remember all of us crowding together in a room at the sorority house and sitting in a circle. Someone suggested, "Let's go around the room and talk about a special time we remember having with Kristin." And so we did, one by one. It was so wonderful to hear all the great stories. When it came to my turn, all I could say was that I didn't have any one-on-one memories to share about Kristin. As much as she had touched my life with her bubbly personality, I was a senior when Kristin pledged the sorority during her freshman year.

Several months later, I had another dream. I was walking in the same woods where I had seen Nana and came across the same clearing with the same picnic table. This time, sitting at the table were my grandmother *and* Kristin. Both looked healthy and very content. Calmly I asked, "What are you doing here? You're both dead."

Kristin said, "I'm mad at you." I was astonished. I couldn't believe what she was saying. First off, how could this happy, cheerful girl be mad? And secondly, why would she be mad at me? Kristin continued admonishing me: "I can't believe you don't remember the times we spent together! What about when we were on Student Senate together? What about when we went to the convention together? ..." Kristin went on to name at least seven wonderful times just the two of us had spent together.

"Oh yeah, you're right!" I said laughing, as I reflected on memories long since forgotten. Finally, Kristen said, "Now we have to go Jell-O wrestling, but I never want you to forget those great times we had together." The dream ended. I woke up amazed. As instructed, I took Kristin's words to heart. Along with never forgetting to tell my grandmother my innermost secrets, I have never forgotten the happy times I had with Gizmo or how confused I was about the idea that my eighty-four-year-old grandmother was going to go Jell-O wrestling with my sorority sister!

Time passed. I married my wonderful husband, Ken, and we now have two beautiful daughters, Jessica and Rachel. Our younger daughter, Rachel Beth, named after Nana, was born with Canavan disease, a devastating life-limiting neurological disorder. Even though seventeen years had passed since Kristin's funeral, I had not been back to the sorority house, especially with all that had been going on in my life.

However, in the fall of 2002, I received a phone call from my sorority. Some of the girls at Bryant College had read a newspaper article about my family's research fundraising efforts to help find a cure for Canavan disease. My sorority sister called to let me know that the sorority had decided to do a fundraiser for our research fund called "Rachel's Hope." I was so moved by their thoughtfulness, generosity, and efforts on Rachel's behalf. The sorority sister went on to inform me that they had selected a Jell-O wrestling match as their fundraiser! The match was scheduled for a few weeks later. Interestingly enough, none of those sorority sisters knew anything about the two prior dreams I'd had with Nana and Gizmo years earlier.

My whole family, Ken, Jessi, and Rachel drove down to Rhode Island for our first-ever Jell-O wrestling match to show our appreciation. On the ride home, we couldn't help but notice a white station wagon driving ahead of us on the highway with the license plate "BERTHA." That was Nana's name! The wagon remained ahead of us and turned off the highway onto the same exit ramp we took. We followed the white wagon as it drove ahead of us toward our neighborhood and, in fact, all the way onto our dead-end street!

Just before we turned into our driveway, the white station wagon pulled into our neighbor's driveway, three houses down. By the time I had parked the car and unloaded the kids, the station wagon was gone. Suddenly it all clicked—Nana, Gizmo, and Jell-O wrestling! I knew Nana and Gizmo had something to do with all this. Nana had told me in the first dream eight years before Rachel was born that she needed to go Jell-O wrestling. In the second dream, Kristin mentioned it as well. Was it their turn to share secrets with me, as each mentioned something years in advance that no one could have known? And how was it that we happened to follow a car with my grandmother's name on the license plate all the way home from the Jell-O wrestling match, an event predicted by both Nana and Gizmo?

Later, when I questioned my neighbors about the station wagon that had stopped by their house, they told me they had no idea who it could have been. They didn't know anyone who owned a vehicle of that description nor did they know anyone who owned that license plate. I have not seen the white station wagon since.

As I face Rachel's short life expectancy, it gives me great comfort to know that, just like Nana and Gizmo, my daughter, Rachel, will be all right. At first when we received her diagnosis, I was petrified. However, as time has gone on and thanks to Nana and Gizmo, I am more confident than ever that there is life after death. And when her time comes, my sweet little daughter, Rachel, won't be far from me. In fact, she will always be with me... and will be one more precious loved one with whom I can share my innermost thoughts and secrets.

Sherri H. Epstein, wife and mother, works at University of Massachusetts Medical School in geriatric research. Advocacy chairperson for the National Tay-Sachs and Allied Diseases Association (NTSAD), she has devoted her life to finding a cure for Canavan disease.

A Potted Plant and Puppy

Kim Jin-woo

⎯⎯⎯⎯

Late one evening in June of 1994, I returned to my apartment from a college festival. I was a student attending a university in Tokyo, Japan. Before turning on the living room light in my tiny apartment, I noticed the blinking red light on the answering machine signaling that someone had left me a message. I had just moved there a few weeks earlier, so very few people knew my phone number. I was excited to receive a message.

I pushed the red light on the answering machine to listen. The sound of a mechanical female voice announced that the phone message had been left at 10:30 PM. Next, I heard breathing and gasping sounds followed by another female voice. "My dear son, be calm, and listen carefully. Your older brother is in the emergency room now. He is in very bad condition. Please pray for him. God bless you." It was my mother's voice calling from the countryside of Korea. Unable to make sense of her message, I replayed it over and over, listening carefully to her words.

Finally, I realized something was wrong. I tried to reach my immediate family members and relatives, but no one picked up the phone. I was becoming increasingly anxious and angry, but I could not stop calling. Finally, one of my young cousins, Young-hi, answered the phone. She was an elementary school student. I told her that I wanted to speak with her parents. Young-hi said, "Nobody is around here."

"Where are they?" I asked.

She replied, "My parents went to the hospital, because your brother, Jin-su, passed away." She continued, asking, "Why are you still in your apartment?" I hung up the phone. I could not believe what she had just said. My brother was thirty-eight years old and healthy. How could he have died?

The next morning, only a few hours later, I flew from Narita Airport in Tokyo to Kimpo Airport in Seoul, Korea. As soon as I arrived at my parents' house, I could tell that someone had passed away. From outside, I could hear the distinct sound of voices mourning. Through the wide-open front door, I could see that many people were dressed in white. In Korea, family members and close relatives wear white clothing and mourn loudly when attending a wake.

I walked into my home. All of my family and relatives were wearing white cotton clothing. I walked farther inside the house, only to find an open coffin in the living room. The body inside the coffin was completely wrapped in white bands of cotton cloth. I couldn't tell if it was my brother. A few seconds later, I noticed a picture of my older brother, with incense burning next to it, on top of a pedestal stand in front of the coffin. The room was filled with many beautiful flowers, mainly white chrysanthemums. It was true. Jin-su had passed away. He had died from a heart attack. And my mother was nowhere to be found.

In the Korean tradition, family members of the person who has passed must mourn with loud voices at the wake to show sadness. They must also provide lots of food and beverages (mostly alcohol) for the mourners who attend. Family members must also stay up for most of the night. This time of grieving is very difficult emotionally and physically for the bereaved. I finally found my mother lying down in another room, exhausted, with a pale, sad face. I did not say one word to her; I did not want to make the situation any more difficult. I stayed for a few moments, and then turned around to leave. With my back to her, I heard the sounds of very deep sighs and crying coming from my mom.

The next day was Jin-su's funeral, which was held at our home. The weather was sunny. Afterward, all of our family and friends went to the mountain to bury my brother. He was buried near my grand-parents' graves. According to Korean tradition, those who have died are buried on the same mountain as their ancestors. This way, every-one will know the future sites of their family members' graves. While grieving relatives and friends bowed respectfully and offered their last words to my brother, my three-year-old nephew and two-year-old niece ran around their father's grave. They were too young to under-stand their father's death.

After all the guests had left, my family members and I kneeled on the ground in front of my older brother's grave. We were ready to give our last words, but my mother kept saying to my brother, "I'm so sorry, my son. I forgot to water the potted plant and feed the pup-py. Please forgive my laziness." I did not understand what she was talking about.

When we returned home, no one spoke a word. My mother wa-tered a potted plant and fed a little puppy that I had not seen before. She picked up the puppy and lovingly held it in her arms. It seemed to bring her comfort. When I saw that scene, I felt a little relief. I didn't know what my mother was talking about at the grave. It made me worry about her health, but it wasn't appropriate for me to ask questions at the time. A few days later, my mother explained to me that the potted plant and the puppy were Jin-su's last gifts to her on her birthday only a couple months earlier. Those gifts were a part of my older brother's love. She wanted to take good care of them.

I still miss my brother. Since his death, I have dreamt of him a few times. In my first dream, Jin-su was taking a puppy for a walk while holding a potted plant cradled in his left arm. He seemed calm, peaceful, healthy, and happy. I felt empty.

Every year within a few days of the anniversary of my brother's death, I dream of him. The same puppy and plant are always in my dreams. Sometimes Jin-su is holding the puppy. Other times the pup-py is on a leash. Still other times the puppy is running around freely.

The first time it happened, I really didn't pay much attention to it at all. But by the second year, the dream grabbed my attention.

When I first shared my dream of Jin-su with my mother, I was amazed. She had been having dreams of him, too, and they were identical to mine! My brother also comes into her dreams with the same potted plant and puppy that he had given to her for her birthday. Since then, my mother and I share our identical dreams of Jin-su every year. It is comforting to be able to share them with one another. It helps a lot to know that my older brother lives on. Whenever I see a potted plant and a puppy, it reminds me of my brother's love for my mother, and my mother's love for him.

Kim Jin-woo shares his story to help heal the sadness of others. He is grateful that his mother's deep sadness was healed through her spiritual dream and gifts from her son. Kim enjoys watching movies and listening to jazz.

IN PAPA'S CARE

Debra Sue Richters

In November of 1991, I went into labor with Danielle, our first child. When my husband and I arrived at the hospital, there was no heartbeat. Sadly, our first daughter, Danielle, was stillborn. A few weeks later, I had the most inspirational dream. Someone was handing a beautiful, healthy, newborn baby to my great-grandfather, Papa, who had died many years earlier. My papa was one of the most amazing people I have ever met. In my dream, he was sitting in a chair, with a few people standing behind him. My great-grandfather looked healthy and strong, just the way I remembered him. Then, a person, whom I believe was God, asked Papa, "Are you sure you are able to care for this child?" My papa said without hesitation that he could.

During this time, I wanted to die; I wanted to be with my baby. The dream helped me get through this very difficult period in my life. I've always thought the dream was God's way of letting me know that Danielle was okay and that she would be well cared for. How reassuring to know that Papa would be the one caring for her. That was twenty years ago. My second daughter, Holly, just graduated from high school, and my son, Kevin, will be a junior this fall. Just think how many lives would have been wasted if I had never dreamt that dream.

Debra Sue Richters and her husband, Darryl, live in Plymouth, Massachusetts. She has two children and three stepchildren. Debra thanks God every day for all that He has blessed her with, however big or small.

Miracle Moment

Laura Alcazar-Vizcarra

It was such a blessing to be expecting a child after waiting eight years to start our family. I bought baby shoes, clothing, and all the sweet things a new mother looks forward to while she is pregnant. During my one-hundred-fifty-mile commute to finish my college degree, I played the Phil Collins song "You'll Be in My Heart" for my baby, because I had heard babies could hear music in the womb.

When I went for my four-month doctor's appointment, I was told the baby was dead. Crying and heartbroken, I felt like the earth needed to just open up and swallow me so I wouldn't feel any more pain. I went home, grabbed a plastic trash bag, tearfully pulled out all the baby's clothes I had organized in the closet, and threw them in the bag. I wanted no memories of the pregnancy, and I dumped the big bag in the garage. I crawled into bed, curled up in the fetal position, and cried myself to sleep.

Hours went by and I could hear whispers in the living room. My sister entered my bedroom and said, "I'm sorry that you are feeling this pain, but only God knows why things happen. You might not understand it right now, but one day you will." I was so upset with everyone, including God. I replied, "Well, if God didn't want me to have my baby, why did He give him to me? Why did I get pregnant? So that He could take him away from me?"

"I understand your pain," my sister said, "but don't be mad at God. You don't know what you are saying."

A few days went by, and I heard the same Phil Collins song I had played for my baby on the car radio. My gut reaction was to turn it off, but some part of me had already tuned in. And then, like a ray of light, I remembered a dream I'd had two weeks prior to losing the baby. That dream is still as clear and vivid in my mind today as the day I had it.

In the dream, there was darkness, and all of a sudden a strong earthquake shook the earth. I got down on my knees and prayed to God to make it stop. As I looked down, I could see the ground pulling apart, with a river of lava and fire below. Terrified, I continued to pray. Then I looked up at the sky, and I saw white clouds parting and a being so monumental that I knew it had to be someone from heaven. I believe it was our Lord God Almighty, but I couldn't imagine why He would want to communicate with me.

This enormous being came very close to me. Sitting on His golden throne, He had long white hair and a long white beard and wore a white garment. He was so bright I couldn't even look at Him. Then He lowered His right hand and extended it to hold mine. The earthquake calmed, and the darkness became light. With a baby now resting in His left arm, He rose back to the heavens.

I woke up from the dream in total shock. Although I never thought about the meaning of the baby in His arms, I did feel tremendous peace and comfort. Little did I know that this dream would be the instrument God would use to heal my pain. On the day the doctor told me my baby had died, I asked how long she thought the baby had been dead. She said about two weeks, which would have been the same time I'd had the dream.

I had originally played the Phil Collins song to comfort my baby, yet God used that same song to comfort me. I will never forget God holding my hand and letting me know that things would be okay. He would protect my baby and me. Whenever I speak about the loss of my child, I can do so without tears in my eyes because I know God has my baby in heaven. And one day when I die, I will see my baby, and we will never be apart again.

After my first pregnancy, I lost a second baby and then became pregnant for a third time. I miscarried my third baby in the doctor's office. The nurse said, "Let's do an ultrasound to make sure everything came out and that you won't need a D&C."

"Why?" I asked. "You were with me, and you know there is no point in doing one because I just lost baby number three." After a little coaxing, she walked me to the ultrasound lab and handed me over to the technician. During the ultrasound, the tech said, "Wow!" I asked myself, "Now what?"

The tech informed me that everything was okay, the sac was still intact, and my baby's heartbeat was strong. I said, "You're kidding, right? I just miscarried my baby in the doctor's bathroom. This can't be." The tech told me I was probably carrying twins. The good news was that the second baby was okay. The bad news was that when you lose one twin, the second one is usually miscarried as well. So the doctor prescribed bed rest for the remainder of the pregnancy, and on October 17, 2002, Mikael Vizcarra arrived at nine pounds, four ounces—my miracle baby! He arrived two years later on the exact due date of my first child.

I am now the proud mother of two healthy boys, Mikael and Gabriel. I had always wanted three children, but I am blessed to have two. I know that God has a plan for all of us, and I look forward to seeing what He will do with my boys.

Laura Alcazar-Vizcarra is the mother of two beautiful boys. Married to her best friend, Laura most loves the time she spends with family and friends. She also enjoys her newfound hobbies of gardening and photography.

Meeting an Unborn Son

Brent Ledgerwood

My eldest brother, Steffan, died as a result of an automobile accident on October 28, 1977. Having recently moved to Mesa, Arizona, Steffan, his pregnant wife, and two boys were traveling on the interstate. My brother slowed the car down because of an accident up ahead. Because the driver of the pickup truck traveling close behind didn't see the accident or Steffan's car in time, he slammed into the rear of their car.

The resulting fire caused my brother's death. There were no injuries to his oldest son. His pregnant wife was burned on her hands and face as she worked frantically to rescue their boys from the back seat. The youngest suffered severe burns on his back from the vinyl seat that had melted. His injury occurred well before car seats were designed for young children. At the time of the accident, Steffan was twenty-nine years old, just two weeks shy of his thirtieth birthday. Each of his five surviving siblings, myself included, sweated out those last two weeks before turning thirty ourselves. We all made it through without incident.

Steffan was a drummer in several rock and roll bands in the '60s and '70s, which included, in one instance, being the only white guy in an all-black band. He was a cave explorer and a college graduate, even though it took him seven years to obtain his bachelor's degree in science. My brother loved NASA and the excitement of the space program. He frequently reminded me that I worried about all the wrong things. Steffan loved life, and he never met a stranger. I remember his wife complaining that she could never keep a Bible in the house because Steffan kept giving them away to anyone who wanted to know more about Jesus.

On February 12, 1978 at 4:00 AM, I had a vivid dream about my brother. We were standing outside in a green field surrounded by trees dappled with sunlight. Steffan and I were in the middle of the field facing one another. My brother was communicating with me telepathically rather than verbally. The main thing I remember about the dream was the extreme range of emotions that I felt...intense happiness and intense sorrow...both of which were a reflection of Steffan's emotions.

I was well aware that my brother was a spirit. Wearing a long white robe, Steffan told me that since his death, he'd had such a unique experience. He had met his unborn son. What a joy it had been to meet him, and what a joy it had been to get to know the child *before* he was born. Steffan was very sad, though, because he knew his son was getting ready to enter my world, the earthly world. His son would go from a world of no pain and suffering to a world filled with both. There were almost no words to describe the intense extremes of happiness and sadness I felt.

Once the vision was gone, I was wide awake. I reflected on this extraordinary experience. I don't commonly have those kinds of dreams, but I had been missing Steffan quite a bit. At the time, I kept a diary. I pulled it out and wrote down every detail of the dream. Then I rolled over and went back to sleep.

The next thing I knew, my telephone was ringing. It was my mother calling to let me know that Steffan's wife had gone into labor that morning. She had driven herself to the hospital and had given birth to a healthy baby boy. Less than six hours had passed from the time of my dream to the time that Steffan Jr. was born. Since ultrasound diagnostic testing was not yet being utilized routinely in the field of obstetrics, no one knew the sex of this child prior to his birth. In the dream, my brother had referred to his unborn baby as his third son. In addition, I was unaware of his wife's due date. Steffan's wife had a perfectly natural delivery; everything went fine. I know that my deceased brother, Steffan, came to visit me in this dream.

Time went on. Several months passed, and I had a similar dream about Steffan. Again, the emotions were very strong. It was midnight when I woke up. I wrote in my dream journal as I had done before. The details didn't seem as elaborate as in the first dream. However, I hadn't had another dream about Steffan since the first one. I looked at the date. It was February 12, 1979. I asked myself, "Now, why does that date stand out?"

Suddenly, I remembered the first dream of Steffan, and I pulled out my old journal. I quickly flipped through the pages and found my first dream entry about my brother. When I looked at the date, I discovered that it was exactly one year to the day from my last dream. That day, the day that Steffan visited me a second time, was Steffan Jr.'s first birthday! How amazing!

Since that time, I've had a few dreams about Steffan; however, none of them have been as intense as the first. There isn't a day that goes by that I don't think of my brother. I am so thankful for all the great years we had together.

Brent Ledgerwood, husband and father, is a semi-retired nuclear power instrument technician. An avid bicyclist and pianist, Brent enjoys being active in church, volunteering at a local hospice home and food bank, and spending time with his family.

Our Children Live On Forever

Elissa Al-Chokhachy

———

I will never forget the Russian physician who sadly shared with me that she had been forced to terminate her third pregnancy. Societal pressures dictated that Russian couples limit their family size to two children, and Alena already had two healthy children at home. She pleaded with her husband to keep their third child, but he adamantly refused to have their family face the financial penalties that would result from doing so.

With great reluctance, Alena went through with the abortion, but she felt heartsick afterward. She believed she had lost a part of herself and her family forever. However, from that night on, Alena regularly saw her unborn baby boy in her dreams. She held Igor, nursed him, and loved him. As the years progressed, Alena inwardly watched her beautiful little son grow up to be a fine young man. Miraculously, she interacted with him as he passed through all the developmental stages of infancy, toddlerhood, youth, and adolescence. Alena even disciplined Igor at times, as she had done with her other children.

On the day that I met Alena, she shared that Igor, now in his twenties, still visited her on a regular basis. Yet her heart still ached for her son. Without Igor's nighttime visits, she would not have emotionally survived his loss. How remarkable that these two souls were able to continue their relationship in such an extraordinary way. Physical bodies temporarily house our souls, which are eternal. No matter the circumstances or even the brevity of one's life, one thing is clear: our children live on forever.

AUNT MICKEY

Michelle Zaccaria

⌒

My whole life I have struggled with cystic fibrosis (CF), a chronic genetic disease affecting the lungs, digestive system, liver, and pancreas. Diagnosed with a mild form at three years old at the same time as my four-month-old sister, Lisa, the two of us have lived different lives than most. Especially as a child, I remember always feeling different. I needed to take enzymes before eating to help me digest my food. At school, I would have to step out of the school lunch line to go to the nurse's office to take my medicine. The kids always wondered what I was doing. Plus, I've always had a CF cough, and kids would repeatedly ask if I had a cold. Sometimes I would say yes, and other times I would tell them it was my allergies or asthma. Only three of my closest girlfriends knew I had cystic fibrosis.

I also had daily physical therapy, which I despised and still do to this day. As a child, I hated coming home every day after school to a physical therapist waiting to pound on my chest. This prevented me from going out after school with my friends, going to their houses, and even doing afterschool activities, because I had to do my treatments. I was very angry that I had CF. Even though I knew I had the disease, I really didn't understand it. It made me different than other kids, and I just wanted to be normal.

Those feelings changed when I was hospitalized at nineteen years old. I met so many people diagnosed with cystic fibrosis who had been taking the same medications and going through the same treatments. Immediately I felt a special bond with them, and it was great. I no longer felt isolated; I no longer felt ashamed of my disease. It was then that I started accepting the disease and learning more about it. Meeting all those people in the hospital with CF was great. But one thing really bothered me. Some of the people I met were dying; in fact, too many to name. I found myself becoming scared. I was afraid to die. I questioned the existence of God and heaven. Death had become too real.

A few years after this realization, I had three significant dreams of Aunt Mickey, my great-grandmother's sister on my mother's side. She was an extremely religious woman who was very devoted to God. Described by Kevin M. Cronin in his book *A Friar's Joy*, my great-great-aunt Mickey was a "little, old, withered, Italian lady ... a parishioner of the church before Abraham. Her tiny, stooped frame held a face with a mass of wrinkles and an almost sorrowful expression." Yet I remember my Aunt Mickey as a beautiful, thin, frail, petite, gray-haired lady who was the kindest, most caring person you would ever want to meet. This quiet woman who prayed constantly attended Mass daily.

My first dream of Aunt Mickey occurred shortly after she died. Although I forgot to write down the exact date in my journal, the memory is a lasting one. On that night, I dreamt that Aunt Mickey came down from heaven. After telling me that she and God were praying for me, Aunt Mickey asked, "Is there anything special you want us to pray for?" I answered, "Pray that I never have to go to the hospital again. Pray that they find a cure for cystic fibrosis." Aunt Mickey told me not to be afraid of heaven. "Heaven is a beautiful place," she reassured me. She also told me that I was going to die soon. Then she told me she had to return to heaven. I cried and cried because I didn't want her to leave me.

A month later, I had a second dream about Aunt Mickey. In the dream, she called me on the telephone. My mother and grandmother were with me, but I am not sure where we were. I remember hearing the telephone ring, picking it up, and saying, "Hello?" I heard Aunt Mickey's voice say, "Hi, Michelle. I'm glad you answered the phone. I want you to know that I am praying for you."

"I know you are, Aunt Mickey," I said. "I know."

"I have a message for you. You have to figure it out on your own after you hang up the phone." My aunt began to spell out letters. Although her muffled voice made it difficult to hear, it sounded like L - G - I - T- H. I repeated those letters back to her. Then Aunt Mickey said, "I love you." I replied, "I love you, too." I started screaming and crying in the dream, but this time they were tears of joy and happiness. I woke up and immediately figured out Aunt Mickey's message—the letters spelled LIGHT. That night, I happened to be watching a program about Mother Angelica on TV. The show featured author Joan Anderson, who had written about people's experiences with their guardian angels. Before I went to sleep, I had a long talk with God. I asked Him to please give me another dream with my guardian angel, Aunt Mickey.

Two and a half years later, I had a third dream involving her. This time I was at my Aunt Josie's house looking for nice pictures of her sister that I could frame. As I looked through the pictures, Aunt Francis, another one of Aunt Mickey's sisters who had died, came down from heaven. I asked Aunt Francis if heaven was scary. She replied, "Heaven is beautiful, calm, and peaceful." I asked where my aunt was, and Aunt Francis replied, "Aunt Mickey is guiding someone right now and couldn't come down." That's when I woke up, feeling a sense of calmness and ease.

In fact, after all three dreams, I remember waking up feeling very much at peace and not so frightened anymore. Even though I have issues surrounding death, losing loved ones, and wondering what heaven might be like, I can easily say my three dreams of Aunt Mickey were deeply peaceful and comforting...and the best dreams I have ever had.

I still struggle with CF. Although my condition continues to be classified as mild, I now receive more medical treatments than before and am hospitalized twice a year. Sometimes it scares me, but I think that's only normal. However, I am no longer angry at God or the disease. I know God didn't give me CF. God gives me the love, strength, and courage I need to keep fighting.

In counseling, I talk about the things that still bother me, such as what it feels like to see friends who are dying from cystic fibrosis, as well as the fearful feelings that sometimes arise, especially when I become ill. But I have to remember that God is watching over me. He is the one in control. I also understand it is the people on earth who experience suffering, not the ones who die. I am grateful to know that deceased loved ones like Aunt Mickey and Aunt Francis are truly at peace and doing well, and will reunite with me one day in heaven.

Michelle Zaccaria lost her battle to cystic fibrosis on May 3, 2010, at the age of thirty-five. Originally written by Michelle, this story has been lovingly shared by her mother, sister, and grandmother. They feel comforted in knowing that Michelle is being cared for by God and their family in heaven.

Our Treasure

Ann Morelli

⌒

Our daughter, Kim Morelli, our shimmering sunbeam, introduced herself to this world on June 21, 1956, the first day of summer. Her identical twin, Jo-ann, did not survive. We had no idea that I was carrying twins, since only one heartbeat had been detected. The doctors thought Kim's sister had been dead for about six weeks, probably crushed from too little room inside my belly. My grandmother was also a twin, and her sibling had been born dead as well. At my husband's request, the doctors allowed him to delay telling me the heartbreaking news until after we arrived home from the hospital. We had an angel here on earth and one in heaven.

When Kim was just four months old, my mother and I realized something was wrong with her. She was sick, and in those days, doctors still made house calls. After the doctor examined her in our home, he said matter-of-factly, "Children like this always get sick."

"Children like what?" I asked. He told us that Kim had cerebral palsy. From that time on, I brought my daughter to many doctors in search of ways to help her. One doctor, who sat with his feet on his desk leaning back in his chair, told us, "Do what the Chinese do when they have baby girls. Put the baby on a mountainside and forget about her." Behind him on his credenza was a picture of his two children, healthy and normal. He had no clue what I was feeling.

Whenever I had contact with doctors, all they did was patronize me. At that time, little was being done to help affected children. All the doctors could see was that I had an extremely handicapped child who had nothing to offer. The sad part about it all was that Kim's brain worked fine, which wasn't acknowledged until she was twenty-one years old. I remember the day that happened, walking out into the sunlight saying, "Thank you, God, for this much."

Kim tried to be independent. Whenever I placed my daughter in the swing, holding her hands onto the ropes, she would try to hold on by herself; Kim didn't want me to help her. Also, when her younger siblings were playing games, she would crawl over to the game board, mess it up so they couldn't play, and then laugh; if she couldn't play, no one else was going to play either. Kim loved watching soap operas and would put her head down during the commercials. She also enjoyed music, children's programming, and especially the show *American Bandstand*. Her dad and I would hold her in our arms and dance with her, which she absolutely loved.

When Kim was five years old, we tried placing her in a rehabilitation facility. The people in charge there told me I couldn't see her for six weeks because she needed to get acclimated to the place. I just couldn't wait; I had to see her. So I visited her after three weeks, and I was shocked at what I found. Not only did Kim have impetigo on her face, but she now had secondary wound infections on both her legs from the leg braces; the infections were being treated with alcohol. I took my daughter home. She was a changed child. Her spasms had increased so much that I needed to sleep with her on the floor at night because she would wake up screaming.

Kim also attended Camp Pohelo (Potential through Healing and Love). Many of the young people in our neighborhood volunteered there. Because they had grown up with Kim, they felt comfortable helping others like her. Kim's sisters, Jill and Lisa, volunteered there, too. It was such a wonderful experience. The director of the camp, Mary Lou Morris, was great with children, and she was the first person to recognize that Kim had great potential and knowledge within. It just couldn't come out because of her severe disability. Kim absolutely loved that whole camp experience.

As she grew older, Kim was placed in various rehabilitation facilities based on her age. She also visited the hospital frequently with respiratory problems and would be placed on life support. Each time, my husband and I would have to make a decision about what to do the next time it occurred—what would be the most loving thing to do for our daughter? During her stay at the Lennox Hill Nursing Rehabilitation Center, a wonderful facility we discovered at the end of her life, we made the decision to just keep her comfortable. In the end, Kim went to sleep with a smile on her face. She passed on May 29, 1984.

My family and I are certain that Kim has not left us. She still watches over us and sometimes lets us know that she is near. The first time this became evident was when Kim's younger sister Jill misplaced her emerald ring seven months after Kim had passed away. Having searched her bed, bedroom, clothing, and everywhere she could think of, Jill was beside herself because she could not find the ring. I suggested that she try asking Kim for some help. After saying a quick prayer to her sister, Jill returned to her bedroom only to find the missing emerald ring lying right in the middle of her bed!

Jill and her husband were married on a wet and rainy day one year after Kim's passing. As the bride and groom walked out of the church, Jill said longingly to her husband, "I wish Kim were here." In that moment, the clouds parted and a beautiful ray of sunlight appeared. Jill knew it was Kim. Her sister was right there sharing in her happiness on that special day.

Although I've had fleeting dreams of Kim over the years, I had one dream in particular that was extremely vivid. Kim and I were outdoors in a field of wildflowers, and it felt so peaceful there. It was bright and sunny, and the flowers seemed to go on forever. Kim was wearing my favorite outfit of hers—a wool, navy blue skirt with a white sweater. Instead of running through the fields, Kim seemed to be flitting through the fields, playing with another child. The two girls seemed to be having so much fun together, happily dancing among the flowers, not playing any game in particular. Kim looked so beautiful and so healthy. I'm crying as I describe this. Kim was moving freely and without limitation, something she could never do in this life. The child she was playing with looked just like her, with the same brown eyes and the same short, dark brown hair. Then I awoke from the dream.

My first thought was that the other child looked identical. Over and over I kept saying to myself, "She was identical … she was identical." Then I realized the other child was identical to Kim! It was her twin sister, Jo-ann! How incredible! The dream confirmed for me that Kim had gone to heaven, and she was there with her identical twin sister. I was so elated and so at peace! Also, there are no words to describe how happy Kim appeared. It was as if she had come to say, "I'm fine, Mom. I can walk, and I can talk. I can do all the things that you wanted for me. I'm doing just fine." That dream left me with such a warm feeling inside that all was well with my girls.

My niece Julie also shared a dream about Kim. In the dream, Kim was smiling as she and her identical twin walked across the front yard of Julie's parents' home. Wearing a pretty white dress and some of the jewelry that I had given her over the years, Kim appeared very happy. She told my niece, "Tell Mom and Dad that I'm with my sister. I'm very happy. I'm safe and at peace." That dream occurred on either Kim's birthday or the anniversary of her death.

My daughter Kim taught me unconditional love. She taught me strength. But most importantly, she taught me about faith and to hold on no matter how difficult life might be. Kim wasn't handicapped; we are. Kim loved and never hated. She gave herself fully and completely to everyone; she never asked for anything in return—only to be loved, and loved she was and still is. Kim will always be a part of our family, leading us in the right direction. My exquisite dream of Kim let me know that she is completely healed and whole, as is her twin sister, Jo-ann. It makes my heart so happy to think that my twin daughters are joyfully playing together in heaven.

Ann Morelli and her loving husband of fifty-eight years, Al, have raised five wonderful children together. She has chaired Operation Friendship, taught Sunday school, and raised money for the Cerebral Palsy Foundation. Ann enjoys time at home, church, quilting, and crafts.

FINALLY FREE

Elissa Al-Chokhachy

———

On Memorial Day of 2010, I woke up from a dream involving a special little boy, Benjamin Orton. He had passed away two days prior at the young age of eight. This beautiful little boy had been born with a small head and a small brain, otherwise known as microcephaly. Despite the multiple medical challenges he'd faced, Benjamin had brought love and light wherever he went. Adored by his family and surrounded by love, he lived far beyond most people's expectations. I had met Benjamin and his mom several years earlier at a craft fair in New Hampshire. He was just a baby at the time, but one baby that I knew I would never forget. I felt honored to sign a copy of my first book, *The Angel with the Golden Glow*, in honor of this special little angel in our world.

I learned of Benjamin's passing in an e-mail from his mom, Becky. Ten hours later, I actually shared a dreamlike experience with her son. In the dream, I found myself holding a close-up photograph of Ben being hugged by a little girl, who I thought might be his sister. I had the awareness that he had passed, and I felt the urge to hold him. Suddenly, Benjamin was right there with me inside an open, cardboard mailing box along with a butterfly and a half-filled baby bottle of formula. As I lifted him out of the box, I thought, "Oh my, look at how long your body is! You have grown so tall." Yet as I cradled him in my arms, his body was more the size of the baby boy I had met years before. Benjamin was so happy, smiling and making goo-goo baby sounds. His head and face were both perfectly shaped, and his hair was thick, dark brown, and wavy.

As I held him in my lap, Benjamin reached for his baby bottle with his left hand. "No, honey, I'm sorry. You can't have that right now,"

I said as I pushed the bottle away. "I first need to check with your mommy because I know you've been on a special formula." Benjamin didn't seem to mind at all. He just kept smiling, almost giggling, and looking around at all the people in the room. At one point I repositioned Ben on my left hip in the same way that I had held my own children when they were babies. Amazingly, Benjamin held up his head entirely on his own, something he could not do in this lifetime.

I became aware that I needed to let Becky know that Benjamin was right there with me; I also wanted to find out if he still needed any special formula. First, I searched to locate Becky's telephone number. Then I attempted to call her. But every time I reached for the wall phone, someone else seemed to grab the handle the second before I got there. Finally, I decided to shift gears and use a nearby cell phone instead.

With the cell phone in hand, I began dialing Becky when I noticed the butterfly start to fly away. "Oh no, Ben, I need to get the butterfly that your mom sent with you!" I definitely wanted to be able to return the baby, bottle, and butterfly to Becky. Quickly, I asked someone else to hold Benjamin, with special instructions to support his head. Having just said that, I also remembered that he had just been able to hold his head up on his own.

By this time, the butterfly had flown into the right-hand corner of the room and halfway up the wall. It was now huge, almost a foot in size. I didn't want to hurt the white butterfly, so I tried to grab it carefully by the back of its body and legs with my right hand. But this enormous butterfly was extremely strong. The harder I tried to hold on to it, the more the butterfly fought to get away. Finally, my right hand cramped, and I was forced to release it. As soon as I did, the butterfly quickly flew out of sight.

I awoke with the awareness that Benjamin just wanted to be free. This beautiful little angel was not meant to stay here on earth any longer. Just like the butterfly released from its chrysalis, Benjamin was finally able to spread his wings and fly without being encumbered or limited by an earthly, human form. I smile when I think of him. I know Benjamin is a happy, healthy, and playful little boy. I'm sure he's having so much fun now with all his little friends in heaven.

8

Angels

Angel of God, my guardian dear
To whom God's love commits me here;
Ever this day be at my side,
To light and guard, to rule and guide.

—TRADITIONAL CATHOLIC PRAYER

ANGELS ARE IN OUR lives every day. They bring us hope. They intercede on our behalf in times of danger. Angels also come and comfort us in our dreams. While some appear in human form, others have wings of light. But make no mistake: angels are real. They are God's invisible helpers here on earth. Have you ever been visited by an angel? Has an angel ever interceded on your behalf?

I remember one time I was driving down a highway in my little silver Subaru with four brand-new tires on my car. The tires had been on less than a week when all of sudden my car started to wobble.

Then I lost control of my car completely! As the car started to spin to the left, time slowed, and I remember thinking, "But I didn't think I was supposed to die yet...Angels, HELP!!" In slow motion, my car was lifted into the air as it slowly spun a full 360 degrees while crossing three lanes of moving traffic. The car landed in the same direction I was originally headed on the tiniest patch of green grass right next to the metal guardrail dividing the highway. The car didn't touch the guardrail nor did it hit any of the cars speeding by. As I got out of my car, I could barely walk. My legs were shaking so hard because I knew that I could have easily died. What a close call! Thank goodness, I was safe. Other than my right rear tire being ruined from having no air in it, the car was fine, too. It truly was a miracle that I walked away unharmed from that near miss that day. I am convinced that the angels came to my rescue.

Some of the angels who intercede on our behalf are our dear loved ones in spirit. Love transcends death; our love once shared now spans heaven and earth. Eleven stories in this chapter talk about angelic intervention here on earth. Our beloved angels come close in times of need. They bring hope and healing to those who are hurting, comfort to those who are suffering, and messages of love to those in need. Thank heaven for all of God's angels!

HEAVEN

Elissa Al-Chokhachy

⌒

Have you ever contemplated heaven? Have you ever wondered what heaven might be like for your child? I believe that God's precious children who left this world prematurely are now enjoying earthly activities with deceased loved ones in their new heavenly home. And for those sweet souls who never had an opportunity at childhood, I believe they are also happily engaged and lovingly supported in those same childhood activities in their new, perfectly healthy, spiritual forms. I have heard too many moving, life-affirming stories from the dying and the bereaved to think otherwise.

One bereaved mom shared with me that she had seen her eight-year-old daughter in a dream riding a horse and galloping through a field. Her daughter was radiantly smiling and waving at her. What comfort the vision brought this mother since she knew her daughter loved horses. Two other bereaved moms saw their daughters skipping, running, and joyfully playing in a field of flowers in dreamtime. Another woman shared about her neighbor's seven-year-old son, who was dying of a brain tumor. He briefly woke up before he died and said, "Mommy, please don't bury me in a suit. An angel told me that I'm going to be playing, and I need to wear sneakers and sweats."

Finally, one private-duty nurse felt from her years of hospice work that children have an easier time of letting go. She described a poignant moment with a young girl dying of AIDS. The girl, struggling for breath, asked, "Am I dying?"

"No, you're not dying," the nurse replied, trying to reassure her.

Then the young girl continued, "Because if I am, please get out my Holy Communion dress. I am going to be with my grandfather, and we are going to plant the most beautiful garden!" Tearfully, the nurse listened as the young girl eagerly described the garden that she and her deceased grandfather would be planting together. Shortly after that, the child quietly and peacefully passed from this world.

ICU Angel

Laurin Bellg

———

In our three-hundred-bed Midwestern hospital, the intensive care unit (ICU) typically receives trauma victims from all kinds of accidents. One winter night, injured family members from a very bad automobile accident were rushed to our hospital. Their car had hit a patch of black ice and had run off the road while they were returning home from an evening event.

The driver of the car was not speeding, no one was intoxicated, and the children had all been safely buckled in. It was just a freak accident—an unforeseen and unfortunate encounter with black ice. All three children—two boys and a girl—were killed. The father, also the driver of the car, was hospitalized with minor injuries, but the mother, in critical condition, was transferred to our ICU.

Our telemetry center monitors the data of each ICU patient, and the video screens display what is happening in each room. The telemetry technician, also a nurse, is responsible for monitoring patient data and observing everything that occurs. After this mother was transferred to our ICU, the telemetry tech noticed something unusual on her room's monitor screen around one in the morning. She saw a little boy wearing a baseball cap standing next to the nurse who was working in her room.

So the tech said to the nurse over the intercom, "There's a little boy in there with you." The nurse in the room looked around and replied, "No, I'm in here by myself. It's just me and the patient."

Then another nurse walked up to the telemetry center and also saw the little boy with a baseball cap on the screen. More than a little puzzled, one of these nurses went quickly into the patient's room, which was only a few yards away. Sure enough, no little boy could be found. The nurse caring for the patient, also dumbfounded, had not seen the little boy in the room either. As soon as both nurses returned to the telemetry center, they could see the little boy on the monitor.

Other nurses and staff started to gather inside the telemetry center to witness this mystifying event. Over the next six hours, up until the shift change occurred that morning, the little boy disappeared and re-appeared on the monitor screen about half a dozen times. Sometimes, even when the nurse went into another room to care for a different patient, the little boy stuck by her side and followed her.

Shortly after this incident began, the nurses heard from a respiratory therapist who had helped in the emergency room after the ambulances arrived with this family that all three children had been pronounced dead upon arrival. One of boys that had been killed in the accident had been wearing a baseball cap. Naturally, the nurses started to wonder, "Is this the spirit of that little boy who's watching the nurse take care of his mother?"

So it became poignant; it became sweet; it became fascinating. Five nurses—some of them very skeptical nonbelievers and non-embellishers—were able to see the boy on the monitor but not in the room. I know one of the first nurses who saw the little boy quite well. She is a huge skeptic of anything that she cannot see with her own eyes. She is a no-nonsense nurse who is all about trauma and no fluff. I've known her for years, and she'd be the first one to say that the unseen doesn't exist. However, she was also one of the first nurses to see the boy that night.

While it is not unheard of to occasionally encounter the unexplained when working in an environment where there is death and dying, this particular event is still talked about in our ICU and with such tenderness. It is comforting to think that this little child, once he was no longer confined to his physical body, lingered at his mom's side, attending to her just like the nurse he was following—a sweet little boy angel looking after his mom at a time when she needed him most.

Laurin Bellg, MD, works as an ICU physician at two large medical centers in the Midwest. Writing and speaking about her experiences is as much a vital part of her journey in medicine as the care she provides for her patients.

Pink Carnations from Angel

Vinette Silvers

⎯⎯⎯

The sky was blue, and the air was filled with the scent of freshly cut grass. I was sitting high up on the hillside, visiting my dear friend Angel. On his gravestone was the name Alan Friedman, but to his friends he was known as Angel. At twenty-eight years old, his life was cut short, taken unnecessarily in a senseless act of violence. It had been five years since his passing. Although I would love him forever, I had been able to move forward in my life. Thankfully, I met a wonderful man by the name of Gregg, and I fell deeply in love with him. We were married shortly thereafter. I knew Angel would be happy for the two of us. In fact, I often talked to Angel about what was going on in my life.

On that day, I had been discussing with Angel something that had been troubling me. For a few years, Gregg and I had desperately been trying to have a baby. I had sadly endured three miscarriages. I asked Angel to please speak to God on our behalf. "Please, Angel, I need your help. You're with God," I told him. "Ask God to help us to become parents…You know I would be a good mom. And if it's not too much to ask, could you please ask Him for twins?" From the time I was a little girl, I had always dreamed of having twins. So why not shoot for the stars?

I asked Angel, "Do you hear me? If so, could you please show me a sign that you know I'm here, and you're listening?" I waited. Nothing happened. I stood up and turned to leave. As I did, I happened to notice a small red Pacer driving toward me. It was traveling on a road that separated two hillsides. There was the one on which I had been sitting and the other hill, where several people were gathering for a burial ceremony.

The red car stopped and parked on the road between the two hills. I watched a blond man in his twenties get out of his car and open his hatchback. Underneath the hatchback and inside the car was a huge basket filled with beautiful, freshly arranged flowers. I fully expected the young man to lift the basket out of the car and deliver it to the funeral site. Instead, he pulled out one flowered stem from the arrangement, closed his trunk, and began walking up the hill in my direction. Surely he must have been headed for someone else. Yet this man walked straight toward me!

He stopped directly in front of me and extended his right arm. In his right hand was a gift—two pink-and-white-striped carnations joined together on one stem. He smiled and said, "God bless you!" I was stunned. Why had the man come to me? I was just a girl walking alone in a cemetery wearing ripped jeans and a bandana on my head. I thanked him. Then, just as quickly as he had come, the man was gone.

I stood there for a moment pondering what had just happened. Was the gift of the two pink carnations a sign of twins to come? Had I just received a gift from an angel? I realized Angel must have sent the angel. He had heard me. My dream of twins would come true after all. I discovered on the Internet that pink carnations represent Mother's Day, and the stripes mean "I will never forget you." Angel couldn't have picked a more perfect sign. I broke off one of the flowers and laid it on his gravestone as a thank-you; I placed the other one in a water bottle inside my car. I rushed home to tell Gregg about my wonderful experience. My soul was content knowing our babies were on the way.

Two months later, I discovered I was pregnant...with twins! God had surely blessed Gregg and me. We were going to be parents. My first trimester went along perfectly. All of us were healthy, and I felt like the luckiest girl in the world. I proudly showed off my belly, swam every day, and ate organic food. I also followed all of the doctor's orders.

Then Gregg and I discovered that we were having twin girls. I was having one girl for each pink carnation I had received. We couldn't have been happier. Every day I would write to my little girls in a journal. I would tell them all about the life Gregg and I had planned for all of us. I also excitedly counted down the days until their arrival.

Sadly, their arrival came far too soon. I went into preterm labor at only nineteen weeks and spent the next month in the hospital. The doctors tried everything to keep my babies inside me for as long as possible. They needed to grow big and strong enough in order to survive being born premature. We lost our battle when our girls were born at just twenty-three weeks.

Angelena Cecelia Silvers was born on September 3, 2001, and her sister, Isabella Cecelia Silvers, followed two days later on September 5, 2001. At only one pound each, they were both so tiny and so beautiful. Each of the girls had their papa's mouth and toes. Those days were by far the most heart-wrenching days of our lives. Yet it was also a great blessing to be able to have had at least one day with each of them before they passed on to heaven. I was able to hold them and tell them how very much we loved them both and that we would love them forever.

Afterward, I was faced with going forward again without my babies. I needed to find a way to heal from the ongoing grief and loss. Fortunately, my mom flew in from Milwaukee, Wisconsin, to help me through that desperate time. She lovingly held me for the hardest cry of my life.

Only days after returning home, I was lying in my bed staring through the archway connecting my bedroom to the girls' room. Their bedroom was overflowing with baby paraphernalia from the twin baby shower I had just been given. As I stared into what should have been Angelena and Isabella's bedroom, I was simply distraught. I was so angry. I remember thinking there would never be babies in that room. It was so unfair. Just then, the ceiling fan in the girls' room turned on and began to spin all by itself! Other than Mom, who was lying right next to me, holding and comforting me, no one else was in our home. I got out of bed and walked into their room to find the remote. When I stepped inside their bedroom, the fan light turned on! Then, I felt them ... *I felt my girls* ... I knew they were right there with me.

I immediately telephoned Gregg to tell him what had happened. He suggested that maybe there was a short in the electrical wiring and said he would check into it as soon as he got home. My mom also thought the wiring was faulty. To all of our surprise, as soon as Gregg arrived home and walked into his office, the ceiling fan and light turned on in that room again. I chuckled. Our girls were playing tricks on their papa.

That was the first of many unusual occurrences in our home. On a daily basis, the fans would start randomly spinning, or the lights would brighten and dim, especially if I was having a difficult time. I felt so comforted that my girls were letting me know they were there with me, and no one could tell me any differently.

Finally, Gregg decided to hire an electrician to come to our home. The electrician methodically checked each and every outlet. He also checked the wiring throughout the house in an effort to explain the odd electrical occurrences. When the inspection was completed, the electrician informed us that everything was "safe and normal"; the only way the ceiling fans could possibly turn on would be if someone were to push the on button. Gregg and I just looked at each other with a knowing smile. Since that time, we have continued to feel the twins' ongoing love and comfort from room to room in our home.

Seven months after the loss of our girls, with the amazing help of my mom, Gregg and I were so blessed to be able to adopt a beautiful, newborn baby girl. We named her Ella Angel after her twin sisters. She has absolutely been the love of our lives.

I remember when Ella Angel was just a toddler and learning to talk. My precocious little daughter would tell me how her twin sisters would sing to her. One day, Ella Angel started singing "Old Mac-Donald." Although I sang to Ella nightly, my repertoire consisted of three songs I had created. No one else had taught her that song, either. When I asked Ella Angel where she had learned "Old Mac-Donald," she said very matter-of-factly, "Angelena and Ella Zabella." I remember other times when I would hear her singing songs I had not taught her. It was so comforting just to think that my three girls were spending time together.

Ella Angel is now five years old. I asked her about the songs her sisters used to sing to her when she was little. She told me that some-times they would sing to her in the morning, and sometimes they would sing to her at night. Each of her sisters sang her own song. Angelena would sing "Rock-A-Bye Baby," and Ella Zabella (Isabella) would sing "Twinkle, Twinkle Little Star." But the two of them sang "Old MacDonald" together. Ella Angel also told me that sometimes she still hears her sisters singing to her from heaven.

Vinette Cecelia Silvers dedicates her story to her precocious Ella Angel, her great-est gift from God, with her beautiful loving spirit and heart of gold. Vinette also gives thanks to her brilliant, dedicated, handsome, and loving husband, Gregg, for making her the luckiest woman on earth.

SURPRISING SISTERS

Eileen Kearney

———

"Eileen, come here. I want to talk with you," my father said.

"Okay, Daddy." I excitedly went to the kitchen to hear what my father was going to say. He was probably going to tell me that our new baby had been born. After all, why else would he be home after school instead of Mommy?

"Here, sit in this chair." I climbed up onto the kitchen chair. When I had seated myself, my thirty-three-year-old father hunkered down in front of me with such a serious look on his face. I was confused. Shouldn't he be happy? I was. At six years old, I was going to be the big sister of a new baby and my three-year-old sister, Cindy.

"Did Mommy have the baby? Is it a girl or a boy?" I asked.

"Yes, she did. It's a girl. But I have some bad news. Mommy is okay, but the baby died." I was stunned. How could a brand-new baby die? My father went on. "The baby had trouble breathing. The doctors couldn't help her, so she died. She's with God now, up in heaven. Sometimes He needs babies more than we do."

"But why does He need babies more than us, Daddy?"

"They become angels and watch out for us," my father replied. I was feeling so confused, sad, and disappointed, but how could I argue with God? He knew everything. Our stunned little family had to regroup from the unexpected loss of Elizabeth. We did our best to get back to normal.

Flash forward ten years, and our family had moved to a new town. My younger sister, Cindy, was now thirteen, and I was sixteen. One day, in my bedroom, as I was brushing my hair in front of the mirror on my bureau, I noticed movement out of the corner of my eye. I turned to see what it was. I saw my sister from the back, quietly going up the stairs, her long brown hair looking pretty as it cascaded down the back of her purple jersey. Just as she was putting her hand on the newel post at the top of the stairway, I turned back to my mirror. *Hah!* I thought. *Cindy's trying to sneak up and scare me. Well, I'll turn the trick on her and give her just enough time to get behind me. Then I'll turn around fast and scare her!* That's just what I did. At precisely the right moment, I spun around and yelled, "Boo!!!" However, the trick was truly on me. There was no one there.

I ran downstairs and confronted my sister about sneaking up on me. As I was telling her what had just happened, I realized she wasn't wearing a purple shirt. In fact, she didn't even own a purple shirt. Exactly who, then, was the girl who looked just like Cindy from the back, only a little shorter, and had soundlessly come and gone from my room? It could only have been our younger sister, Elizabeth. Just as my father had told me all those years before, Elizabeth is an angel. How heartwarming to know our sister is still watching out for us.

Eileen Kearney, librarian, lives on Boston's North Shore, where she has raised two wonderful children, Amy and Brian. She has worked at her public library for the last thirty years and is looking forward to the next chapter in her life... retirement!

GRATITUDE

Elissa Al-Chokhachy

Providing comfort to grieving family members is an important component of hospice work. At times, this can be a difficult task to achieve, especially when their loved one has just died. Probably one of the toughest on-call visits I have ever made as a hospice nurse involved a grieving mother whose adult son had just died from colon cancer in his mid-thirties. For his entire life, his mother had lovingly provided the care he needed at home in order to prevent him from being institutionalized for his severe disabilities. Now, her son was gone, as was her purpose for living.

As her husband stood silently nearby, watching helplessly, I held this mother in my arms as she sobbed and sobbed and sobbed. I don't even know how long I held her; it didn't matter. But the whole time I held her in my arms, I prayed intensely with all my heart for God and the Blessed Mother to please help her, hold her, and grant her solace and peace. Eventually the mother calmed down, allowing me to complete the tasks I needed to do, which involved notifying her son's physician of his death, contacting the funeral home, completing the nurse's pronouncement form, and disposing of his medications. I did not leave their home until everything had been completed and the young man had been safely transferred into the hearse and was on his way to the funeral home.

Afterward, I drove home in silence and in tears with a heavy heart, praying for this mother, child, and family. Sometimes praying is the only thing I can do amidst so much angst and grief. Just before midnight, I climbed into my king-sized bed, pulled the covers over me, and turned on my left side, facing the window. Still needing to unwind before going to sleep, I reflected for a little while longer on all that had just transpired. Then I rolled onto my back, and I couldn't believe what I saw. On my right side, in the middle of the bed between my sleeping husband and me, was an angel—a pure, white, translucent female figure from the waist up lovingly looking down at me in my darkened bedroom.

Although the angel did not speak to me, she radiated incredible warmth, love, and gratitude. I had the sense that she was the guardian angel of the young man who had just died, and was perhaps even his grandmother in spirit; she had come to say thank you for all the compassion and love extended to this family. Also, when I rolled over in bed, my right arm and hand actually went right through her torso. I felt no fear—only peace and love emanating from my angelic visitor.

At that moment, my youngest daughter, Andrea, cried out in her sleep from her nearby bedroom. I quickly turned my head to the left to listen for any further cries. There were none, and when I looked back, the angel was gone. Gone but surely not forgotten. I will always be grateful for the compassion extended to me on that night from God's angel of mercy who had made a difficult night a memorable one of love.

God's Messenger

Rosa Viglas

After we were married in 1970, my husband and I immigrated to America from Greece. I was only seventeen years old, and I found myself homesick living so far away from my parents and siblings. Fortunately, we were blessed with two beautiful children. From the moment I gave birth to my first child, Andrew, the intense loneliness I had been feeling for months went away; four years later, I gave birth to my sweet little girl, Alexia. Our home was very happy and blessed. I gave thanks to God every day for His greatest gifts to me—my two children.

Andrew seemed to grow up quickly. He filled everyone's lives with joy and love. In addition to being a good student, Andrew attended Greek school and Sunday school and played all types of sports. His favorites were baseball and basketball. Winning the state baseball championship was one of the highlights of his high school career. Also, Andrew always saw the good in people. Never a complainer, he was mature, self-confident, loving, and very kind. Andrew spent time with people of all ages, and he always reached out to help others in need. Surrounded by friends, his trademark was his big, beautiful, ever-present smile.

When Andrew graduated from college with his bachelor's degree, the whole family was so proud of him. His sister, Alexia, especially loved and admired her big brother. Whenever his friends visited him at our house, everyone would laugh like little kids. I often wondered how I would manage when Andrew finally left home. Things turned out quite differently than I ever imagined.

On February 18, 1995, my twenty-three-year-old son, Andrew, and his friend Jimmy left our home in the middle of the night on their way to meet their friends in Montreal for a bachelor's party later that day. Around 6:30 in the morning, their car veered off the road in St. George, Vermont, and crashed into a huge concrete rock. They were ten miles from the Canadian border. Jimmy was driving; no other cars were involved. Both young men lost their lives.

My husband, along with two police officers, arrived at my place of business at nine in the morning with the news. I went crazy. In total shock and disbelief, I couldn't see; I couldn't hear. I was devastated. My pain was so heavy, so hard, and so deep. My son, Andrew, was such an exceptional man in the world, and now he was gone. I desperately needed to know he was okay. I prayed to God continuously, asking, "Is Andrew happy?" Fortunately, an answer to my prayers came two days later.

My family and I had gone to the funeral home to see Andrew for the first time, and he didn't look like himself at all. What struck us most was the odd way his hair was brushed to one side. Andrew was always very particular about the way he groomed his hair; it just didn't look right, so I instructed the funeral director to please fix it. As soon as we returned home, we found Andrew's pregnant cousin anxiously waiting for us by the door. We had asked her to remain at home rather than accompany us and stress her unborn baby any further. Yet we were shocked to find her smiling and at ease.

She explained that once we had left for the funeral home, she had lain down on the couch to rest. When she looked up, there was her cousin's beautiful smiling face looking down upon her. Andrew said, "Please don't cry. Don't worry. Everything is fine. They just messed up my hair." That message from Andrew was a gift from God to give us strength and hope to go on.

I never lost faith in Andrew's eternal existence, thanks to my strong belief in God. As each day passed, I waited for my son to let me know he was happy. Because I wanted to help his soul elevate higher, I prayed constantly and made special efforts on his behalf to help others. In every prayer, I asked God and the Virgin Mary for a sign to show me that Andrew was happy. God, who loves all children in His own way, began answering my prayers.

When Andrew's sister returned to Bentley College two weeks after the accident, Alexia was still distraught. I was so worried. With Andrew gone, I now feared something would happen to my little girl. One day, Alexia called me from school crying hysterically. She missed her brother terribly and told me that she would do anything to see him again. I tried to calm her down; I told Alexia not to worry because she would see Andrew that night in her dreams. She asked how I was so sure, and I replied that I just knew. Sure enough, Andrew came that night in her dreams.

In the dream, Andrew explained how the accident had happened. Although Andrew had driven most of the way, they had just stopped for a Coca-Cola because he was feeling pretty tired. Jimmy took over the driving; they had both fallen asleep at the time the accident occurred. Andrew also told Alexia that he was right next to me on the day of the funeral, and he was so moved and surprised at the number of people who had attended.

The moment that I heard Andrew had died I experienced severe pain in my chest; the heartache lasted for four months, day and night. I felt completely lost, and I blamed myself for what had happened to my son. Maybe if I had stayed awake that night, I might have been able to stop the boys from leaving so early. One morning while at work, I actually felt the pain leave my body and be replaced by some happiness, which worried me. What kind of mother could ever feel an ounce of happiness after losing her son? Yet, during my prayers that evening, I realized I had finally come to accept that God had taken my Andrew, and I knew I would be able to cope. "God," I prayed, "I accept that you have my son, but please show me a sign. I'm asking in particular to please see my Andrew." Since God had taken him, I needed to know that my son was all right in His hands. I was hoping to finally have a dream of Andrew that I could fully remember.

That night, Andrew came to see me in a dream, and he was totally healed, with all of his injuries gone. I held him in my arms and asked if he felt any pain at the time of the accident. "Only a little," Andrew said, "just before I passed on." When I awoke the next morning, I felt enormous joy in my heart. My prayers had finally been answered. Seeing my son brought me a deep feeling of inner peace. I continued to pray for his soul, hoping that one day I would understand more about what happens in the next life.

Six months after Andrew's passing, I had the most wonderful dream. I was standing in a huge room filled with people when I saw Jesus in the distance. He was bearded and dressed in a dark, maroon robe, with a slim build, exactly like his icon. I wondered how I could possibly reach Jesus to talk to Him about Andrew. Suddenly, He was right next to me. I looked straight into His eyes and began sobbing. "Jesus," I pleaded, "I ask you to please pray to your Father for my son." Jesus asked for his name, and I answered, "Andrew." He nodded, and with so much happiness in his eyes, Jesus gave me the most reassuring, loving look. Telepathically, He said, "Don't worry, Rosa. Everything will be taken care of." I watched Him go to speak with the high priest of the Greek Orthodox Church, and then He left. The following morning, I woke up feeling extremely happy and proud. It was the first time Jesus had ever visited me in a dream. His visit gave me strength and hope and reaffirmed my faith. Since that time, Jesus and many saints have visited me in dreams.

My heartbroken mother and siblings had begged me for months to visit them in Greece. As soon as I arrived, I went straight to the Metamorphosis Sotiros Monastery near my hometown of Agrinio, where I spoke to the priest and his mother for some time. Father Athanasios Patis's life mission was to help as many people as possible. In memory of my son, I donated a large framed icon of Saint Andreas to the monastery. Andrew's father, sister, and friends all had dreams of him while I was away; Andrew told them that he was happy and did not regret passing at such a young age.

Then, on February 18, 1996, exactly one year after the accident, our family held two memorial anniversary services in honor of Andrew, one in the States and one in Greece. That evening, while Father Athanasios was praying for Andrew and Jimmy at the monastery, a young man appeared in front of him. The priest asked the angel who he was. The young man replied, "Andrew." He had come to thank the priest and his family in America for everything that had been done in his honor; all the prayers from his mother and loved ones had helped elevate him to higher levels. When the priest asked if Andrew was happy where he was or if he was upset that he was no longer here on earth, Andrew replied, "Life continues on in heaven."

Any mother who has lost a child is left with questions about where the child is and if the child is happy. Andrew answers these questions whenever he visits our family, friends, and the Greek priest; also, the priest now sees both Andrew and Jimmy. Prior to my son's passing, my faith in God was strong, but now it is even stronger. I believe in miracles, and I also know that God tests each of us in His own way. Through the help of His son, Jesus, the Virgin Mary, and all the saints, God answers any problem that may arise for all who are able to keep their hearts open to Him.

Andrew continues to do God's work. Whenever his faithful friends pray and ask for help, Andrew is sent as God's messenger with the answers to their prayers. This fills my heart with great happiness and peace. God gave me Andrew for twenty-three beautiful years. Although there still are days when I miss him and cry myself to sleep, Andrew now appears in so many ways. I know that my son is happy; I know he is alive and well, and I want to share that knowledge with everyone. I promised God that I would do anything for Him if He would simply let me know that Andrew is happy. God has clearly answered my prayers. Sharing about Andrew is my way of keeping my promise to God. As Andrew's mother, it makes me very happy and pleased to be able to share these experiences.

Rosa Viglas, proud mother and grandmother, is a native of Greece. The messages she receives from Andrew through the Greek priest let Rosa know that Andrew is always with her. Rosa looks forward to seeing her son again one day.

AND THE CRADLE ROCKED

Ami & Matthew Romero

———

Finding out we were pregnant was truly a miracle. I had been fighting infertility for over four years, and the doctors felt that my chances of conceiving a child were slim. Little did my husband, Matthew, and I realize what a long road of faith, despair, and enlightenment this child growing inside of me would bring.

January 19, 1998, sits like a hard rock in our stomachs. I had an ultrasound performed at twenty-nine weeks. Although it was a routine sonogram, the news we received was not positive. Our baby had a cleft lip and was missing ventricles in her brain. Even before the ultrasound, I had been troubled with repeated unsettling dreams about my baby. Knowing how difficult it was for me, Matthew prayed often for spiritual assistance to help get me through.

The doctor scheduled a procedure three days later to determine a more definitive diagnosis of what was going on. The night before my amniocentesis, my husband awoke out of a sound sleep with a sense that someone was close by and watching over us. As he rolled over from his right side to his back, he very clearly saw a tall male angel standing over me while I slept. The angel had short, dark, curly hair and enormous wings. He was wearing a long white robe and emanated a very gentle and calming presence. Apparently, the angel looked startled, as if surprised that Matthew could see him, but never said a word. The angel maintained eye contact while Matthew very slowly sat up in bed. Then the angel took three slow steps backward, and his image began to fade away. It became paler and then opaque, until it completely disappeared. My husband had the sense that the angel was our baby's guardian angel assigned to help in some way. The next morning, the results of the amniocentesis showed that our daughter had an extra thirteenth chromosome. Trisomy 13, we quickly learned, is a fatal chromosomal disorder. Our little girl was destined to die.

The next six weeks were a blur. We had been so busy planning for her birth, and now we were beginning to prepare for her death. Planning our little girl's funeral while she kicked inside of me left an indescribable ache. We had been told that it was unlikely she would live through birth, and if she was born alive, she would die shortly after. Mattison Marie was born one month early. To our amazement, she not only lived through the birth, but we also were able to take her home.

Mattison lived for twenty-six days. She died on her scheduled due date, March 22. Those twenty-six days were the longest and shortest days of our lives. Our faith was greatly tested. It was a time when we reached out to God, praying that He would give us strength and acceptance of His greater plan. Born in Pueblo, Colorado, my husband, Matthew, had been raised Catholic in a strongly religious family. His father was Hispanic, and his maternal grandmother was Cherokee Indian and spoke fluent Apache. She was an "abweller," or herbal healer; she always had a cure for everything. Matthew's family traveled annually to the Santuario Church near Española, New Mexico, where many miraculous healings have occurred. His family's strong spiritual influence and cultural beliefs enabled Matthew to find peace in knowing that Mattison would still be able to "visit" us and watch over us. However, I had been raised in St. Joseph, Missouri; I was a conventional Methodist who believed that when a person dies, he or she enters either heaven or hell. I struggled with the idea that our daughter could be near my family or me.

Miraculously, God made Mattison's presence known to us the night following her death. We had just gotten home from the visitation services held at the funeral home. I had stayed up late with my sister, Meredith. I remember asking her if she believed Mattison was with us. For two days, everyone around me kept talking about how they felt Matti's presence, yet I felt completely removed from this awareness. Meredith quietly replied, "I think you will feel her when you least expect it."

Later that night, after everyone else had gone to bed, I was sitting in the living room with our yellow Labrador retriever, Lazer, looking at pictures of Matti. Lazer had bonded with Mattison, and he was very protective of her. For forty-eight hours before her death, Lazer had refused to eat. After that, he had moped around the house for the longest time, obviously grieving her loss. Intensely missing my daughter, I began desperately praying, "God, please send me a sign that Mattison is in heaven and is safe in Your arms." Lazer lifted his head toward Mattison's empty cradle, and to my amazement, her cradle began to rock back and forth! I was paralyzed, wanting desperately to call out to my sleeping husband to confirm that I was not losing my mind. I sat still for fear of ruining the moment, watching the cradle rock. After approximately five minutes, it stopped. Her wooden cradle had been given to us by a hospice volunteer who felt Mattison might feel safer sleeping in a small cradle instead of her crib.

The next morning, I shared with my husband what had happened. Matthew didn't seem surprised at all. Very nonchalantly, he told me that he had been feeling her presence all along. Whenever Mattison was around, he got a very warm, fuzzy feeling, that same feeling you sometimes get when you arrive home after being away on a long trip. Mattison brought a smile to his face whenever she was near.

The next time the cradle rocked was one hour before Mattison's funeral. We were getting ready to leave for the church when Meredith saw the cradle rocking, and she called out to us. This time, Matthew, Meredith, her husband, Tom, and I all witnessed this miracle. The cradle rocked for a good three minutes. All four of us checked the room to rule out any logical explanation for the phenomenon. Yet no air was coming out of the floor heating vents. Moreover, the ceiling fan was off, and all the outside doors that could have caused a draft were closed. We were convinced that Mattison was with us! After that experience, I made a promise to myself to leave the cradle up for one month in hopes that it would rock again. Sadly, it did not. At the end of the month, Matthew disassembled the cradle and put it away.

Two years later, as we were awaiting the birth of Mattison's sister, TobiAnn, my husband got the cradle out of storage and prepared it for our baby. I was eight months pregnant. We decided to set up the cradle in our bedroom. While we were getting ready for bed the first night it was up, I noticed Matthew's eyes open wide as he looked in the direction of the cradle. I turned to see what he was staring at and was astonished to find the cradle rocking again! We quickly did a room check, making sure the heater was off, the ceiling fan was off, the dog was not under the cradle, and the bedroom window was closed and locked. Together, we sat on the bed and happily watched in amazement as the cradle rocked for several more minutes. How incredible! Mattison was with us!

Mattison proved her presence and provided assistance to us one more time shortly after her sister's birth. Twelve hours after TobiAnn was born, she was flown by Flight for Life to Children's Hospital in Denver, Colorado. TobiAnn was deathly ill with a respiratory infection. The doctors were baffled as to its cause. TobiAnn was not responding to the antibiotics she was receiving. I began to envision myself burying another child. Even Matthew struggled with the image of carrying another baby's casket to the grave. No one knew if she would survive.

Four days into TobiAn's illness, my husband went to the hospital chapel to pray for our daughter's life. He told God that we both surrendered TobiAnn to Him, and he asked that His will be done. If TobiAnn was to live, Matthew pleaded, "Please, God, guide the physician's hands who are caring for her." Then he prayed to Mattison, asking her to please watch over TobiAnn and give her strength. The following day, TobiAnn showed signs of improvement. Seven days later, she was released from the hospital with a clean bill of health.

One evening a week after we brought TobiAnn home, I placed her in the cradle while Matthew and I were getting ready for bed. TobiAnn was fussing, and we had been having trouble consoling her. I looked up and noticed the cradle beginning to slowly rock. But this time it swayed side to side, rather than back and forth, which was a completely different direction than we had witnessed before. It was as if TobiAnn were being rocked in someone's arms. The movement quickly soothed her. The cradle has not rocked on its own since that night. We leave it up as a reminder of the presence of our little guardian angel. Although two years have passed since Mattison entered our lives, our hearts still grieve. Yet amidst the grief, we have found room to live, love, and laugh again.

Matthew has dreamt about Mattison occasionally since her death. Whenever he sees her, Mattison is totally restored and healed. She has no cleft lip, her eyes are wide open, and she is giggling up a storm. Mattison is usually playing with her guardian angel, the same angel that Matthew saw standing over me when I was pregnant with her. The angel bounces Matti on his knee or plays games with her in the park next to a lake with lots of different kinds of baby animals, such as ducklings and lambs.

Mattison has taught me so much. There are so many ways I now see and feel her in my life. Sometimes I find a bathroom faucet running full blast when nobody turned it on. I might hear a noise-activated toy start to play music in the baby's room when our whole family is in the next room. I smile when I find my Christmas window candle lights turned on inexplicably. And I feel so blessed whenever I have the incredible sensation of smelling Mattison's familiar baby scent. Sometimes when TobiAnn is giving me the biggest smile, she seems to be looking just beyond my head, as if there is someone else standing behind me making her smile.

Matthew and I are so grateful for the gift of Mattison Marie. Our sweet little daughter has taught us what it means to be bereaved. She came into our lives and left a legacy that will never be forgotten. As a tribute to Mattison Marie, we chose the middle name "Esperanza" for TobiAnn, which means "hope" in Spanish. Without hope, we would have never had the strength to conceive TobiAnn. Although she will never replace Matti, she allows us to experience the many dreams we had held for our child.

Ami Gorsky-Romero, MSW, Matthew Romero, RN, and their family reside in Pueblo, Colorado. As administrator and VP of Sangre de Cristo Hospice Family Services, Ami facilitates grief groups including Shattered Dreams, a pregnancy and infant loss group, and Hopeful Dreams, a group for those experiencing a pregnancy after a loss. Thanks to Mattison, Matthew pursued a career in nursing and now works for a local home health agency.

ANGEL VISITORS

Elissa Al-Chokhachy

⌒

Raphael was a six-year-old boy diagnosed with cancer who was referred to the hospital for chemotherapy. He was responding well to the treatment, with all parameters pointing to a positive outcome. Two weeks into the chemotherapy, while still at the hospital, Raphael awoke and told his aunt who had stayed overnight with him that the angels had visited him. The angels told him they were going to bring him home to Jesus.

The aunt, puzzled, mentioned it to his mother as soon as she arrived. The family was not particularly a churchgoing family. Hours later, Raphael spiked a high fever and died unexpectedly from septic shock later that day. No one had expected his sudden, premature death. Yet the experience reminded the pediatrician who cared for the child that we touch each other in ways we sometimes don't realize, and also that God loves each of us. How comforting for the child's family to know that God's angels and Jesus were now caring for Raphael.

Baby Cherub Healing

Andie Hight

⌒

Shortly after we married, my husband and I moved to a quaint seaside town in Maine where we rented an antique Cape home. Whenever the snow fell lightly outside, it felt as if we were living inside a handheld snow globe that one would buy at Christmas. The combination of the cold winter nights and the warm, glowing fires found us expecting a baby before we knew it. At six months along in the pregnancy, I saw a miraculous vision; little did I know what solace this vision would one day bring.

I had just climbed into bed early for the night when a tiny, shimmering light began to twinkle in the ceiling. I couldn't figure out how a light could be shining when the lights in my room were off. I thought perhaps it was a reflection from the hall. It began to grow bigger and get brighter and eventually took the shape of toes—tiny, glowing toes coming through the ceiling! I shook my head in disbelief, hoping it was a momentary blurriness that would correct itself. However, soon toes were followed by chubby little calves and thighs, as if the ceiling were giving birth. It wasn't long before a fully formed baby cherub glowing in the most extraordinary light emerged and floated before me, reaching his little hands out to me in love. He was transparent, but I could clearly see all of his features. He was adorable and looked to be around four to six months old.

There was a pause as I took in the situation. It was one of those moments in life when everything suddenly slows down. I asked myself several questions over the span of the next five seconds before I heard myself scream in utter terror. Was it an angel? Was it my new baby's spirit? Could it be the spirit of another baby? For a split second, my mind contemplated these possibilities with a sense of wonder until the flight-or-fight response took over and I let out a bloodcurdling scream. My husband bounded up the stairs to see what was wrong. By the time he arrived, the baby spirit had exited the same way he had entered, and I realized nothing was wrong. Everything was right. I sensed that the little baby cherub knew me and loved me. It was the most amazing thing I had ever witnessed.

Soon thereafter, I gave birth to our healthy baby boy, and my husband and I were delighted. I found myself pregnant again two years later, but this time things were different. The pregnancy was worrisome from the start, with spotting and a pregnant belly much smaller than expected. One morning at six months along, I awoke to an alarming sensation—I didn't feel pregnant anymore. I told my husband I was going to run in for a quick check, even though we had just heard the baby's heartbeat a week earlier.

The doctor's initial happy expression turned dour upon pressing the stethoscope onto my pregnant belly. He then uttered the words every pregnant woman dreads: "I can't find the heartbeat." The ultrasound afterward confirmed my worst fears—my baby had died. In an effort to comfort me, the doctor explained that we were lucky our child had passed now, as he had been terribly deformed and would have suffered greatly in life. Words cannot describe the overwhelming heartache and grief I felt over the loss of this child.

That was such a painful experience. One of the things that gave me strength was thinking back on that exquisite baby cherub who had come to visit me in the night. He had shown me just what my little baby's spirit would look like in heaven. Instead of worrying that my son was deformed and crippled, I could easily envision him as a perfectly healthy little baby angel, which made all the difference. The glowing baby cherub has been such a blessing and a comfort in my life; he has been instrumental in helping me to heal and move on.

Andie Hight, wife, mother, and spiritual intuitive based in Oakland, California, is completing her first book, Whispered Wisdom, *which chronicles her experiences with and lessons learned from the spiritual realm. Andie also hosts her own radio show,* Wisdom Radio.

Isabella's Kiss

Angela Amoroso & Drew Skinner

My husband, Drew, and I decided to celebrate what would have been our infant daughter's first birthday. Born three months premature on Labor Day, Isabella had died in my arms from sudden infant death syndrome at ninety-six days old with her daddy right beside us at our home. As we approached this significant milestone in our lives, Drew and I knew we needed to acknowledge our daughter's special day. We invited several of our friends with September birthdays for a unique celebration; even Drew and my dad shared a September birthday. My girlfriend Katy made a big cake, and we invited some of Isabella's baby friends and their parents, too. It was a magical evening. We sang songs and told Isabella stories all night long. We shared successes of the non-profit organization we had established in her honor, called Isabella's Giraffe Club, which provides support for preemies and their families. Then my girlfriends surprised us with a birthday gift for Isabella.

The Hurricane Katrina disaster had been weighing on all of our hearts. My girlfriend Lori had seen a television news report from a neonatal intensive care unit in Louisiana with an unusual backdrop. Behind the reporter was a four-foot stuffed giraffe, seemingly looking down at all the babies, just like the one in our living room from Isabella's memorial service. Lori sensed that Isabella was speaking to her through the eyes of the giraffe, saying, "Look at these babies. Can you see them? You have to help them."

The forty preemies had been precariously evacuated to another hospital as a result of the hurricane. Nurses had hand-carried each of the tiny babies in canoes to a safer location. Lori located them in Baton Rouge. Together with a dedicated team of volunteers, they created preemie packs: orange canvas bags containing an outfit, diapers, a "Lessons from Isabella" bookmark, and a beautiful, cozy, handmade giraffe blanket. Lori and our friends presented Drew and me with this prototype in honor of Isabella's first birthday. There was more love in that room that night than I could ever possibly describe.

My husband and I keep Isabella's ashes in her bedroom inside a red wooden heart that her daddy made for her. When it was time for the birthday cake, I impishly said to my husband, "Let's go get the baby." Drew mentioned that it might be viewed as inappropriate or perhaps even a little morbid. "Nonsense," I said. "They're our friends." So Drew brought out Isabella's heart-shaped wooden urn, held it next to him, and stood behind the cake as our friends sang "Happy Birthday" to everyone with a September birthday.

As the birthday candles were blown out, my girlfriend Carla snapped a picture, gasping afterward when she looked at the camera screen. "What's this?!" she asked. There, in the photograph, in front of my husband's smile, was a brilliant ball of white light. We all stood there, amazed. Then we uploaded the photo to our computer and enlarged the area around Drew's face. To our further surprise, we could see the profile of a baby's face inside the ball of light! How incredible! Scientists who study these photographic balls of light call them orbs or emanations from spirit. My husband and I refer to what came that night as "Isabella's kiss." How special that our little angel somehow showed up for her birthday party!

Although my husband and I initially believed that the birthday ball of white light was a one-time occurrence, we have since learned there are thousands of people who see this photographic phenomenon in pictures every day. When we looked through older photographs taken since Isabella's passing, we discovered many more brilliant balls of light; we had just never noticed them before. Since then, my husband and I have taken hundreds of photographs, and lo and behold, we continue to be blessed with hundreds of these same sightings. As a result of Isabella and her special birthday kiss, we truly believe that we *all* live surrounded by angels!

Angela Amoroso and Drew Skinner, award-winning authors, composers, and inspirational speakers, founded Isabella's Giraffe Club in 2004, raising hundreds of thousands of dollars for the UCSD Medical Center. As Infant Loss Peer-to-Peer Parent Contacts for the San Diego Medical Examiner's office, they also help train emergency workers and medical staff. Their presentation, "Sudden Love," is an eternal reminder that they live partnered with their angel Isabella.

Inspiration Angel

Elissa Al-Chokhachy

⌒

I remember the first day I met Vail, a sweet, fourteen-month-old toddler with a rare, life-limiting neurological disorder. With a beauty beyond words, this extraordinary child exuded pure love and light. As his private-duty nurse sixty hours a week at night for the next four months, I had the privilege of helping his parents and family lovingly care for Vail in their home. Each time I went to work and laid my eyes upon him, I would inwardly say, "Oh, my God. He's an angel." Vail possessed an inner knowing and profound wisdom that could be perceived. His all-knowing eyes radiated such amazing healing and peace. And even though Vail never spoke a word, he knew that I sensed his angelic nature, and that was all that mattered.

Caring for Vail and having the opportunity to love him was one of the greatest honors of my life. Not only was I blessed to be in his presence, but his parents were some of my greatest teachers. They taught me the truest meaning of unconditional love. Their every waking moment was spent focused on making their child's life the most beautiful it could possibly be. Whether it was singing to him, caressing him, reading to him, or lying next to him, they loved him beyond measure. How do people love so completely and fully, know-ing that in the next moment the one they love could be gone? I was in awe. And, like them, I couldn't help but love this child each day even more than the day before. His chubby cheeks were so irresistible to kiss. And his eyes, though they never held my gaze, drew me into his essence; they took my heart places I never knew it could go.

At night, when his parents were asleep, I often sat near Vail with a pad of paper and pen in hand. It was as if I could almost hear him quietly speak to me. Before long, I was writing poetry to his parents from their son. In fact, one of the poems of comfort I wrote became the song "A Parent's Lullaby: A Song of Hope for Bereaved Parents." That poem appears at the end of this book.

Vail also inspired me to write my first illustrated children's book, *The Angel with the Golden Glow: A Family's Journey Through Loss and Healing*. Within hours of his passing, I was awoken from a sound sleep. With my eyes closed, I saw Vail and the beautiful golden light that radiated from him. One picture at a time, I watched the story unfold. Rushes of goosebumps ran across my body whenever I correctly interpreted the impressions I saw. The next morning I was awoken a second time to receive the rest of the story. Tears streamed from my eyes at Vail's joyous reunion with his best friend in heaven. It was such a beautiful story. Now, I've heard of creative inspiration before, but this was simply beyond words. I carefully wrote down each impression I received, knowing it was important to capture such an exquisite experience in the moment. Within three weeks, I had the story, the illustrator, the publisher, and the graphic designer for this book without even trying. What a magical journey I was on.

Then, a few weeks later, I found myself waking up every morning with yet another story, this time about a nine-year-old girl and her terminally ill grandfather. I remember saying, "God, I don't need another story. I already have Your beautiful angel story to share." But every morning, the visions persisted until I wrote them down. Once I did, the visual images did not return. As I look back, I feel certain that Vail helped me create that story, too, which became my second children's book, *How Can I Help, Papa? A Child's Journey Through Loss and Healing*.

Although my vision for a *Miraculous Moments* anthology had been in my heart for almost twenty years, I had never contemplated writing a lullaby, much less two illustrated children's books, to help with loss and grief. I do believe these creations were part of God's plan and Vail's plan. Remarkably, these works of hope inspired by Vail continue to help many grieving individuals to this day. I am so blessed to have been touched by an angel. Thank you, Vail, for all that you are and for the many gifts of healing you bring. You are my inspiration angel. I am eternally grateful.

9

Near-Death Experiences

There is no death. Only a change of worlds.

—CHIEF SEATTLE

NEAR-DEATH EXPERIENCES OCCUR FOR people who have been resuscitated and brought back to life. They can also occur for individuals who are critically ill or teetering on the edge of life and death. Although every near-death experience is unique and personal, commonalities exist. Firsthand knowledge and experiences of the other side are life altering; they permanently erase any doubt about the existence of life after death.

Sometimes the near-death experience will just involve hovering above one's body, looking down and watching all the events that are transpiring. This is commonly known as an out-of-body experience. Some people can describe everything that happened to them during resuscitation efforts, including instruments used, medications given, and conversations of emergency responders.

The individual who has died may have seen "the light," felt God's expansive love, or even had conversations with angels, spiritual beings, and loved ones in spirit. Sometimes they may have been shown a boundary, such as a river or a bridge, and been told that if they cross it, they will not return. Some individuals are given a choice to stay, while others are told to go back because their work on earth is not done. Others report a panoramic life review in which they re-experience every thought, word, and action throughout their life; they also simultaneously experience the impact of those thoughts and actions on others. Still others are given a preview of what they have left to do on earth. Six of the seven stories in this chapter describe the near-death experiences of children; the seventh is about a mom's near-death experience with her child in spirit.

This unexplained phenomenon and mystery is profound, life changing, and transformative. Individuals are instilled with the knowledge and awareness that consciousness survives physical death. While on the other side, physical limitations no longer exist. Struggles and pain are gone. Any fear of death dissolves. As a result of the near-death experience, the individual is blessed with infinite wisdom, compassion, and unconditional love.

Walking the Rainbow

Theresa Burke Melnikas

My husband, Dennis, and I had four beautiful daughters together. Our third daughter, Allison, died four days after being diagnosed with a brain tumor. Alli was three years, three months, and thirteen days old. Yet our adorable little blond-haired, blue-eyed daughter was filled with faith. At three years old, Alli drew a picture of a rainbow and told me that she was going to walk it.

Alli thought our pastor, Father Keyes, was God. At Mass, she would always say, "There is God." Eventually, she learned that Father Keyes was not God; he was related to Him. When Alli was hospitalized, she asked Father Mike where God was. Afterward, matter-of-factly, Alli informed him that she was going home to see God. My little daughter was *going home*, even though her doctors and nurses had not discussed discharge plans with any of us.

The night before Alli died, I had a dream about an angel who lovingly wrapped his arms around a small child. As he did this, the moon shone brightly behind him as if it were a clock with the hands pointing to four o'clock. Early that morning when I arrived at the hospital garage, my pager went off with the message "911." I knew it had to be about Alli. I ran to the elevator, where I happened to meet the neurosurgery team on their way to help my daughter. We all rushed to the pediatric unit together. Dennis was holding Alli in his arms. Because her brain was hemorrhaging, Alli's condition was deteriorating rapidly. She was rushed to the CT scanner and then transferred to the pediatric intensive care unit (PICU) for closer monitoring.

In the PICU, Alli touched Dennis's face. Then, she pushed him away and reached for me. She mouthed, "I love you" and "A is for Allison." Dennis and I sang her favorite song, "You Are My Sunshine," but this time, we asked God to take our sunshine with Him. Then we told Alli to walk the rainbow; it was okay. God would take care of her, and she would be safe.

The following morning at 4:00, the moon came out from behind the clouds and shone brightly. Alli died at that exact time, just as the angel had foretold. It was snowing outside, yet with the sunrise came a beautiful double rainbow that lasted all day. Even the television news broadcaster mentioned it. Dennis and I knew our young daughter had walked that rainbow.

Since that time, I have received numerous signs from Alli. Sometimes I will hear a small child giggle and then run by a window, only to find no one there. Afterward, her smell will completely permeate the room. Her giggle and the memory of her smile are so uplifting. Also, tiny, downy white feathers appear everywhere. I find them all over the inside of my car, in my home, and even if I go for a walk in the snow. These feathers appear out of nowhere, especially when I am in need of my daughter's support. Alli's help and guidance are amazing. Her memories fill me with warmth. Whenever Alli is near, I feel complete and fulfilled.

The year after Alli died, my husband and I conceived a fourth daughter. In my sixth month of pregnancy, I became critically ill. As a result, Julia Allyse was born fourteen weeks premature at twenty-six weeks gestation. The doctors did not feel either of us would survive. However, during that time I had a vivid dreamlike experience of Alli. She was healthy, vibrant, and beautiful. Alli was in front of me, almost as if she were sitting in the grass and leaning over to tell me a secret. As she reached out to touch my right shoulder, her hair fell forward. Alli said to me, "Go home, Momma. I can do it myself!" I remember the sky being a vivid blue and the trees a brilliant green overhead. Back in my hospital room, one of the nurses brought in Alli's prayer card for the two of us, and my newborn baby immediately responded. Julia's condition dramatically improved, and we both survived that precarious time. However, one year later, my dear husband, Dennis, died in a motorcycle accident. Somehow I have found a way to go on.

Despite the combined losses, I know that Allison is with me, as is her dad. I truly believe that God protected the two of them from the horrors of illness and sorrow. They are both watching over my three girls and me. Whenever something is lost, we just ask for their help, and the lost item is found right away. Whenever we bring our problems to Dennis, the problems don't seem so large anymore. And all the feathers that Alli leaves around keep us grounded. They give us hope and keep us all connected. Feathers are Alli's signal to let us know that she is "doing it" herself.

Even though Allison had only four days from diagnosis to death, hers is a story of survival. Our connection really does exist. When I was dying, Alli helped me and told me to go back. She reassured me that she was okay and could do it herself. Allison is okay. I know that now. I carry her memory with me every day. I can feel her presence. My sweet daughter Alli is my hero.

Theresa Burke Melnikas, DNP, MSN, RN, wife and mother, is a pediatric and neonatal nurse educator. Terry is blessed by her supportive husband, Andy; her daughters, Jennifer, Jillian, and Julia; and her two angels in heaven, Alli and Dennis.

THE LIGHT THAT SHINES FOREVER

Joan Meese

⌒

I was working at hospice the weekend Michael was actively dying from leukemia. Supported by a large family and many friends, this sixteen-year-old young man had round-the-clock nursing coverage in his home to help his parents manage his care. He was receiving morphine through a PCA pump, which was regularly being adjusted to help alleviate his steadily increasing pain.

Michael was fearful of dying. At the same time, his mother was not ready to let him go. I was arranging my schedule for patient visits when my beeper went off at 7:00 AM. I answered the page from the nurse caring for Michael, who informed me that he had died earlier. "Why didn't you notify me?" I asked. "But that's what I've got to tell you!" she gasped. "He died! And then he came back! You'll never believe it!" She told me that Michael was still in a lot of pain even though the nurse had increased the morphine as much as allowed. I told her I would be right there.

When I arrived at his home, Michael's Uncle Harry, who had just returned from an errand, met me at the door. "You're never going to believe what happened here today," he declared. "Michael died a couple of hours ago. He just stopped breathing, and his mother became hysterical. She was holding him, crying, yelling, and asking him not to go. Of course, we were all upset. And then he started to breathe again. He looked up at his mother and said, 'Mom, it was *beautiful!* The light in this room is so dull compared to the light I saw! It was *so bright and so beautiful!* See that light?' He pointed to the ceiling fixture. 'It was a hundred times ... no, a thousand times brighter! There was so much peace, and there was no pain. I wasn't afraid. I asked if I could come back and tell you that I would be the light that would shine on you forever.'"

At that point, Michael's mother, who had been clinging to her son's shoulders, released him and quietly sat in the chair next to the bed. She picked up Michael's hand and looked into his eyes. "I love you, Michael," she whispered. "It's okay for you to go."

One by one, Uncle Harry had gone to everyone present to verify the details. Each person described the situation identically. They used the same words and mentioned the same unmistakable beauty in Michael's face. There was such peace in his eyes as he spoke. Then the whole atmosphere in the room shifted when Michael suddenly grimaced. His entire body stiffened as the intense pain returned.

While escorting me into the house, Uncle Harry turned to me and said, "That's where you come in. The nurse called you for help." In her Irish brogue, Michael's nurse had joined us and concurred by saying, "Joan, it happened just like Harry said."

The three of us went into Michael's bedroom and found him in excruciating pain. I called his physician and increased the dosage on the morphine pump accordingly. I tried to reassure Michael and his parents, letting them know their time together would be brief.

My beeper went off again. This time it was concerning another pain crisis, another overwhelmed family right down the street from Michael's. I knew I had to act quickly but was undecided about what to do. Inwardly I said a quick prayer, "Lord, please help me make the right decision." I went back into Michael's room, and in an effort to offer spiritual support, I suggested that we say a prayer together. Michael's mother was holding his right hand. He made a rough gesture to shake her hand off in order to hold mine and said, "Okay." At that moment, we all joined hands with Michael to recite the Lord's Prayer. With the room filled to overflowing, the memorable sound of all those prayers surely must have flooded heaven's gates with so much love for this boy. I asked Michael if it would be okay if I left for a short time, and I assured him that I would return very soon. With the continuing care nurse still there, Michael and his parents were comfortable with my leaving. They knew I would be right back.

As I walked into the new patient's home, my beeper went off again. In my heart, I knew that Our Lord had called Michael home. I called the answering service, which confirmed what had happened. Thankfully, the second pain crisis was easily managed, and I was able to return quickly to Michael's home.

Miraculously, his mother was calm, and there was peace through-out the entire house. Michael was at peace. There was no more pain. I embraced Michael's tearful mother and father as I told them what a brave young man their son was. I felt so blessed to have shared this time with them. I offered parting words of comfort and hugs to fam-ily and friends. I said one last goodbye to his mom and dad.

Even though I've had the privilege of spending similar moments with other families, I was deeply moved by Michael's intense love and sacrifice. He willingly left a place filled with peace and free of pain to return to tremendous pain in order to ease his mother's burden. He needed her to know that he would always be her guiding light. Michael's love was truly incomprehensible—an incredible gift given with all his heart by a very remarkable young man.

Joan Meese, RN, hospice nurse, learned from her parents that death, as well as dying at home, are natural processes. All the chapters in Joan's life, including marrying her husband, Jim, have been directed by her God, a power greater than herself.

Passing into the Light on the Isle of Guernsey

Renee L. Collas

A deafening noise droned on, hidden by a dark cloud in the overcast sky. My little brother, Richard, and I looked at each other. "What's that?" he asked. We raced to stand on the attic window seat that overlooked our blue slate roof. We could see across our neighbors' coal-burning, red chimneys, lanes snaking between browned winter hedges, and the rocky Bordeaux beach on little Guernsey in the British Channel Islands. Suddenly we looked up and saw broken crosses stenciled on black outstretched wings. German planes flew low over our house, shaking all within. Pilots searched for a small airstrip four miles away. It was early in 1940 when they brought us death, shootings, starvation, concentration camps, deportations, and evil. However, all through the war, the angels protected our family. My parents, neighbors, Richard, and I grew vegetables, kept cows, chickens, and rabbits, and helped one another.

There is little written about the sufferings that the old and young bore during the five years of World War II on those islands. All our military-aged men had joined up and gone to England. In addition, our school-aged children had gone there, too, evacuated with their teachers. So close were the islands to northern France—only ten miles across the sea channel—that Hitler immediately ordered their occupation after his troops rolled their tanks into Paris. Nazi socialist governance had arrived. A battle for the lives of the Guernsey people ensued.

As a chronic asthmatic with persistent pneumonia, the fight for my own life began. Coughing would rip and tear at my lungs. No prescription medicines were available, since all cargo ships and small boats to and from England had been halted. Activated land mines along the whole coast blew up those who dared to pass through or to fish, sail, or swim. Cement bunkers with wide slit eyes hid the aircraft guns peeping out with their long, tubular snouts through green camouflage. Air raid sirens wailed on.

Finally, I wheezed and choked until I could breathe no longer. I fell back into my soft bedclothes. My five-year-old body had had enough. Having slipped into a coma on more than one occasion, I happily joined my angelic teachers in another dimension. These trips foretold events I would experience in my future. From the bedroom ceiling, I would silently watch my still body below. Sadly, I would view my mother and my doctor at the end of my bed, shaking their heads in disbelief, with my mother in tears. The doctor considered me dead. Yet my mother would bring a cot into my room to keep vigil by my side, for she knew I would eventually awaken from the comas.

During those years, I didn't want to stay in my sick body. Instead, I would place my small hand into the soft, silk hand of my angel guide dressed in a flowing, white silk gown. It took me several days to learn to fly. I was anxious, but my sweet angel guide was patient with my frustration. With her repeated instructions, I finally got it. I completely relaxed, let go, and emptied my mind of all thoughts, which then automatically enabled me to focus on my purpose. Exhilarated, I soared on the wind with my angel guide through the heavens. In a state of pure ecstasy, I felt the cool breeze on my face and the air on my body.

Together, we soared over green fields, valleys, hills, Swiss mountains, and even the Rocky Mountains. We flew along Paradise Valley, now known as U.S. Highway 89S, dotted with houses, mobile homes, and farms, which led us to the town of Livingston, busy with people. Precipitous dry riverbanks scarred the earth where the Yellowstone River had long ago changed its course.

My angel taught me about events that had not yet come to pass, knowing of my reluctance to return to earth. She showed me people I would spend time with, as well as the important things I still needed to do. Together, we traveled to several places I would live in this life-time. Because all of these things were shown to me, I understood why I couldn't die then. I had to return to earth, which I did. Still, when-ever the pain became unbearable, I would go on visits with my angel guide.

Finally, with a fond goodbye to my teacher, I slipped back into my body to stay. A quiet, deep sleep ensued; the blinding headaches were gone. At noon on May 8, 1945, I heard British Prime Minister Winston Churchill give a radio speech: "My dear Channel Islands are liberated." British ships took away 40,000-plus Germans, and the Yankees arrived on Guernsey to give candy to the children. Our soldiers returned home; then, in September, the teachers and their island children returned home to their parents.

Later on, when I was well, I practiced disappearing through the light tunnel once again. Given a rare gift by the angels to see my future, I now teach others and write about who we really are—spiritual beings.

Renee L. Collas is founder and executive director of Saint Germain's Children Foundation, a small 501(c)(3) tax-exempt charity in Winthrop, Massachusetts, for needy families and children in the US and Colombia.

Second Chance

Robin Frank

My kind, lovable father died of a massive coronary when I was only ten years old. His heart had been damaged years earlier by an untreated case of strep throat and rheumatic fever at a time when antibiotics weren't available to the military. Although he had been told by his physician not to exert himself, my stubborn father did not always follow his doctor's advice. Dad was shoveling snow outside our home on a cold, snowy January day when his fatal heart attack occurred. My mother was widowed at the age of thirty-four, and my life was changed forever.

Two years later on Christmas Day, Mom remarried an acquaintance of Dad's and left for a honeymoon. With Grandma in charge of my nine-year-old brother and me, we stayed at her home while they were gone. Three red poinsettias decorated Grandma's family room. My younger brother dared me to stick my finger inside one of their sappy centers. At twelve years old, I knew they were poisonous and that I shouldn't do it. But I foolishly decided to stroll around the family room and boldly stick my right index finger inside the gooey center of all three anyway. Within a half hour, I had a splitting headache. I told Grandma about the headache and lay down on the sofa. After she placed a cold compress on my forehead, Grandma left the room to find a thermometer to take my temperature.

My next memory was of me hovering over my body. As I looked down, I watched the doctor examine me while my grandmother sat calmly off to one side. I remember thinking, "Why isn't Grandma upset that I'm so sick and floating above my body?" Instantly I felt myself being sucked up, head first, into a narrow shaft of light, which was shaped like a tube and not much wider than my body. Looking directly up into the warm, white light, I traveled quickly for several seconds through this silent tube of bright light.

As soon as I reached the end, I entered a wide-open space of warm, soft, brilliant white light. I remember feeling overwhelmed with so much warmth and happiness. I didn't see any people. Instead, I saw a few fuzzy, white forms. Then, a strong, authoritative mass of energy spoke to me and said telepathically, "It's not your time. You have to go home."

The next thing I remember was waking up in my bed feeling very cold and also quite disappointed that I'd had to return. Unsure whether the experience had been a dream or reality, I never mentioned one word about it to my grandmother. My headache was gone, and Grandma was so happy that I was better. I could never bring myself to tell anybody about what had happened to me even though I had almost died on my parents' honeymoon. However, I no longer feared death, and I lived my life with open-mindedness about the whole concept of life after death.

Many years later while in my thirties and raising young children, I helped Mom nurse my stepfather, who was dying of cancer. A week after he passed away, my mother suffered a serious heart attack, which required a quadruple bypass. Mom moved in with our family to recuperate for a while, and then she suffered a serious medical setback. I worried terribly that I would lose her, too. Caring for Mom and my family was exhausting. Many a night, I went to bed in tears.

After one particularly difficult evening with Mom, I was awakened in the middle of the night with the sense that someone was standing in the room. I thought that it must be my husband or one of my children. Instead, lo and behold, there stood both my biological father and my stepfather smiling, side by side, at the foot of my bed! They told me that Mom would be fine. "It's not her time," each of them said reassuringly. "Your mother has many more years to spend with you and your family." Although I listened intently to each and every word, I couldn't help but stare in disbelief at the two of them. I kept opening and closing my eyes as they spoke to me to see if they were really there. Finally, feeling tired, I rolled over, fell into a deep sleep, and woke up in the morning feeling refreshed and renewed.

The sense of relief I felt the next morning was exhilarating; I could breathe again. I knew that both of my fathers had spoken the truth; I felt it in every part of my body. Not only had I been given a second chance at life, but so had my mother. Here it is ten years later, and she is still doing fine. My fathers were right. It really wasn't Mom's time. Forever thankful for their reassurance, I appreciate every single day I have with Mom even more.

Robin Frank, mother of two grown children, has been married to her husband and best friend for thirty-two years. A former social worker, she loves gardening, hiking, and traveling with her husband. Robin also enjoys spending time with family, friends, and especially her mom.

INTO THE LIGHT

Mary J. Wasielak Skaggs

Imagine having your life changed forever in only a moment. On the evening of December 28, 2002, that is exactly what happened to me. I was in the middle of winter break from my classes at Fordham University. I had just spent a relaxing day with my friends at an all-day rock concert in Worcester, Massachusetts. The concert took place in an original, old theater being used for various types of performances. While drinking beer out of a plastic cup, I was sitting in one of those comfy old chairs in the back of the theater enjoying the music. The bartender who sold me the beer had transferred it from its original glass bottle into the cup to prevent any glass from being broken at the concert.

Suddenly, I felt a strange feeling come over me . . . and something told me to get up. I quickly grabbed the left arm of an acquaintance sitting next to me. All I could do was stand up and take a few steps down the stairs when all of a sudden I collapsed. It was as if my legs could not hold my body any longer. I have very little recollection of what happened after that.

According to friends and acquaintances attending the concert, I was carried into the theater's bathroom and placed on the floor. The right side of my body began to seize. Before long, my entire body was convulsing. EMTs arrived, placed me on a stretcher, and took me away in an ambulance. I have vague memories of EMTs administering Valium to relax my seizing body.

By the time I arrived at the University of Massachusetts Memorial Hospital, my breathing had stopped completely due to a respiratory arrest. I had been intubated in the ambulance, and EMTs were using an ambu bag to help me breathe. Also, my clothes had been cut off in order to attach the electrodes, IVs, and various paraphernalia needed to monitor my critical condition. The rest of the night's memories were my own unique experience. These memories have changed my life forever...

I remember being in a still and silent place. I had the sense that I was hovering over my physical body. It was as though a part of me had levitated. I was aware that my physical body was lying beneath me on a hospital bed, but my soul, my spirit, the only part of me that felt alive in that moment, was rising above my physical form. I felt calm. I was not just relaxed, but at *complete peace*. There was no pain or suffering there... There were no sounds, no words, just calmness... a calmness and peace that was beyond words, and like nothing else on this earth that I had ever experienced before.

As I looked out, all I could see was a grand, all-encompassing bright light. It was brighter than any light I had ever seen. It felt similar to staring at the sun, except this light was brilliantly white, without any shades of yellow in it whatsoever. My eyes didn't have to squint as I looked at the bright light, but rather I *absorbed* the light as I took it all in. This brilliant light extended as far as I could see and completely filled my field of vision; I felt at ease and relaxed. My body, emotions, and mind were at total peace.

Then I noticed my grandfather in front of me. How could this be? My Dziadziu, the Polish term for grandfather, had died nearly a year earlier. Yet he was standing right in front of me wearing his dark-colored suit, the same suit we had buried him in. I sensed pure tranquility in my grandfather's face. He did not show any emotion; rather, Dziadziu emanated stillness and peace. He was a strong yet silent presence, just as he had been in life. I felt almost relieved to see him. For some reason, I was not shocked or startled that Dziadziu was with me.

My Dziadziu was holding Speckles, my white rabbit with black spots who had died five years earlier on Easter Sunday. The last time I had seen Speckles was just before he died, when he was in so much pain and discomfort. Yet Speckles was in front of me in Dziadziu's arms, looking very much alive, with his fur thick and healthy once again. Just like Dziadziu, Speckles was filled with contentment, peace, and tranquility. What an incredible experience!

No words were spoken. This moment that we shared did not need words. We just gazed into one another's eyes, almost as if Dziadziu and Speckles were perhaps waiting for me to come closer... In this place, time stood still. A second may have passed or it may have been several hours... All of it was *beautiful*, simply beautiful. I had never felt this way before and I haven't since... Eventually, I emerged from the stillness.

I awakened to an exasperating sound being emitted from a machine off to my left. I slowly oriented myself to my physical surroundings. There was a tube down my throat, and it was difficult to swallow. I became aware that the loud noise I was hearing off to my left side and behind my shoulder was a ventilator. It certainly sounded much louder in person than it did on television or in the movies. I could feel and see all sorts of tubes and wires attached to every part of my body, monitoring my medical condition. I was unable to speak, as the tube in my throat prevented me from doing so.

Within minutes of my returning to full consciousness, the nurse removed my endotrachial tube after determining I was capable of breathing on my own. Another nurse telephoned Mom, who had been working overnight as a charge nurse at Saint Francis Hospital. We shared very quick "I love yous" on the phone. Mom was so relieved to know that I was okay. I remained in the intensive care unit for a few more hours until my heart rate stabilized and returned to a normal rhythm. While lying in my hospital bed, I struggled to make sense of everything that had transpired.

The nurse told me that I'd had a seizure. How could that be possible? I was a healthy, twenty-two-year-old woman with no prior history of seizures. I was told that I'd been on a ventilator for several hours, unresponsive throughout the night until awakening on my own in the early morning hours. Despite everything that I had just been told, I still felt calm—a little scared, but calm. Then I comprehended the magnitude of the situation ... I had almost died!

Just after the early morning shift change, I was finally discharged from the hospital after such a horrific and traumatizing night. One of my friends was kind enough to drive me home. I was so tired. My body felt like I had just run a marathon, but I had to stay awake. I needed to process what had happened. There were very few words spoken during the ride home to Connecticut. Too many thoughts were racing through my mind for me to be able to talk.

We pulled into the driveway, and my mom came running out of the garage to greet me with open arms. I became so full of emotion. I think it was one of the tightest hugs I have ever received in my life. Through all our tears, my mother and I hugged with such joy, love, and relief, thankful that I was alive and that I had been able to survive the whole ordeal.

The three of us went inside the house, and I lay down on the couch. Mom pulled up her chair right next to me, and my friend sat on the couch beside me. I so wanted to share all the memories from the night before. First, Mom asked a few questions. Then she listened intently as I described the remarkable experience of seeing her deceased father and our beloved deceased pet rabbit, Speckles.

Mom and I shared how much Dziadziu meant to both of us. He was so fully present in our lives, hearts, and memories. We reaffirmed our lifelong belief that whenever someone passes from this world, part of him or her continues to live on in the memory and lives of others. We also discussed Dziadziu's special affection for both my mother and me. Because my grandfather was one of six brothers with no sisters, his heart had always held a special place of pride for his only daughter, my mother, and his only granddaughter, me. Later on that night, as soon as my father returned home from his Vermont ski trip where he had been unreachable by phone, I shared my experience with him. Dad was clearly amazed. He held me and affirmed his love.

Over the next few days and weeks, I no longer struggled to accept the events of the fateful evening of December 28, 2002. Instead, I embraced them. As I tried to get back into the swing of things in my senior practicum work for my master's degree in social work, I went through extensive medical tests and follow-up appointments. All the tests came back normal, with nothing conclusive. The doctors said it was possible that I could have unknowingly ingested a club drug, not tested for in the ER, which precipitated the whole event. No one will ever know for sure.

As time passed, I continued to process what I now refer to as my near-death experience, an experience that made me feel so much more alive than I ever had before. I decided to disclose to my Fordham College professors what had happened to me over winter break, as I also wanted to be able to educate others. When I did, my practicum supervisor validated my thoughts and feelings. Having done research into near-death experiences himself, my supervisor was extremely supportive and encouraged me to go forward and continue to tell my story. As I began to share my experience more and more, I was surprised to find that no one looked at me strangely when I talked openly and freely about dying. Instead, I felt truly comforted and supported, more than I ever imagined.

This amazing experience has been a catalyst for my personal growth. As a result of what happened and the research I did afterward, I now provide educational training to my colleagues on the use, abuse, and treatment of club drugs. Additionally, I feel blessed to be able to work with adolescents who have abused substances in the past; I work diligently to educate them on the risks of such behavior.

Sometimes when I think back to that pivotal and critical night in my life, I cry for so many reasons. I cry when I think of all the things that I've accomplished thus far that would have never happened. I weep as I think of how hard it would have been for my loved ones if I had died. I also cry tears of joy because *I am alive* today!

My life has changed forever. I live for each day and appreciate every single moment I have. I am eternally grateful to those who saved my life and also that Dziadziu and Speckles were there to welcome me into the light. It is so incredible to know they are alive, healthy, well, and watching over me. Thanks to my grandfather, my pet bunny, and my near-death experience, I know that my spirit will live on.

Mary J. Wasielak Skaggs, LCSW, lives with her husband and son in Oldham County, Kentucky. She is a licensed clinical social worker practicing at a psychiatric hospital in Louisville, Kentucky. Mary feels so blessed to have her guardian angels.

MORGAN AND JESUS

Marlene Leeds

My niece Morgan has the sweetest disposition. One of my most memorable moments occurred while babysitting her when she was four years old. While happily playing with her dolls, my niece looked up at me and asked, "Aunt Marlene, do you know Jesus?"

"Yes, I do know Jesus," I replied, smiling. "Do you?"

Morgan said, "Oh, yes. I went to visit Him, you know."

"You went to visit Jesus?" I questioned, surprised by her response.

"Remember when I was little and sick? I went to visit Him," she said very matter-of-factly.

"Did he talk to you?"

"Of course," she said confidently. "He ran up to me. He laughed. He hugged me. He kissed me, and He rubbed my head. Then He said, 'Morgan, I love you, but I am sending you back home to your mommy because she needs you.'" Then Morgan said, "I have to love Jesus because He sent me back to my mommy."

At only four years old, Morgan had already been through several kidney operations as a result of renal problems at birth. I always wondered if she had been given a glimpse of the other side during one of those surgeries. Not only did she go to the other side, but I truly believe that my niece was in the presence of Christ.

Marlene Leeds, retired flight attendant of thirty-four years, lives with her husband, Bob, a retired pilot. They both love traveling, reading, and their cute little dog, Tucker. Marlene especially enjoys her work as a hospice volunteer at a residential hospice in Knoxville.

Saved by the Light

Owl Medicine Woman

———

My family and I spent our summers at a little cottage on the beach when I was growing up. As a young girl, I spent the majority of those summers swimming in the ocean. From morning till night, I was a water baby, and the ocean was my playground for hours of fun. My father's good friend, who worked for Converse Rubber Company, provided us with durable flotation rafts made for maritime use. These navy-blue canvas and rubber rafts were as strong and comfortable as a mattress. My sisters and I would laugh uncontrollably as we piled on top of one another onto a raft to ride the big waves in together. The bigger the waves, the better the ride. However, I soon learned that the power and force of the ocean demanded my attention and respect. One close call in particular changed my life forever.

I had been daydreaming on a raft, floating on the ocean without a care in the world. The rhythmic, calming motion of the waves and the warmth of the summer sun soothed and relaxed me. Without even realizing it, I had drifted out to sea. Only the faint sound of voices yelling from a distance brought my awareness back to the present. Much to my surprise, I found myself a long way out from the beach.

I began to paddle in, but no matter how hard I paddled, the raft went nowhere. So I decided to swim to shore, holding on to the rope while towing the raft behind me. Once I slipped into the water, I felt myself immediately pulled under by the riptide and entangled in the long rope. The current's unrelenting force and momentum somersaulted me over and over and over again. The water was freezing cold; everything was pitch black. A captive of the riptide current, I had no control. A sense of panic set in. Struggling, I got my legs free from the rope, but the ocean continued to toss me around. I thought

I was going to die. Unable to see, I lost all my bearings from tumbling through the darkness. I tried one more time to save myself. The last thing I remember was banging my head on the hard, sandy ocean floor.

An incredible tunnel of brilliant white light appeared through the depths of the dark water and reached for me. This cone-shaped tunnel of light expanded up into the whiteness of the sky, the vastness of heaven, and the calmness of eternity as it guided me upward toward the surface. There are no words to describe this infinite, open, expansive white light without boundaries that came for me. I have no idea how I breathed through all of this or how I made it to shore. All I know is that the light lifted me in slow motion from the depths of the ocean fully out of the water and beyond. From above, I watched a crowd of people gather around me on the beach. I could hear my mother, who was eight months pregnant at the time, screaming hysterically in the background. It was so hard leaving the calmness of the light to return to my body and the feelings of sheer panic from my loved ones all around.

I was later told that I had drifted out on the raft and was drowning, and a man had saved my life. Yet I know it was the light that saved me. The light guided me to the water's surface so the man could find and rescue me; but it was God's light that had pulled me up and out of the riptide current to beyond. In an instant, I went from tumbling through the cold, dark, tumultuous ocean water into the warmth and brilliance of God's loving light and peace. The contrast was stark; both existed at the same time and in the same physical locality. How is it possible that the light had come to show me the way?

Despite everything that happened, I do not have a fear of death, nor do I fear the ocean. I respect the mystery of the ocean and its strength, yet I know that the strength of the light is even greater than that. I still look at it in awe and in tears. The experience changed the course of my life. I know with certainty that there is so much more to this vast universe than we could ever imagine. I am grateful for all the blessings received. And until the light comes to beckon me home, I embrace every opportunity to be fully present with my loved ones here on earth.

Owl Medicine Woman's experience has been a gift. It has led her to a lifelong practice of healing throughout New England. Her soul connection with the light allows Owl Medicine Woman to be a beacon of light during times of darkness for others.

Conclusion

Life is eternal, and love is immortal,
And death is only a horizon;
And a horizon is nothing save the limit of our sight.

—ROSSITER WORTHINGTON RAYMOND

THESE PAGES HAVE BEEN blessed with the heartfelt stories of numerous parents, grandparents, family members, and friends, as well as those in the helping professions. They have willingly shared their journeys of love, loss, hope, and faith. May their words help heal the hearts of those who are suffering; may their journeys help guide the way. May their experiences bring hope and reassurance that love and life are eternal and that the souls of all children truly live on.

I only wish that I could provide answers for all those parents and grandparents who wonder why their children left this earth far sooner than they had planned. What I do know is that these children, no matter how brief their stay, have changed our lives forever. They have left their imprints indelibly written upon our hearts, our minds, and our souls. I also know that one day we will be reunited again.

In closing, I would like to share a poem that I wrote while caring for a young toddler with a life-limiting neurological disorder. The words came to me while sitting quietly next to him during the night. It felt as though somehow his little soul was speaking to me through the silence. The loving words I heard were surely a message of hope for his parents.

Then, a few weeks later, I woke up one morning with a melody playing in my head that I had never heard before. I immediately got up and hummed it onto a tape recorder to make sure I wouldn't forget it. Later that day, I decided to try combining the melody with the words I had written earlier. Sure enough, they fit together perfectly. Eventually, accompanied by harp music, they became "A Parent's Lullaby: A Song of Hope for Bereaved Parents." May these words bring hope and comfort to those who have lost a child or young person in their lives. May this book and lullaby bring you solace, healing, and peace.

A Parent's Lullaby

A Song of Hope for Bereaved Parents

———

Mom and Dad, here I am! Your child I'll always be
Loving you both with all my heart through all eternity.
Will you love me even though on earth I could not stay?
There were things beyond control that called me on my way.
Sometimes when you miss me, I know it makes you cry.
Know that I am still with you and will be by your side.

If you sit quietly with me, I'll share with you my thoughts.
Ask me what you'd like to know. Then listen with your heart.
Be open to the subtle ways I will say to you,
"Thanks for being my mom and dad, for loving me through and
through."
I want to make you happy. I want to make you smile.
Know each time that you think of me I'm loving you all the while.

I'm sorry I'll never accomplish the things you'd hoped for me.
God and I had other plans. Search and you will see...
I came to earth to be your child, to be a teacher true.
There's so much I've been teaching since I've come to be with you.
You've learned to live in the moment and cherish each day we have.
It's the little things that mean the most, like a smile or touch of the
hand.

You know it doesn't matter the things that will never be.
True love is a gift that is given unconditionally.
If you'll share this wisdom and pass it on even after I am gone,
You'll see that I am still with you for I made you wise and strong.
Together we'll be doing the work that I came to do...
Spreading love and joy and wisdom to special parents and people like
you.

Remember I'll always be with you in the memories we share.
Remember the love we treasure and the ways in which we care.
Thanks, Mom and Dad, for bringing me into this world with you.
Thanks for all the memories, for loving me like you do.
After I am gone from here, remember to look for me
Perhaps in the song of a cardinal in the breeze as it wafts through the
trees.

I'll be your guardian angel to lovingly guide you
To assist in troubled times when you don't know what to do.
Just call my name and I'll be there, for love is what I am.
It's what I was before I came. It's all a part of the plan.
If you feel a gentle touch or sense that I'm close by,
Know the last lesson I am teaching is that love can never die.

Dear Reader,

If you would like to share a true, firsthand experience affirming the continuity of life with the author, please send your brief description along with your contact information to: stories@MiraculousMoments.com.

Every submission will be read and reviewed. You will be contacted if your story could potentially be used in a future book. Thank you in advance for your willingness to share. May we bring much comfort, hope, and healing to many.

Blessings,

Elissa Al-Chokhachy

www.MiraculousMoments.com

To Write to the Author

If you wish to contact the author or would like more information about this book, please write to the author in care of Llewellyn Worldwide Ltd. and we will forward your request. Both the author and publisher appreciate hearing from you and learning of your enjoyment of this book and how it has helped you. Llewellyn Worldwide Ltd. cannot guarantee that every letter written to the author can be answered, but all will be forwarded. Please write to:

Elissa Al-Chokhachy
c/o Llewellyn Worldwide Ltd.
2143 Wooddale Drive
Woodbury, MN 55125-2989

Please enclose a self-addressed stamped envelope for reply, or $1.00 to cover costs. If outside the U.S.A., enclose an international postal reply coupon.

Many of Llewellyn's authors have websites with additional information and resources. For more information, please visit our website at www.llewellyn.com.